DEVA

DEVA

Our Relationship
with the Subtle World

JACQUELYN E. LANE

FINDHORN PRESS

Findhorn Press
One Park Street
Rochester, Vermont 05767
www.findhornpress.com

Text stock is SFI certified

Findhorn Press is a division of Inner Traditions International

Disclaimer
The information in this book is given in good faith and intended for
information only. Neither author nor publisher can be held liable by any
person for any loss or damage whatsoever which may arise directly or
indirectly from the use of this book or any of the information therein.

Cataloging-in-Publication data for this title
is available from the Library of Congress

ISBN 978-1-64411-074-4 (print)
ISBN 978-1-64411-075-1 (ebook)

Printed and bound in the United States by Lake Book Manufacturing, Inc.
The text stock is SFI certified. The Sustainable Forestry Initiative®
program promotes sustainable forest management.

10 9 8 7 6 5 4 3 2 1

Edited by Michael Hawkins
Text design and layout by Anna-Kristina Larsson
This book was typeset in Garamond and Myriad

To send correspondence to the author of this book,
mail a first-class letter to the author c/o Inner Traditions •
Bear & Company, One Park Street, Rochester, VT 05767, USA
and we will forward the communication, or contact
the author directly at www.jacquelynelane.com

Contents

Part Two
Who's Singing Your Song?

Part Three

Symphonies

Bibliography

Introduction

The Song

Life is a great song. From the rocks that seem to be still to the bubbling water of the stream that flows over them. From the uncurling leaves of small plants to giant trees. From quiet hamlets to teeming cities. It's all singing—notes within tunes, tunes within themes, themes within symphonies. We usually think of sound as something that happens in our ears but that's just one way of recognizing the phenomenon we call "sound".

From soil to stars everything vibrates, everything has its own resonance because inside every atom there is energy. In fact, quantum physics tells us an atom is *nothing but energy*. So, at its very heart physical matter is *only* energy; vibrating fiery light that emits or "sounds" different notes.

How does the fiery energy inside the atoms and molecules that make up a leaf know how to be, how to respond to the elements of air, water, heat and light that surround it, bombard it, caress it and pass through it? How does that matter know how to be a leaf and not something else, a caterpillar for instance?

We can reduce everything to chemical analysis or explain the universe in mechanical terms but these are not the only avenues open to us. We've already been there, done that, when Descartes and Newton, enamoured by the new inventions of their time, found it convenient to see our entire universe as a giant machine. How we choose to see or think about things fundamentally decides how we treat them. The consequences of treating this living, breathing,

11

growing, dynamic planet as a machine has had disastrous consequences. It has also led us to ignore countless thousands of years of observation, knowledge and wisdom of entirely different sorts. We will discover that seen from a different perspective, knowing *how* to be a leaf (or a caterpillar, a rock or a stream) is both the task and the joy of deva.

Are There Faeries at the Bottom of Your Garden?

"Faeries at the bottom of the garden" is an English saying that was in vogue amongst the grown-ups when I was a child. It was usually accompanied by a tolerant smile. Perhaps for me, it was a seed thought. The word "deva" however, was not in use until the Eastern philosophies began to disseminate in the West in the 1960s and 70s.

You may have heard that deva are nature spirits, faeries and elves for example but the deva kingdom is about *all* matter in, on and surrounding our planet. Furthermore, deva is not *just* in what we normally consider to be physical matter. You may, however, have picked up this book because you thought it would be about faeries, so we won't leave them out.

So, are there faeries at the bottom of your garden? What, you don't have a garden? No matter, I'll show you they don't just live in gardens so if your back yard is a concrete jungle you may still find them. (Though I confess, I find it easier in a garden.) From the faeries at the bottom of the garden or in the concrete jungle, to the mighty deva of landscapes, deva are known for their joy and humour, so they've asked me not to get too serious. That goes counter to my natural inclinations but for their sake and yours, I'll try. To stay as true to them as I can, this book is full of deva encounters and wherever possible I have let them speak for themselves.

While this is not a textbook, we need a framework to help us better understand this kingdom that is both so vital and vitalizing to our world and ourselves. Woven with our journey into the deva realms will be attempts to answer some of the what, how and why questions about deva. Let's start with a few short questions, and some short answers . . .

What Are Deva?

Deva is an ancient Sanskrit word from India meaning "Being of Light". I am told it is pronounced "day-vah". Because it is not an English word, we can use "deva" as a collective noun, just as in English we use the word "sheep" to mean a single animal or a flock.

Deva are not to be confused with "diva"—those female celebrities of opera—though deva *are* singers. They sing ideas into form. It is deva that cause us to exclaim, "Wow, this is a special place. It feels so alive!" At the lowliest level, they are within each atom. Deva are the faeries in the grass. They are the vast energy of sea, wind and mountains and as we will see, the deva kingdom is not confined to what we call nature.

In this book, I am using the term "deva" to refer to the entire range of beings that come under the domain of the "deva kingdom". Just as the term "animal kingdom" includes millions of different life forms at varying stages of evolution—bacteria, insects, birds, animals, fish etc.—the deva kingdom includes a huge variety of beings. They range from the tiny elemental lives associated with "the elements" right up through faerie or nature spirits to the great angelic beings that are most appropriately called "deva"—beings of Light. Hence, in Western countries, deva is often referred to as the angelic kingdom and its higher ranks are included in the major religions. In other traditions, they are referred to as "the gods".

To really "get" deva (in the sense of understanding what they are really about), we need to realize that deva is the *kingdom of substance and form*—the world of matter both solid and subtle.

What Do Deva Do?

Deva infuse all matter in our solar system with intelligence and respond to us from the spaces inside everything we see, feel and think.

Intelligent matter? Now don't drop the book in horror, thinking you have entered that controversy between religion and science over a "designer God". Knowledge of deva has been around for many thousands of years in various guises. Many other writers have shared their experiences, as have uncountable sane, sensible human beings who may or may not belong to a particular religion.

We could go through the rest of this book without talking of God again. To some people even mentioning the word can be intensely annoying. To others it is a word of power that expresses the Oneness of Being and brings meaning into our small lives. North American Indians use the term the "Great Spirit". Islam says there are ninety-nine names for "God". Judaism likewise has its own names. There are thousands of paths and perceptions around what we think of (or are at pains to deny) as "divinity".

If you are so inclined, you can see the deva kingdom I describe as an expression of divinity. It may just expand your definition of God far beyond the one you are used to. The major world religions claim that God is omnipresent, and that means He/She/It is every-where, in everything, even in what may not seem very God-like to us. So, putting prejudice aside, here's what deva do. Wherever there is purpose, deva gather to carry it out. We think we are the Masters in this world but we can do and experience *nothing* without them.

Deva are in all substance regardless of how dense or subtle it is, so everything is alive with their intelligence. Some of this intelligence is so infinitesimally small it is way below our level of awareness and some of it is so enormously large we can barely begin to comprehend it. We can also describe deva as Creation's engineers and mechanics because they are the beings that get things done on Earth. They produce all the phenomena we see and experience so our relationship with deva is one of interdependence. Without them we might still Be but we would have no *experience* of our Being. If you are new to such concepts, they can be hard to get your head around. Don't let that put you off; it will become clearer as we journey together.

Above all, deva have revealed to so many of us, a universe of joy, love and respect for a Being-ness way beyond what we can physically see with our eyes or deduce with our machines and instruments.

The Sea of Deva

Both inside and outside, we live in a sea of deva that surrounds us as water surrounds a fish. We are so *in* it that most of us are not aware of it. The deva kingdom infuses *all* substance and because of our lack of awareness, we do not realize that such substance surrounds us in multiple levels of density. Here, "subtle" and "subtler" means it's less dense than solid and that for us, it is accessed as different levels of consciousness.

A heaving body of ocean, a liquid, flowing river, moving, changeable clouds, they're all expressions of an elemental life we call "water". The same element sloshes, flows and gurgles within our physical body. Its higher counterparts form the subtle "waters" of our astral/emotional body. In Chapter Seven, we acknowledge how water affects us emotionally. When the water elementals interact with the rocks of a streambed or fall as rain, their song stimulates our own watery astral elementals, delighting us with its musical tumbling and soothing us with the gentle patter of rain or, as a raging sea or a flooding river, instilling us with fear. Water is also traditionally used as a symbol and metaphor for our emotions, for obvious reasons.

Like our emotions, water is a changeable fluid. When it is cold enough, water freezes into crystalline forms of snowflakes and ice. When our emotions "freeze", we become emotionally cold, uncaring and unresponsive to the needs of others. Toxins can be created by emotional turbulence that triggers the release of chemicals that flood our physical body. Whether in sadness or joy, when we experience strong emotions, we can cry spontaneous, watery tears that help to remove those toxins from our bodies. As well as being a receptacle of emotions then, water is also a natural cleanser. Water can have a quality of clarity and stillness just as our emotions do when we are calm or meditating deeply but physical water can also become stagnant. Tears can wash our emotions clean, getting them out of the body whereas harbouring them can lead to an unhealthy negative accumulation or to a stagnant emotional life.

The Nature of Reality

If there is intelligent deva life in every atom of physical matter, what of the more subtle layers that make up the vehicle you, as a human personality inhabit? What of your emotions? Does your emotional body have matter or substance? Of course! You may not normally see it with your physical eyes but yes; it is composed of substance that is finer than solid, liquid, gas or etheric (look ahead to Fig 8 on page 100 for those layers). So, the substance of your emotional body (sometimes called a "sheath") is above the etheric plane. You'll find it in Fig 9 on page 118 where it is called by its usual name, the "astral body". It may be less dense but it's no less *real* than the physical matter you can see with your eyes.

To the trained eye, the emotional body *is* visible, changing colour and form in a heartbeat. It spreads outward or contracts, flares, sparks, floats, soothes, expressing pain or pleasure. While not all of us can see it, we can usually *feel* it or *sense* it via our own or other people's emotions. Yes, our emotional body *is matter*, emotional/astral matter and what is infused into every "piece of matter" at every level of density? Deva—a kingdom of responsive intelligence that at each level of being has its own quality. The qualities of fluidity, changeability, seeping into things, flooding, thirsting, crystallizing, becoming solid or evaporating into "thin air", these are all characteristics of both water elementals and the astral elementals that constitute our subtle emotional body. Unruly little devils at times aren't they, causing problems whether we're two or eighty-two. Now there's an evolutionary challenge; how do we get those emotional/astral elementals under control?

Shakespeare's Hamlet was right, "There are more things in heaven and earth, Horatio, than are dreamt of in your philosophy." The esoteric philosophy in this book aims to open us up to those things not dreamt of or just plain avoided, in orthodox Western philosophy.

The nature of reality is not just a subject for investigation by the physical sciences but the field of metaphysics, the study of what is behind, beyond "normal" human sight in the physical world. Metaphysics can include religious, philosophical and spiritual teachings and is often given other labels like "esotericism" and "occultism". "Occult" is a word that has been hijacked by misuse and confined in recent times to the realm of superstition, witchcraft and devilry. Its *real* meaning is used in astronomy to describe a celestial body (e.g., a planet or moon) that is hidden or unseen *behind* one that can be seen. So, it's a very apt word to describe the subject matter of this book.

Metaphysics seeks to explain what is hidden behind or beyond the physics of the "real" world and to explain what *causes* the physics of this "real" world. To the esotericist or metaphysician, the discovery that atoms are just energy is hardly surprising since one of the fundamental ideas of metaphysics is that the manifested world (the world and universe of physical form) is in fact, nothing but *energy of different densities and qualities.*

The solidity of our world only holds together in a narrow band of perception. Its apparent solidity is merely the result of our human physiology—our eyes, ears, touch etc.—and of course, the way our brain functions. Outside of this band, our world is just patterns and qualities of energy. The solidity we humans perceive is the illusion that holds us prisoner but also enables us to make "sense" of the buzzing, sparking shifting energy that is our universe—the creation in which we "live and move and have our being". We'll come back again and again in different ways to this tricky business of the nature of reality and between the stories of deva we'll gradually build a framework that helps us to understand it. The anecdotes will give you a sense of how we can consciously experience the deva realm.

On Landing

When I returned to a mortal human life again, this time in a personality to be named by my parents "Jacquelyn", I already knew this planet was very beautiful. That didn't stop me being afraid as I stood upon the departure disk for I knew there were many challenges to face in this world. The bright colours of spirit dimmed to a dull grey as an opaque, swirling fog surrounded my little island. I felt as if I were in a tiny field of long grass that swooshed and swayed with the force of a violent wind. Only later did I realize it was the swishing sound of amniotic fluid that added a note of terror before the descent into denser matter.

It wasn't as if I hadn't been here before. I had, quite a few times in fact and I knew there were compensations. The abundant plant life of the vegetable kingdom clothes our planetary Being in a love blanket of rich greens—beautiful, nurturing and constantly giving. This greening began in the oceans before spreading to the rocky land where water, pressure, shifting and grinding had created small particles. Amongst these particles new plant forms could take root and over time create a rich soil through their decomposition. Soil gave the plant kingdom more opportunities to grow and change, setting the cycles of growth, decay and rebirth. What was originally barren land, gave rise to countless new forms of life. After millions of orbits around the sun, building and building, the great deva of nature grew huge forests to cover the lands with their splendour—nurseries of life of a scope and complexity beyond our human imagination.

I love forests but I love the deserts too, even where there is seldom green of any hue. The desert deva are large and powerful. Their processes are subtle and their effects majestic. Their vast space gives quietude to the mind if one has the chance to be alone with them. It mirrors a little the glorious stillness of the space between the stars.

Earth is evolving, necessitating constant change. We say that water symbolizes emotions. Does that mean when the planet has mastered its own planetary equivalent of emotions, that the seas will dry and the colour of Earth will shift from watery blue when seen from space to the colour of mind? What *is* the colour of mind? Perhaps it's like polluted air; dim and filled with particles of illusion until it too has evolved to resolution and clarity to become a clear bright diamond, folded by the pressures of its own mastery into a thing of sharp beauty.

Mineral, vegetable, animal—how large must the thoughts of a planet be to create such magnificent lives as these! And how high and tuned to love those thoughts must be to make such beauty as the forests and the seas. But how do these thoughts of a planetary Being get turned into the things I see, that we all see, touch or feel when we stand and gaze upon this Earth?

Learning to Drive Our Vehicle

It takes a while, in an unfamiliar body, to master its sensory equipment. It doesn't help that those who are teaching us to take care of this new body don't have knowledge of all the sensors our human bodies contain. It's like buying a computer that no-one shows us how to use so we try different things, lose a few files now and then, pick up tips here and there, eventually becoming familiar enough with its capability to do some essential stuff. Yet it's only a small fraction of what the computer is capable of but we don't have the time or the patience or let's be truthful, the inclination, to discover the rest.

So, like an underutilized computer, only a few of our body's sensors get used—eyes, ears, nose, taste buds, muscles, skin—the usual ones that are obvious to everybody. But what if someone taught us, when we were very young, that we have so many more sensors than these? What if we knew that our ears have a subtler counterpart, as do our eyes; that there is a field of subtle stimuli around us that is picked up by a subtle body, of which our physical body is just an out-picturing?

That's the challenge when landing on this planet Earth—how to get the most from this physical instrument. Not to get it to run faster or jump higher but go ahead and do those things if that's your want. I'm talking about using our own subtle body to sense the subtle field of all that makes life on this planet special, beautiful and rare, so rare. Have the great big telescopes trained upon the stars found another planet in the galaxy such as this? No (not yet), so the Earth *is* rare and if you want to know how it gets to be this way, stick around.

Growing Up with the Inner Eye Open

I had a friend called Carron. She had long brown hair and eyes so large and round that when they moved, lots of white showed below the iris. Her hands were neatly formed as if they'd come from a Renaissance

19

painting. Always expressive, she waved those beautiful hands through the air as she talked.

Carron grew up in a family that knew about faerie. Nobody said, "Don't be silly, faeries aren't real." They knew the nature spirits were there where nature is able to flourish and faeries are nature spirits.

When I began writing my eco novel, *The Children of Gaia*, it was Carron who offered to help. "Am I imagining things?" I asked myself. She took me for walks around the lagoon. We watched the water and she asked me what I saw. When I discovered a soil gnome beneath a big flax bush, feeding energy to the roots and emitting its heat through the earth, she nodded and smiled her bright red lipstick smile and grew my own confidence in what I could sense and see.

A woman called Dora Van Gelda grew up in Indonesia in the earlier part of the 20th Century. Her parents were part of a group of esotericists that included the famous theosophist, C. W. Leadbeater. Born with clairvoyant abilities, it was many years before Dora discovered (to her surprise) that not everybody saw the nature spirits. It is significant that Dora's abilities were accepted and reinforced by her parents and their peers. There are many who begin life being clairvoyant but who lose their abilities when those gifts are not acknowledged or encouraged, or are openly denied or derided. How often, we may wonder, is a child's clairvoyant experience dismissed as imagination?

It was my heart that drew me to the idea of faeries when I was very young. It is the trees that have always beckoned my heart to come and play. When I spied Paul Hawken's book, *The Magic of Findhorn*, I knew I had to read it. At first, I thought it was a novel but it was actually the true story of a community in Scotland that still exists. The three founders took their instructions from deva and created a garden that defied soil science in the quality and size of its produce.

These were just some of the tugs on my heart and finer senses that have led me to write this book. Over the years, I have met many people who have communication with the nature spirits or faerie as they are often known. These humans come from many walks of life but they have in common a deep appreciation and love of nature, two attributes that help us pass through the gateways to the deva kingdom.

The Scope of This Book

I intend to go beyond nature to include the dance between deva and ourselves, a dance that gifts us the experience of being human here on Earth. We'll look at the challenges deva present us with, along with how our intentions and inventions actually create new kinds of deva. Above everything else, the world of deva gifts us the indescribable sensation of being connected to *everything* through the medium of substance, everything from our favourite tree to that star twinkling in our night sky.

Where appropriate I shall let deva speak for themselves. I have set these passages from deva apart, indented from the main text, so you will know deva are the authors of that information and I, for better or worse, am simply the scribe.

How can we claim deva speak to us? And in our own language? Of course they are not using the words of our languages be it English, Japanese or Swahili. They communicate via a transmission or exchange of energy that our brains, mental and emotional bodies translate into words or feelings. One of my university lecturers quoted research claiming that even human to human, our communication is around eighty-five per cent non-verbal. We don't just pick up visual clues from each other but emotional and other subtle signals. Rightly interpreted or not, we *feel* attitudes, judgements and emotions emanating from another person. Behind smiles and politeness, we can sense disdain or irritation.

These emotional and mental states flow out of us as surely as words do but they flow from finer layers or "bodies" than our flesh and bone physical body. These finer layers are made of substance too but substance of less density and different qualities of energy than our physical body. It's these less dense bodies or layers that enable us to connect to similar layers in the world around us. Our less dense or "subtle" bodies are connected with each other and with our physical body via spiralling vortices traditionally called "chakras". In their book, *Superlearning*, Sheila Ostrander and Lynn Schroeder tell how blind people have even been taught to use the chakra between the eyebrows to "see" the placement of furniture in a room. It is via our subtle, less dense bodies and their chakras that we communicate with deva. How deva-human communication works should become clearer as we journey together and put this whole subject into a wider context.

This book is certainly not intended as a complete text on deva, even if it were possible to write such a book at this time in our evolution. Many great writers go before me who can tell you just what this faerie, nature spirit, landscape angel or greater deva look like and what their hierarchies are. You'll find reference to some of these works throughout the book and listed at the back.

My aim is to present a framework that will help us to understand the bigger picture of deva and how this kingdom is so intertwined with our lives at all levels, not just in nature. In no way is this framework intended to be a religion, a cult or a fixed, unbendable perception. Rather it is intended as a helpful philosophical perspective designed to integrate and expand our understanding of deva rather than see it as an isolated folklore tradition that does not fit with our current worldview. I see *science* and *spirituality* as being necessary partners in our understanding of both the natural world and us. I do not see how we can solve our multitude of problems without such integration.

Above all, this is a personal journey. It may or may not resonate with your own encounters with the deva kingdom. Either way, I hope that in my sharing, you will be both entertained and to whatever degree, informed. When we're done, you can go find the faeries at the bottom of your garden, your asphalt or your concrete. If it's the latter, maybe encourage your fellow citizens by writing your own story "My encounters with apartment deva" or "Life with the city gnomes". No, I'm not being facetious, I'm perfectly serious, it's my nature, you see.

Talking of which, the nature spirits are drumming on the desk now, waiting for me to leave these ponderous word elementals and join them. I'll see you again in Chapter One.

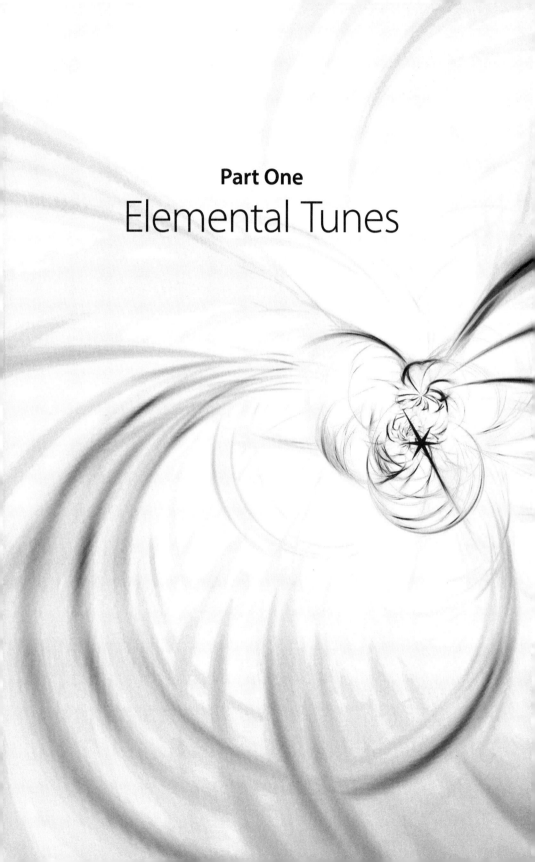

Part One
Elemental Tunes

Chapter One
Density

Sensing Faerie

Many children, especially girls, love the thought of faeries. Perhaps that's because they are depicted wearing very pretty but distinctly human dresses, fluttering, gossamer wings, have long hair and slender bodies. Often children will go looking for faeries, enchanted by the idea of them as if a distant knowing has tapped upon their minds and said, "Remember us?" They may look for them, as I did, in the grass but saw only flickers of light instead of gossamer-soft dresses and wings. Our human brain wants to make sense of what it "sees" and so it will turn the flickering, fast light of faerie into a tiny humanoid figure with a pretty dress and wings. After all, how could a faerie creature move so fast if it didn't have wings?

Science tells us that matter is not actually solid at all. The parts of an atom are no more solid than the flicker of light in a distant electrical storm. Matter, they say, is just energy, a fizzing spark of light. Sounds a lot like that slithery light of a faerie to me . . .

Faeries, the wise tell us, are part of an order of being called "deva". The deva kingdom is everywhere, say the ancients—an *Intelligence infused into matter at every level of density.*

What Does "Level of Density" Mean?

Isn't liquid less dense than rock and gas less dense than liquid? What of light and the wavelengths of light that we cannot see or the sounds that only certain animals or specially designed machines can "hear"? Some lights and sounds can be registered by our "normal" senses and some can only be inferred from collective experience or understood through reaction of instruments or machines. Such things are even "less dense" than gas.

Metaphysicians say we have many senses and that some are subtler than our physical ears and eyes. There is life, movement and consciousness beyond the three dimensions of our space-time model of the world. This way of understanding the world says there are many levels of density.

It's deep into this less dense world we are going, deep into the heart of matter and no, faeries do not wear human dresses nor butterfly wings though the flowing light of their movement may seem like flight and suggest these things. But what we call faeries *do* exist and I'll show you they are only a tiny part of a kingdom so vast, so joyful and so close you use it with every step you take and every thought you have. It infuses the air you breathe and the body you inhabit all day and take to bed each night. It's called deva and it's a kingdom of natural joy and light.

From Simplicity to Complexity

No scientist has actually seen an atom with their eyes (because atoms are way too small) but they believe they have proved these tiny sparks of energy exist, so let's begin right there. Deva is intelligence, so the devic life within an atom is a very tiny intelligence indeed. We could fill this entire chapter with a discussion on what intelligence is, probably a whole book. No doubt, someone has already done that. Instead, we will let intelligence define itself, not by limitation, for a definition by its very nature must limit the concept under scrutiny to one thing and exclude it from being another. We will liberate intelligence from the constraints of old thinking and look instead at its dynamic, moving nature that is directly related to that topic so central to today's thinking—energy. For now, we'll just say that intelligence knows stuff—what and how. The atom knows how to be an atom of whatever kind it is.

"An atom is so small, what use is that?" we may protest but if an atom joins up with other atoms, it makes a molecule and collectively a molecule knows how to do much more than a single atom alone. Now here's a mystery; if two atoms of hydrogen (a gas), team up with just one atom of oxygen (another gas), it becomes water, which is not a gas at all!

A team of three can do wondrous things and water is a most magical team of three. It can freeze into a solid crystal of ice, melt into a liquid drop to quench a thirsty plant or make an ocean. Or it can become so light it floats upon the air to obscure the sun or sail across the sky as part of a fluffy cloud on a bright blue day. These three invisible atoms, when they get together can do these wondrous things, increasing the complexity of the intelligence they hold by far more than just 3 x 1. For a start, by combining, they can become visible to our eyes as an "object" in the world.

Everything on Earth is built this way, through cooperation and unity. Molecules dance together to create a new song—a single cell— then cells join together to make a more complex song—a microbe, a plant or a tiny animal. Each joining creates something more complex, more powerful, more *intelligent* than the simpler parts of which it is made. A plant knows how to be a plant and the body of a beetle knows how to live and move and be a beetle. Everything on Earth is a buzzing, orbiting, sparking collection of intelligence that knows how to be what it is and how to do what it does. We call this mystery "life" and the intelligence within that knows *how* to be—a drop of water, a beetle, a leaf or a mighty ocean—*is deva*.

Everything on Earth is organized like this into hierarchies of complexity. The human kingdom is not immune. Put a group of humans together and someone will emerge as leader. They'll allocate each other jobs to do, form a committee, then an organization, then a bureaucracy, a government, and a nation. It's the same throughout our Universe—little things combine to make bigger things that can do more, be more, experience more. So, life is organized from the bottom up, right? Well looked at this way, yes but things are never quite what they seem . . .

Why a Kingdom?

Deva is a kingdom, just like humanity is a kingdom. Why do we call them kingdoms? Because they are hierarchical—they have each evolved from the simple to the complex, from the "lower" form to the "higher". This is true for all of them—mineral, vegetable, animal, human and deva. Or is it?

It's true for the physical *bodies* that express each of those kingdoms in this world—rocks, plants, animals and humans. Physical *evolution* goes from the simple to the complex. Higher up, in the less dense planes of our world, the same thing happens. Our feelings evolve into emotions and the birth of thought evolves into complex mental processes that produce a plethora of thoughts. But where does the idea for these physical, emotional and mental forms and their function come from? Where does the idea for a cell come from or the idea for a bee or a human being? Where do they *originate*? Deva hold many of the secrets to understanding how things come to be here, how life is top-down *before* it is bottom-up, but for now, we need to stay with the bottom-up, simplicity to complexity view before we dive into these heady questions of origin.

The Elementals

From rock to human and beyond, for each level of being, there's a level of deva. Why? Because deva are infused into matter at every level of density. We've talked about the basic, most simple intelligence within the atom and how, when these basic building blocks of physical life join together in greater and greater combinations, they create more and more complex forms. At the lower levels, we generally refer to the devic intelligence within these forms as "elementals". "Elemental" could refer to the scientific table of elements but let's use a more symbolic way of suggesting different qualities. If we take the elements that we talk of in popular culture—earth, air, fire, water, for instance—these elements are said to be infused with their own characteristic elemental intelligence of the deva kingdom.

As more and more complex forms evolve, a devic intelligence emerges that is overseeing the overall function of that form, for example a plant. Now we start seeing what we generally refer to as "Nature Spirits", though they still retain an elemental nature. The following passage given to me by deva for a chapter in *This World of Echoes* sums it up:

They appear to you as light, ethereal beings, yet this belies the activity of them. That they are called elementals is no accident and you would learn much of the importance of these creatures if you would ponder this other name. Nature Spirits are elemental.

The elements are their vehicle and their parentage for it is through the elements that the deva work, just as it is through your body you work on Earth. There are those that are a direct product of the energies of nature you call the elements and these exist as raw expressions of the air, the fire, water etc., whatever in their raw form these phenomena are. But as each element has gathered, combined and functioned in more complicated form, as flowers, plants, trees, there you will find that sophisticated collaboration between the elements expressed as a sophisticated creature, uniquely combining the elements of its being as the plant has done. The two are inseparable just as your manifestation is a product of what you are.

They are driven not by individual but by collective will and only in the highest forms, like trees, will something like an individual will be found. *(WE I)*

There are quotes from *This World of Echoes* throughout this book. From here on, you'll see them identified with the letters *(WE)* at the end of the quote followed by the volume number I, II or III.

What Do Nature Spirits Do?

Faerie in all its categories and varieties is an energy of Life. Faeries and other nature spirits exist, as your emotions do, in finer layers of the physical strata of the world. These strata or planes are finer than air but knowable to senses designed for a level that is less dense.

What do faeries do, you may ask?

Just as your emotions impact upon your body, via hormones, heartbeat rates and the production of chemicals that set off chain reactions, stimuli and responses in your body, so the presence of nature spirits affects the quality of life and functioning of plants. The tiny elemental lives inside every part of the plant are responding to the *vitalizing and coordinating energy or song* of the nature spirits. What we humans see as faerie is light, emitted by a being composed of fine substance that seems to us to be a body.

Nature spirits are aware of humans. For them there is no barrier but remember they are responsive, playful beings so it is supposed that when a human senses their presence, they use the fluidity of their bodies to mimic the human form. Maybe they do it to put us at ease but I suspect it's also to amuse themselves. Over different times and places they have appeared as mythological creatures, part human, part animal; whatever fits the psyche and expectations of the humans who see them and whatever (to us) expresses their nature.

Faeries gather in multitudes as hovering clusters of light. After all, that's what a deva is, *"a Being of Light"*.

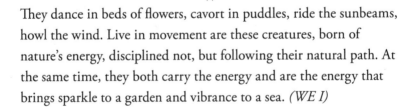

They dance in beds of flowers, cavort in puddles, ride the sunbeams, howl the wind. Live in movement are these creatures, born of nature's energy, disciplined not, but following their natural path. At the same time, they both carry the energy and are the energy that brings sparkle to a garden and vibrance to a sea. *(WE I)*

The key phrase here is that they "carry the energy and are the energy". Their vibrating energy is both their light and their song. They and their song are one. In a forest or a garden, nature spirits feed life into and through all that grows. They both *are* light and travel *on* light, lacing the plants within and without. Their light *sings*. Their work is subtle, like a master of music coaxing beautiful strains from her violin. It's a partnership that dances between the player and instrument, a subtle form of love that coaxes beauty seemingly from nowhere. The dance between the nature spirits and the plants is just that—loving and subtle.

Deva Hierarchy from the Bottom-Up

At some point on their evolutionary path, we start referring to certain nature spirits as being "transitional elementals". This fancy term just means they are gradually evolving into something even higher—overlighting deva. It is this higher level that people often think of or are referring to, when they use the term "deva" (particularly in Western cultures). This higher level is also known as "angelic". Here we find the deva that overlight larger systems like landscapes, rivers, etc. Higher still are deva that oversee the great systems of Earth—ecological systems, great landscapes like the deserts, large forests, oceans and so on.

So here's a simple schema to help us put this lower to higher deva hierarchy in perspective:

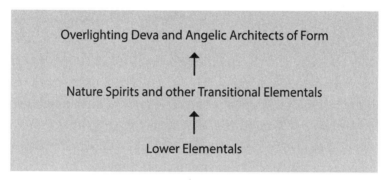

Figure 1 Deva from the Bottom-Up

At the angelic level, we also come to a range of deva that govern species, be they flowers, trees or whatever. They are known as the "architects of form". Here's how they describe themselves . . .

———————✶———————

We hold the thought of all created form, hold the patterns seen
by you as flower, bird or tree. For matter is intelligent, and we the
children born of that infusion of solidity with mind. And in this
great spawning of our lives, over aeons of years this Earth came alive
and we have retreated not. We, both children and creators of the
Earth, exist as you do in solid "natural" form and in mind aware,
singing our songs and playing Earth's tune. *(WE I)*

31

Originally, we explained how, as Life sets out on an evolutionary spiral, small things cooperate or collect to become groups to make more complex forms. That's the bottom-up view of the Universe. Now we have come to that other important idea we need to understand.

Humans talk variously of an overriding Creative force; the Great Spirit, God, Jehovah, Oneness, etc. These are ways of expressing the top-down view of the Universe, which is equally essential to our understanding of deva. It's the idea that there is a singular commanding Will or Entity from which all the *parts* that make up this universe flow. So, we can now follow the formation of life's forms from the *opposite* direction.

Deva Hierarchy from the Top-Down

If we think of the vibration of the Universe as sounding one grand note, a note that contains everything that the Universe *is*, we can use this idea to explore all the parts that make up the Universe.

Inside that seemingly constant Universal note are held the notes of all the planets, suns, comets, etc. The Ancient Greek philosopher, Plato, took up Pythagoras's earlier assertion that bodies in space like planets and suns, each sound their own note. Astrophysicists now confirm that from a scientific perspective, large bodies in space do indeed sound their own note in the sense that they each vibrate and that vibration or resonance can be "heard" as sound. In Metaphysics, sound can also be thought of as *the unique resonance of a particular state of Being*. So, here we are using the word "sound" in a broadly descriptive and symbolic way that may or may not be acceptable to the physical sciences. Metaphysically, we say that if we were to look inside one of these planetary notes, say the note of our Earth, we would find it is composed of many notes or tunes.

Let's explain what that can mean by a simple analogy. A rose bush has a particular quality to it—its own note. That note is made up of contributing notes—the stem, the leaves, thorns and if there is a flower blooming, it has a different note from all of these others. As a whole, the rose bush has its own note but within that note are the tunes that change as the plant grows, as parts of it form, bloom and die to make way for new growth. The song of the rose bush is constantly playing out as the seasons come and go. The plant sings out its life cycles from seed to maturity and eventual death of its form. The song of our rose bush comes from its species and that species has a note of its own, a note that *contains* the unfolding tunes of every potential rose bush that species produces.

We can understand then that our Universe is comprised of large notes within which there are tunes or songs. We can choose any level as our point of perception and what we hear or see will appear as a self-contained universe, system or unity. To a microbe in a droplet of water, that droplet may as well be the extent of the Universe. It contains all the songs of Life, as far as the microbe is concerned.

Who then, are the singers? By the time we get to the end of this journey with deva we'll have a better sense of how to answer that question. Let's start with how you, personally, set a song going.

Your House As a Song

Take your house as an analogy. Whether humble or grand, it began as an idea that became a design and a plan. Let's pretend you were the originator or entity that had the idea to build your house . . .

In our diagram overleaf (Fig 2), the substance (shown as a grey background) is less dense at the top where the idea or inspiration happens than at the bottom where the work with physical objects takes place. Our *ideas* exist in a finer layer of density than the physical objects we are using to build our house. What happens is a dance between our *use* of the different layers of density. It's a dance between the higher, less dense level of your idea and the lower, denser level of physical planning needed to turn it into form. Then, to make the design happen, to *manifest* it as the physical form of your house, you need to use the lowest level of all, lots of physical pieces—wood, brick, concrete, metal and so on. Each of these physical parts has their own unique composition, design and function in the whole.

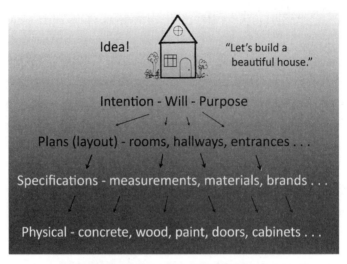

Figure 2 House Building Project

From your *idea* of how you want your house to be, to the parts needed to *build* your house, the flow is top-down, from a plane of substance that is less dense to one that is the densest we experience as human beings—the solid physical. But to actually *construct* your house the flow goes the other way—from the bottom up—because your builder now has to join all those physical pieces together to construct the components of your house and put all those components together according to your plan. Without the intelligence inherent in the design at every level, your house wouldn't come into existence and wouldn't function properly. The process is both top-down *and* bottom-up. Deva is like that too. Our original, simple schema now also looks like this:

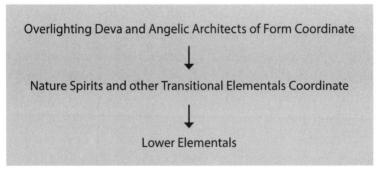

Figure 3 Deva from the Top-Down

Top-Down and Bottom-Up Simultaneously

We're talking now about deva as the architects of all forms like plants and trees so we need to present our levels of deva encompassing both the top-down and bottom-up directions because the higher deva coordinate the collective activities of the lower deva and elementals.

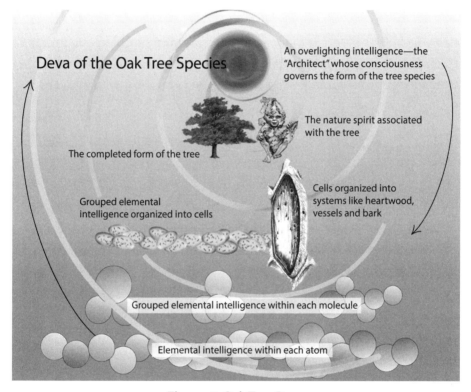

Deva of the Oak Tree Species

An overlighting intelligence—the "Architect" whose consciousness governs the form of the tree species

The nature spirit associated with the tree

The completed form of the tree

Cells organized into systems like heartwood, vessels and bark

Grouped elemental intelligence organized into cells

Grouped elemental intelligence within each molecule

Elemental intelligence within each atom

Figure 4 Oak Tree Deva

Maybe you are joining some dots here? Remember those pieces of timber you needed in the construction of your house? They have come from a tree, which is the *product* of a song of deva—that hierarchy of intelligence infused into matter *at all the levels of density* that it took to create the tree.

Obviously, such diagrams simplify what is actually a complex dance between the different kinds of intelligence infused into every level that's involved. However, diagrams are useful for that part of our brain that wants "order and sense". The deva hierarchies will become clearer as we proceed. Ultimately, we come to realize that our analysis of deva hierarchy is a function of our own experience of separateness and a distortion of what is actually one Being functioning as many.

Naming

There are many books that spell out different categories of deva and name all the different kinds of nature spirits from different cultural traditions, names like undines, pixies, brownies and so on. Taxonomy has never been of much interest to me and here's what deva said when I agonized over it . . .

————————✳————————

Human beings want to name everything and once a thing is named, it is boxed about by limitation by its being named! You do your understanding of nature spirits or all of deva for that matter, no favours by such naming and categorizing. The only use such naming serves is to communicate to other humans what it is you speak of, yet a common name does not ensure you are each relating a shared or common experience of the being you have named.

Your understanding is much better served by speaking in more general terms—what quality of energy does it have, how does it move, who or what was it interacting with?

The nature spirits that inhabit the hills and mountains are very different, are they not, to those that feed the flowers with light or skim the surface of a stream?

With that advice, to concentrate not on categories and names so much as differences in *qualities of energy,* we'll proceed. There is a good deal more to be said about how the deva kingdom functions, why we talk about levels of density and the relationship between humans and deva. How do such things come about? These are some serious questions, which could have our brains really working overtime so first, let's tell some stories. What better place to start than the mineral kingdom, with the earth element itself.

Chapter Two
The Earth Element

The Lemurian

First, I need to tell you how I wound up talking to mountains.

Sometime in the early 1990s, I was invited to an evening with a Kahuna Masseur from Hawaii named Leon Kalili. I knew nothing about this modality and had no idea what to expect but it sounded interesting so I took two young friends along.

Lemuria is said to be the first epoch of humanity's dense physical existence on Earth. It's the long, long time during which we developed, evolved and learned to master our physical human body. "Lemuria" also refers to a continent, now below the sea with only the highest peaks above sea level, namely Hawaii and the other Polynesian islands of the Pacific.

If I ever imagined what a later Lemurian looked like, Leon was it. Heavily, powerfully built, he looked as if he had emerged not from a human womb but from the depths of the earth itself. His hairless skin was the colour of dark, polished wood. His powerful neck, shoulders and arms suggested great strength and his face was as strong and chiselled as a stone carving. He exuded grounded confidence and his movements were fluid and graceful as one by one he picked out volunteers from around the room and performed his art.

After several people were chosen, to my surprise Leon picked me out of the group, though I had not volunteered. "Moi?" I pointed to myself. Leon nodded.

I am slightly built, merely a child's weight to this man's strength. He wrapped me, clothes and all in a sheet and then, moving me about rhythmically in this cloth cocoon, he began a chanting song as he cradled and rocked me about like a baby. Suddenly I was on the ocean, wind whistling about me, yet I was safe, carried on the waves by the Polynesian gods of wind (Tawhirimatea) and sea (Tangaroa). It was an extraordinary experience. As it concluded, Leon leaned closer and said quietly, "You've met the little ones, now it's time to meet the big ones."

I knew he was referring to the deva kingdom. I knew by "little ones" he meant the elementals and nature spirits but what did he mean by the big ones? I sometimes wondered about Leon's words but nothing seemed to fit his prediction and eventually I forgot about it, which probably opened the way for it to happen.

Australian Encounters

My Italian-Australian friend, Biannca, had urged me to meet Elizabeth who lived in northern New South Wales. When I arrived at her home after a train journey from Brisbane, this gentle, generous lady sat me outside on a sunny balcony to drink tea. Elizabeth didn't waste any time on the mundane "get to know you" chitchat. (After all, she was Australian and they usually get to the point straight away.) Beyond the house was a view across grassland to a large bush-clad hill, not what we New Zealanders would call a mountain but in Australia, it qualified to be called such.

"Why don't you meet the mountain?" Elizabeth suggested. Of course, she didn't mean I should get up and walk there. I'd not tried to meet with a mountain deva before but took confidence from her unquestioning assumption that I *could*.

So, I did what I did with trees; looked carefully at it, absorbing its appearance and feeling the quality of its energy. Then closing my eyes to eliminate distraction, I "travelled" along that connection I had made towards the mountain. I greeted it with utmost respect, of course, and asked permission to meet with it. Accepted, I ventured in. There I found what I have since discovered in other such meetings with large hills, that the deva/nature spirit makes its home in what looks to my brain like an ovoid chamber in the centre of the mountain's physical bulk. Of course, it is in the etheric and/or astral plane so digging into the centre of the physical mountain won't reveal it! (We'll talk about the etheric and astral planes later.)

While it might seem to have its cave-like dwelling place deep within the mountain or hill, the more advanced of these beings are certainly not confined there and will often be seen above or as larger than the physical structure of the mountain itself.

Similarly, my first hill deva was both centred at the heart of the hill but energetically through and outside it as well. It seemed to me that there was a lot of dark colour surrounding it but it had a deep ruby-red core. Though self-contained as hill and mountain deva are, it was warm and welcoming and respectful of this imp-sized human that was "knocking" at its front door.

How long I spent communing with the elemental of this large hill, I cannot say. Time disappears on such occasions and it could have been seconds, minutes or half an hour.

When I came back and opened my eyes, Elizabeth was smiling benignly at me. So began the fulfilment of the Kahuna's promise, "Now it's time to meet the big ones." Though I had sensed them before, now I quickly became far more aware of the larger landscape angels. Perhaps it was the big open scale of the Australian landscape that triggered it. Equally important, I think, was Elizabeth's confidence in my ability and the way she treated it as "normal" and no big deal at all. You just do it!

Under Hill and Over Mountain

Since then, I have had many encounters with the deva of both hills and mountains and found some qualitative differences between them.

It has seemed to me, that the beings at the heart of the hills are generally dark in colour and often appear inward-looking as if they are only interested in the earth of their hill and little else. Often, they are shaped somewhat like those wooden ornaments of a human figure so bent over and tucked up that it almost forms a ball. Their energy often feels somewhat heavy and I suspect, gave rise to the idea of trolls that live underground. They often seem unresponsive to human approaches, and usually seem to be in the cave-like space I mentioned above. Sometimes their central cave space is empty and I find them temporarily lumbering along the energy lines within their hill. Perhaps it is their evolutionary path to become more individualized into the great and unique beings that overlight the mountains.

These earthy creatures in the hills move little or rather their pace of movement is to a slower drumbeat from their quicker counterparts that tend beds of plants. Often slow to respond, such an earthy elemental seems a solitary being for its purpose is not to flit around pulling trails of light but to hold and anchor the collective form of rock or earth that we call a "hill".

I have often had a sense of numbers of other earth entities that work within the soil or rock of the hill, and their energy is much like the description of gnomes and brownies. Not being from Northern Europe, however, I don't tend to see these as little "men" in traditional costume as they are often portrayed in storybooks. They are nevertheless, entities with shape, colour and a distinctive quality of energy common to their kind.

All beings on planet Earth evolve, and even a solid seemingly solitary elemental of a hill will, over time and according to what pressures it from beneath, beside and around it, become something else. It is both a product and creator of the form it occupies, responsive to the forces that impact on all such kind.

By contrast, in my experience, most overlighting deva of large mountains have no such indifference to a human approach. In fact, they have generally been both welcoming and willing to communicate.

In New Zealand, one mountain deva struck me as particularly beautiful. It was tracing pale blue light in a shape similar to an infinity symbol above its snowy peaks and down into the mountain's interior. It was a rhythmical dance that went high into the air above the mountain. This weaving of energy in a spiralling, circulating shape is common amongst the nature spirits and higher deva and we'll come across it several times in this book.

I hesitate to call deva "masculine" or "feminine" as I think that's a human projection. Nevertheless, it is an energetic difference we often recognize between deva. I'll use those terms, "masculine" and "feminine" but don't take that as evidence that deva have anything akin to a human gender. The energy of the mountain deva that was artfully swirling blue light from the air into its mountain form was surprisingly feminine whereas the deva of another large New Zealand mountain had a very masculine presence.

Visiting a popular tourist spot in New Zealand's beautiful South Island, I was disturbed by the constant buzz of helicopters around a particularly famous peak. I felt an urge to apologize. To my surprise, I got an immediate, if somewhat aloof response. It described these noisy aircraft as "mere gnats". Their buzzing was of no consequence to "him". I realized I'd been anthropomorphizing, projecting my *own* discomfort with the incessant noise onto the mountain deva, assuming it would be just as annoying to him.

Another South Island mountain deva had a great sense of humour, both challenging and teasing at the same time. Its awareness was very broad, stretching far beyond its individual physical mountain to a sense of networked connections with much of the New Zealand land mass and beyond. Mountains have their roots deep in the Earth's crust so it's not surprising that they are so energetically connected to other such entities across the planet.

Ancient Lands

I love the landscape of Egypt's Sinai Desert east of the Suez Canal. It's so different to the youthful green forests and snowy mountains of New Zealand. The Sinai is old and spent, its mountains bare, rocky, brown and jagged. Their colours are enriched with swathes of coppery green or dark bands of iron. They seem bereft of soil or vegetation yet here too are small oases and enough plant life for some animals to survive, along with tribes of Bedouin. Occasionally there are trees visible from the road, usually festooned with plastic bags, testament to modernity and an endemic indifference to unsightly rubbish.

The mountains were old when the biblical Moses climbed Gabal Musa (aka Mount Sinai) and brought down the Ten Command-ments. Now it is mainly tourists that are coming down after their pilgrimage to the summit where stark mountain ranges stretch to the horizon. Beneath parts of the Sinai there are great centres where lines of energy cross to form powerful hubs. I can feel their throbbing from some distance away and no doubt others have had the good fortune to study these lines and hubs in depth.

On several occasions, I have travelled by bus through the southern Sinai region of Egypt. Every time I have been impressed by the strong group-consciousness that emanates from a particular stretch of the mountains. Individual mountains are discernible within the collective but the overall pulsation is a group one.

The beings of the great mountains of the world seem very different creatures from those enfolded within the lesser hills. The great rocky peaks that thrust toward the sky are governed by intelligence that knows itself as a mediator between the fires that broil in the furnacing centre of Earth and the air above that wraps the planet with a very different form of life. Form can fool us though, and both the fire and the air of Earth express different qualities of the same Life.

As solid as the mountains seem, each is receptive to the finer forces of water and air. Each elemental and deva on Earth is in a dance that continually shapes and changes the outer form they occupy or tend. The large consciousness that is a mountain deva cares not a bit for the loss of stone any more than we care for the dead flakes of skin we shed. These great deva are also joined in song with each other and with the elements of the greater landscape whose surfaces determine the paths of wind and the passages of water. Every inch (25.4mm) of them creates opportunity for other singers, for soil to form in crevices, for plants to find anchor and birds to nest. At their bases lay valleys open or sheltered for rivers to roar or meander, grasses to grow and animals to graze. Yet, these are merely superficial things when seen against the greater flow of shape and diversity of form. Mountains create weather patterns because they force passing clouds to condense and rains to fall. Their roots are strong against the continuous tumults of fire and movement at the Earth's restless core but sometimes, even they have to submit, rising up or sinking lower as the Earth's crust shrugs and shifts.

Anchored in time, the deva of mountains have long memories that go back to their forming when the tiny life within the atoms fused to make stone and stones fused to make rock and rock became mountain. All those millions of minute intelligence within the atoms were harnessed by overlighting deva just as the trillion cells of a human body are harnessed and empowered by a greater overseeing intelligence labelled "you".

Humans see land as solid and water as liquid and truly each form has a different quality. Yet if we could see it as deva do, it would all be a flowing of sound, light and colour. It's an orchestra of sound and light for at a higher level than the physicality we see, that's what all forms are. In this gigantic dance of light, sound and colour, the form is simply a consequence of movement as these forces sing with each other. It is the ignorance of this song that causes humankind to wreak so much destruction.

When we cut the top off a hill to build houses or starve the land of waterways to grow a certain kind of tree or graze a herd of animals, we cannot see the destruction of a long-created harmony, where the intelligence of water danced with that of stone, plain or mountainside to make life abundant.

Why should abundance matter? It is the abundance of deva life that gives rise to the millions of forms that cover the Earth. Without the natural push towards abundance and diversity, atoms would not make molecules or cells that lead eventually to the bodies of plants, animals and humans. It is abundance and diversity that supports us, feeds us and houses us. Our body can exist for a while without a limb or two but destroy too many parts of our body and our spirit cannot keep it alive. Why do we think the Earth any different?

The Old Ones

The last thing I expect when I get on a plane is to have a conversation with rocks. Yet, that's exactly what happened on a scenic flight in Kakadu National Park, Australia. A World Heritage park with its river system entirely within the park's borders, Kakadu is home to large crocodiles and countless birds. Groves of trees grow in lakes strewn with water flowers and in the wet season waterfalls cascade down the face of sheer cliffs.

On the port side of the small plane, I had a perfect view of ochre coloured rocks atop a mountain range. As we flew slowly past it was a few seconds before I registered a sensation of warm communication in my subtle field from my heart region and upwards, surrounding my upper body. Telepathic communication from deva is not in words but thought forms or light-based impressions whose meanings are clearer than words. When we try to tell of what we "hear" all we can do is translate those thought forms via the limitations of our human language.

So, there I was with my two companions, slowly flying past a formation of large rocks, well-weathered and shaped vaguely like coffins standing side by side on their ends, and they were "talking" to me! Not just a conversational buzz, mind you, but something like "It's so good to see you again."

"Again?" I thought, "Whatever can they mean? I've not been here before."

As always with deva I find I cannot convey all the communication in a simple human sentence. The thought-form is complex, containing an entire conversation in one energetic parcel. To recount the "conversation" with these majestic rocks a more poetic style of language, not the analytical, linear language of science is usually more appropriate.

I felt swept into them, embraced like a long-awaited brother who had been known since the beginning of time. They described themselves as the Old Ones, the original "people" of the land who stood fast through change and uncountable seasons. Just as we are not our bodies, emotions or thoughts but something more, they were not their rocky form. They were sentinels with a deep understanding of being, who "saw" and "felt" the coming and going of the quick lives around them. Though they did not move, in the sense that the animals or we do, they emanated their presence into the vast arena around them, deep inland and down into the wide valleys that flattened out to the sea. Just as the large old trees conduct the currents, the waves of life from deep in the ground to the sky above, the rocks of the mountains were doing the same but in a different way and with a different quality of connectedness.

Our Subtle Connectors

Our chakras or energy centres mediate between the outer world and our inner world, between our physical and etheric bodies. The etheric body holds the blueprint for our physical body and sits in the finer layers of substance directly above "gaseous". Together with the chakras, our etheric is the subtle body through which we interact and converse with the subtle bodies of every other thing that occupies the world beside us. The understanding that we have subtle bodies, not just a "solid" physical body is essential to our understanding of how we can sense and see the deva kingdom so we will come back to that topic again.

For me, the sensation of seeing deva is usually behind my head in the region of a chakra known as the alta major near the base of the skull (also known as the "psychic gate"). It's where the skull curves out over the neck. This sensation puzzled me for a long time until I figured that just as our eyes receive light rays that enter our pupil and hit the retina at the back of our eye, waves of etheric "light" enter my ajna centre in the forehead and are projected onto the alta major or psychic gate at the back of my head. This is why I "see" deva from behind my head even though *what* I am seeing may be in front of me. Often however, the general sensation is not so localized and the conversation or connection with deva may resound through the several subtle layers that surround my physical form.

Talking Rocks

Large (and very large) rocks continued to be a keynote of that journey around Australia's Top End. They would call out to me as I walked past, chatting away like old friends who haven't been together in a long while. I began to feel I was living some kind of fantasy movie and half expected the rocks to get up and follow me around.

The overwhelming tenor of their communications was joy, a warmth that has remained in my heart though it is two decades past. Maybe they are used to aboriginal people acknowledging them so they have become accustomed to a chat with passers-by. One even told me its name but I'm sorry to say I have long since forgotten it because it was rather long and the sound unfamiliar. I don't put a lot of store on turning deva "names" into word form because when given, they are a sound rather than a word and by turning it into a word it is both distorted and diminished.

Why should a large rock seem so much more "advanced" in its devic energy than many a hill? I consulted deva for the answer . . .

They (large rocks) were formed by the pressures of the Earth's forming, hardened by force and rain, heated and cooled in the long ages before there was green or life had legs. They are born of the grinding and tearing, uplifting and down falling. They are closer to the beginning than anything that followed.

Why would we not be more knowing than the soil? Were we not old already when plants first colonized the land and ice came to grind it fine? Before there were plants to rot or animals to decay, we were here.

As usual, I have left this communication as it came, despite the change from "They" to "We". It's not uncommon to experience the presence of a number of beings during such communications. Deva are generally excited by our attempts to communicate and delighted to enlighten us. And we don't think of rocks as alive! After all, they just sit there, don't they? Well on our time scale they don't move, but if we were to have a time-lapse movie of the life-span of these large rocks, from their formation to now and speeded it up to a human scale, we would be amazed at how far they have been moved and what changes they have seen.

Quantum physics claims that every atom is a buzzing parcel of energy. It is this inherent energy that keeps the electrons in orbit around their nuclei. Without the bonds of energy holding atoms, elements and molecules in place, the physical world would not have any coherence and would collapse. Viewed from the perspective of an atom, a large rock is a universe of aliveness!

While a small rock, chipped from a large one has only an elemental presence, as do the cells of our hair that is cut and falls to the salon floor, the large rock still has an energetic integrity and often, apparently, an identifiable devic presence. When I put my hands on the surface of a large rock, I get a similar feeling of life inside its solid substance as I do with a mature tree.

A Shared History

The Old Ones of the Earth can give us a sense of belonging as deep as the planet is old. The sentinel rocks atop the range in Kakadu gave out an accepting energy that wrapped me like a warm cloak in a beautiful mixture of friendship and belonging. Why should these ancient Earth creatures treat us as "brothers"?

Our bodies are made of the substance of the Earth and when we hear the call of the rocks or the mountains, we are tuning into some of the oldest parts of Earth's history. Science says that the genes of our human bodies contain a record of a long evolutionary history of earlier animal forms. Metaphysics goes further, saying that we descended or solidified gradually from spirit into matter taking on denser and denser forms until our consciousness found itself in the mineral kingdom—the kingdom of rock and crystal and elements like iron, copper, zinc, etc. The mineral kingdom was our experience of greatest density from which we have evolved through the kingdoms that slowly, successively followed it—vegetable, animal and human.

It is no wonder then that the rock deva wrap us in a comfortable reassurance that we do indeed belong here. Even if we are originally "Star Children" and did not begin our human journey on Earth, the rocks embrace us in the Oneness and stillness of being. The Old Ones don't judge us they just accept us. So perhaps it was simply the love my two companions and I felt for the rocks of Kakadu that elicited their response. Deva delight in our recognition of their being. They respond to our appreciation of their essence and the energy it brings to the forms they inhabit, whether those forms are rocks, trees, a bed of flowers or whatever.

Let the rocks have the last say before we leave them . . .

———————✳———————

We have endured while you have come and gone many times.
What we are you once were. You belong to us and we belong to you.
You are form and we are form,
I am Life. Know Me in all things for I am One.

The Quarry Creature

On friend Joe's farm in the North East of Scotland, there was a small quarry. From here, earth and gravel were quarried out for maintenance of the farm roads. Old farm machinery was dumped there, awaiting the occasional visit of the scrap metal merchant. Sometimes it was the burial place for rubbish too.

I was passing the quarry on my way back from a walk, minding my own business, when something attracted my attention. I stopped to look. There was a rippling in the far bank as if something was emerging from the clay and stones. I became aware of a very large creature slowly emerging. He just sat there, half in and half out of the ground, taking up most of the space of the quarry. His communication was halting and primitive. There was something rather naïve about him. Why, he wanted to know, were these hard things being dumped in his home? He gestured slowly and vaguely to an old farm vehicle and other metal detritus that was gradually sinking into the dirt.

"I can't eat them," he complained, "too hard!"

I wanted to giggle but I didn't. Instead I apologized and told him I would see what I could do about it. Joe quizzed me at length about the encounter and promised to speak to the Quarry Creature, as we dubbed him, and to get the scrap metal man in to remove the offending "hard" stuff the poor Quarry creature could not "eat".

I had another couple of brief conversations with the Quarry Creature that trip. He was pretty docile—a gentle giant' who just wanted to "eat" his dirt in peace.

A year later, Joe sold his farm, happily embracing a new and very different life elsewhere. I sometimes wonder how the quarry creature is now.

Walking the Lines

In Britain, "ley lines" is the name given to lines of energy that criss-cross the land. Their existence has long been known and where they cross, hubs of energy form so where many ley lines intersect powerful energy centres are created. Ley lines can be found all over the world. It is thought they are formed by the collective energy of human habitation acting upon receptive energetic pathways in the earth. Later we'll see how our emotions and thoughts have energy and substance and thus have an impact upon the world at large. Britain and Europe have been peopled for a long time so there has been considerable human energetic input into those lands and consequently their ley lines. Some say ley lines are not fixed but shift their position and according to Hamish Miller and Barry Brailsford (see *In Search of the Southern Serpent*), dowsing evidence suggests their radiating patterns change over time.

We are all constituted slightly differently with more or less predominant energy qualities and patterns akin to the symbolic elements. Joe, the former quarry owner, is an "earthy" type. There were two energy pathways running through his Scottish farmhouse. One of them went right through the kitchen, which led to some interesting meal times. Often Joe would stop eating and turn to greet a "walker" as he called them, a being travelling the ley lines. He said these creatures who walk the lines are compelled to do so and if the line is blocked in some way, the walkers cannot "create" for by walking they create. Presumably that means they are keeping the energy of the lines clear and healthy by virtue of their movement.

Not everyone copes as well with ley line energy as Joe did. They can trigger discomfort, even illness in people whose houses or properties are traversed by such energy pathways. I can attest from my experience that energy lines can attract large numbers of elemental and transitional beings. When blocked lines are cleared it can trigger a great and joyful release of such creatures and a wonderful lightening of the land.

Light Grids

Light grids, on the other hand, are apparently fixed structures. Here's what deva had to say of the grids . . .

Just as you use beams of wood or steel manoeuvred into place for building, so did we use beams of light to form the structures of the Earth. From these grids the business of living can be conducted upon and within the Earth. Our beams of light are like a channel down which energy runs. It is powered and maintained by the sun and the great minds that dwell therein.

There is a good deal to ponder in this statement. How light would be used as a skeleton for greater structures is a subject of study for another time and place. I have merely "dipped my toe in the soil" on the subject of energy lines, which are called by various names, so if you are interested, seek out works by those who have studied them in depth.

A Soil Gnome

In my illustrated novel about the ecology and deva of forests, *The Children of Gaia,* there is a character called "Solum". Solum appeared suddenly and unannounced into my night time meditation and named himself. He gave me a very clear picture of himself, which I quickly sketched on a piece of paper. I knew he was a soil gnome. I recognized his energy as being similar to that of the heat-generating creatures beneath the flax bushes around the lagoon discovered when I was out having my lessons with Carron, who we met in the Introduction under Growing up with the Inner Eye open.

Since he popped into my meditation in such an unmistakable way, I figured he felt he should have a part in the book I was writing. Over the next few months, I obliged and realized that he was in fact critical to the story's completeness. I then drew his portrait in coloured pencil and included it amongst the 178 illustrations in *The Children of Gaia*. My husband grumbled a bit about the name Solum, pointing out that it was too much like "Golum" from Tolkien's *The Lord of the Rings*. Since the soil gnome was very clear about his name, I ignored that objection.

Some months after Solum's inclusion in the story and his depiction as an illustration, I was out in the studio one night typing up a letter. My studio was across the lawn so when I hit a brain-blank over the spelling of a word I hesitated to troop back to the house to hunt out a dictionary. I remembered that a two-volume dictionary was part of a set of encyclopaedias my parents had recently passed on to us and they were currently right there in the studio. I picked up Volume Two to look for the word I couldn't remember how to spell. The book fell open at the "S" section and there at the top of the right-hand page was the word "Solum".

"What?" I thought it was a made-up word, a fancy of the creature who had presented himself to me for inclusion in the book. I looked down the column and there at the bottom was the description:

"Solum: Latin—substrata of the soil."

I ran inside and checked all the dictionaries I could find (we have a few). None of them contained this word, "Solum" even in relation to the word "soil". It was with a somewhat smug satisfaction I showed this dictionary definition of Solum to my husband. He just grinned and tolerantly shook his head.

More mobile and cheery than some of their counterparts in the middle of large hills, I have found that these soil gnomes usually emit a palpable heat. Perhaps their mobility and cheerful disposition (I haven't discovered a grumpy one so far) is due to their working with the soil beneath plants and trees, giving them a different focus from that of their hilly counterparts who are deeper underground and usually surrounded only by soil and rock.

The red blobs emitted by Solum in *The Children of Gaia* were brought to my attention by an artist friend of that time. I had neglected to include this energy dispersal method in the story so Solum came to her during a quiet moment, demonstrating the release of their "hot" energy in big blobs so that she would remind me to include it. I did.

Deserts

I love deserts. The relative lack of vegetation makes me more aware than usual of the great landscape deva. I love the beauty of the light on sand and rock and the deserts I have visited so far are all very different from each other.

In the northwest corner of Egypt is the "sea of sand" that meets the border with Libya and surrounds the large Siwa oasis where groves of olives and date palms thrive in the dry heat. The local Berber women, forbidden to converse with any male outside their family glide by, hidden beneath blue burkas, often accompanied by a young boy.

Much of Egypt's bottled water comes from the Siwa oasis but go inland away from the town and you will find yourself surrounded by a pale sea of soft sand. Then unexpectedly, your feet will crunch on something hard—seashells, great beds of sea shells—and you realise with a sense of wonder that you are standing on what was once the seabed, where fish swam above and generations of crustaceans lived and died on the sea floor. Here we are face to face with the great cycles of the Earth, of lands lifting and lowering, seas rising and retreating, ice, water, wind and fire, and shaking earth.

A couple of hours drive from Cairo there is another desert landscape where great rocks have been left stranded and wind-whipped until they look like space ships or gigantic abstract sculptures. Here there are whale skeletons sitting upon the sand. Yes, truly, there are *whale* skeletons on the desert and the beautiful fossilized remains of mangrove roots in the midst of the sand.

In southern Tunisia on the edge of the Sahara, the sand is pale and fine. It ripples like sand at the beach when the wind carves wobbly lines in a retreating tide. At sunset this desert sand glows softly with gentle pinks and greys. When the wind blows strong and relentless, eyes, ears and every crevice of clothing fill with its swirls of soft grit. There is plenty of life here on the edges of the great Sahara. Shrubs support local herds of goats and sheep and camels find enough vegetation on which to graze. There are beetles and scorpions and sufficient tourists to support an industry of desert trippers while those raised in the desert's vast embrace lament the loss of silence and solitude at the same time as they welcome the employment.

Provided you are not disturbed by the unwelcome and intrusive presence of a four-wheel drive vehicle, a desert can be a place of extraordinary peace. In the silence, it is easy to enjoy the absence of people and tune into the all-enveloping presence of nature. Without the distractions of human noise and interaction you can find a solitary sand hill and feel the life beneath you, in the air around you and in the cosmos of stars above.

As Above, So Below

From above, Australia's central desert is a vast blend of pale fawns, ochre and tints of sienna. Below the plane, an army of small puffy white clouds marched across a bright blue sky. When I looked at my photos, taken both from the air and on the ground, the patterns of nature were writ both large and small. The patterns and textures of the desert seen from the air were larger versions of the colours and patterns seen close up in the rocks below. Nowhere else have I seen the patterns visible from above so clearly repeated on the ground.

The curves and colour of river systems viewed from a plane are repeated in the patterns on rock, stone and land forms. Individual tufts of cloud marching across the desert sky are mimicked in the clumps of pale Spinifex grasses on the ground. The layered turquoise of the coastal seas is captured in opals from the mines. The circles, swirls, stripes and colours created over millions of years as the elementals have obeyed higher devic intent are stamped upon the land and its plants, the imprints of a song solidified. It's a physical demonstration of the metaphysical principle—as it is above, so it is below. It's the same song sung at different levels and in different densities of matter.

Alone with a Red Desert

About forty minutes drive from Uluru (Ayers Rock) in central Australia, is a desert very different from those of the Middle East. The voluptuous curves of a rock formation known as Kata Tjuta (The Olgas) rises from the reddened land. These formations are as feminine in their energy as Uluru is masculine, their forms sensually rounded and their rock darker and scaly looking. They have a peace and silence where nothing but the wind whispers or screams around their forms and through their valleys and trails.

When I visited, there had been an unusual amount of recent rain. Plants were surprisingly abundant and tiny flowers wobbled in the breeze. The unique silvery blue leaves of trees and bushes finds an unusual, contrasting harmony with the orange red of the land.

Left behind by my companions to take photos to my heart's content, I found myself alone with Kata Tjuta. Photography done, I stood still or walked alone, giving up my bodily boundaries to the land. Time disappeared into a seamless present where all the elemental lives danced the tune of their angelic architect. Its presence was felt everywhere—in the wind, the plants, the tiny purple and yellow flowers, the dark orange dirt beneath my shoes. The rocky body of Kata Tjuta held all these parts in a sculptural embrace and for many uncountable moments I knew all these parts simultaneously as both separate and unified. Above all the elemental lives, was the higher deva that held them all.

To be met by the intelligence of the land as "brother" is a wondrous experience, never to be forgotten. This integrated whole we call a "landscape" wrought by intelligent forces over millions of years has a complex song. For me it is deeply tantalising—on the edge of inner hearing and reverberating through my being, both at the same time.

To meet with deva at this level is to be woven into their song. It weaves us into the landscape because the world of deva is totally *integrated*. It's only through the science of ecology that the Western mind has begun to glimpse the intricacy of this integration. More and more it is being revealed; how plants communicate through chemical releases and trees through pheromones, fungi and root entanglements and so on. It's still only a piecemeal understanding but it's a start. I believe that we will not truly feel the impact of this knowledge of how complex and integrated nature truly is until (or unless) it hits us in our heart.

In this wander through the earth element, I have not talked about crystals. There are many fulsome and excellent books on these hard beauties of the mineral kingdom so I'll not add my limited experience of them to this writing.

The Need for a Framework

Several times now, I or deva, have mentioned the "song or songs" of deva. What does that mean? What is the song? Where is it?

Communication with deva gives us an opportunity to reframe our understanding of our Universe and how it works. At this time of transition, from one great solar period (Pisces) to the next (Aquarius) we need to reassess our thinking, to move from the limitations of old precepts be they cultural, religious or even scientific to something more appropriate to this time in our human development. We need frameworks that account for our experiences and help us solve the problems that our own mind-set and actions have created, both for ourselves and for the lives that share this planetary home with us.

Before we continue with our anecdotes, we need to develop our framework further. Of course, it's not entirely new but older known truths need updating now and then. They need to be understood in new ways, in language appropriate to *our* time. Maybe take a break first, get a glass of water or make a cup of tea. Give your brain a rest—you may need it.

Chapter Three
Sound

The Elephant Story

The framework of understanding I present may be familiar enough to feel comfortable. Or, it may not fit with your current understanding or accepted beliefs. Always, when we want to adopt or reject a view of "reality" we need to bear in mind the story of the five blind men and the elephant. One has hold of the ear so he says, "This animal is thin, large, flat and flexible and moves about a lot." The second blind man has hold of the tail and says, "You're right about it being thin and moving about a lot but it's not flat, it's tubular."

The third blind man, who has hold of one of the elephant's legs, snorts and says, "I've never heard such nonsense! This creature is very strong and cylindrical with several smooth plate-like areas near the ground. It's outside is wrinkled and not in the least bit smooth," and so on. You get the point, I'm sure.

Any view of reality, whether it comes from science, metaphysics, religion, legend or wherever, is like the descriptions in this elephant story. They are all right and they are all incomplete. When the subject we are studying is complex and outside our "normal" experience, this problem is almost inevitable. We are trying to break down something that is both whole and intricate and our vocabulary is woefully inadequate to explain it accurately. What is really important is whether the framework we are using to understand "reality" is relevant to our time and useful to us. Until we can expand our language or become proficient at telepathy, we are stuck with these inadequacies.

In the Beginning

"Sound", as we have discovered, is a word that has different meanings. In everyday use, it means something that we hear with our ears. In fact, the sound that we humans "hear" is actually just *pressure* playing variously on the receptors within and behind our ears. It is our *brain* that converts those variations of pressure into the *sensation* we call sound.

"Sound" also refers to a wave form. Everything in our Universe vibrates, sending out its own wave, big or small with its own signature or individual pattern, so everything in the Universe "sings" with its own note.

"Sound" as a metaphysical concept, is the creative force in our major Creation stories. In the Christian tradition, St John Chapter 1 states, "In the beginning was the Word, and the Word was with God and the Word was God." Here we can understand "word" as "sound" or "note".

Our Creation stories also describe the process of the world forming through *sound* acting upon a void. In the Judaic tradition, the book of Genesis describes it thus: "And the earth was without form, and void; and darkness was upon the face of the deep." A later verse says that God commanded there be Light, and that God *divided* the light from the darkness.

Both sound and the void also feature in JRR Tolkien's wonderful description of the process of Creation in *The Silmarillion*. He describes how the Earth was sung into being by the Ainur—angelic singers who were shown a vision of what was to be created by the supreme Being, Illuvatar (the Elfin equivalent of God). The Ainur poured all the effort of their being into realising Illuvatar's vision. Tolkien's angelic singers aptly describe the great planetary deva, the angelic "architects of form".

So how can we understand the role of sound and the void more fully? Think of the void as the still darkness of potential. Sound is the force that penetrates the "void", the "field" or the "darkness of the deep". The void seems to be empty but in fact is full of every possibility. So, when sound (the "Word of God") penetrates the void, the "worlds" manifest. What is *formed* emerges from the void of potential, carved out by its matching sound.

Or we can put it this way: the pattern/quality/frequency of the sound wave determines the nature of the form that manifests from the void. The sound acts like the program in a 3-D printer. It determines the shape of what comes out of the printer.

The Creative Source

Tolkien's Creation myth is very close to what we need for understanding the part deva play in the Universe and in particular, the world we claim to be *reality*. With Genesis, Tolkien's myth, Ageless Wisdom philosophy and *This World of Echoes I, II & III*, we can come up with a very useful framework of understanding . . .

There is One originating source for all that *is*. That Oneness (call it God, the Great Spirit, whatever you like) wanted to know all that it *is* and all that it is capable of *being* and *doing*. So, it looked inside itself and in doing so issued a great sound that was so powerful it seemed to rent the Oneness asunder (aka the Big Bang or perhaps a Gentle Outflowing as power doesn't have to go "bang", does it?). The sound seemed to split that Oneness into two; one "half" is its Purpose (or Will) to know Itself fully and the other "half" being that which it is exploring or getting to know. We shall call the half of itself that it is getting to know, the Substance of its own Being.

That great sound of Creation is the Oneness exploring itself, discovering all the songs, all the tunes that its one Sound contains. Before the sound was released, there was just the still darkness or void of unmanifested Being. As the great sound came forth, it *released* what was contained within that stillness of Being—a great and supremely powerful Light. That Light is the means or tool to explore all those possibilities the Oneness contains. Remember that deva means "Being of Light". We can say that deva are shining the light on what substance contains, revealing the possibilities of Creation that lie in the Oneness of Being.

So, we have two apparent halves—a Will, Purpose or Intention that wants to explore its possibilities and that which it is exploring— Substance or "Matter".

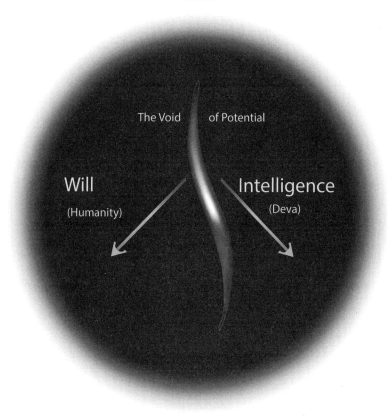

Figure 5 The Apparent Split of the Original Oneness,
Releasing the Light Contained in the Darkness of the Void
(aka The Big Bang)

Infused into Substance is the responsive intelligence that knows *how* to explore that previously unexplored potential. We call that intelligence *deva* (or the Angelic kingdom). Purpose or Will knows *what* it wants to do, deva (Intelligence) knows *how* to do it. You will notice that humanity comes under Will but we are not the only beings on that side of the split.

So, deva is responding to the *command* of Intention or Will, *unfolding the songs that are contained within that One original sound.* The songs are vibrations that penetrate the void of potential substance, exploring it, carving out all those possibilities of what the One Sound contains and, in this process, Light is produced and what was just a possibility is *seen* as a reality.

What's Happening in the Void?

Sound draws the shape of a thing out of the void. *(WE 3)*

It's helpful to think of the void as the "clay of Creation" and sound as the tool that carves out a shape from the clay that matches the intention of whichever Will sent the sound forth. I find it helpful to think of deva as being in the clay (substance) responding to the sound by creating (manifesting) a matching song or "shape" out of the clay. The song may be something we describe as physical, or something less dense, like emotion or thought. (Remember labels like these are metaphors to help us understand processes that seem mysterious, not just because they are so subtle but because we are so much a part of them that we cannot separate ourselves from them.)

But how is half of the One—Will or Intention, that set out to explore its own possibilities—going to find out what's being discovered if the two halves of itself have apparently separated? (As we showed in Fig 5.)

Will or Intention is in a constant dance with deva, that responsive intelligence infused into substance. The song of manifestation is created by their mutual activity; it's the ultimate feedback system happening simultaneously all the time. Will or Purpose sends out the request and deva responds with appropriate intelligence. In that instant of response, the two halves reunite but now they are *conscious* of what that possibility is like because it has been manifested— brought into Light. Thus, a new sound or tune is created and sung.

Consciousness is the *binding* that happens when the Intention (Will) and the result (devic response) come back together. We can call this coming back together *Love* because it is the ultimate fulfilment (at this stage and level) of the original "split". Why? Because Love or Consciousness is the completion of the exploration. It reunites the sound and its light with the original still darkness from which they came forth. So that return to the point of Oneness, however momentary it may be, is a return *with* the knowledge and understanding the Oneness was seeking by apparently splitting in the first place.

Here's how we can represent that Creative interplay graphically . . .

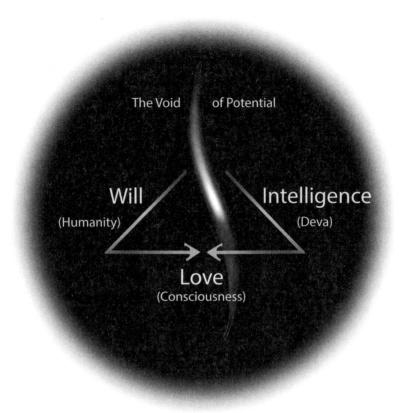

Figure 6 The Creative Trinity as It Applies to Humanity and Deva:
The "Re-joining" of the Apparently Separated Parts of Oneness

That dark disk represents the original, unexplored Oneness of Being. (You can call it "God", the "Originating Source" or whatever you like. It's the *concept* we are trying to understand here not the label we give it.) We are calling it the Void of Potential. That curved slither of Light in the middle represents what is revealed or released by the Sound that is driving this self-exploration. In its effort to discover all its potential that Oneness appears to split into two—the Will to explore and the Intelligence that is actively responding within the substance that is being explored. But those two, Will and Intelligence are still part of the original Oneness so they are constantly drawn back together and the result is Love, which we can also call Consciousness.

Have your eyes glazed over yet? If so, get another drink, maybe coffee this time if you're into stronger stuff. Moving helps, do some yoga poses or dance. In her book, *The Creative Habit,* choreographer Twyla Tharp says moving in unusual ways wakes up the creative side of our brain so try that too . . .

Human Sound and Deva Response

The deva find it very strange that we make such a hard job of understanding how things actually *are.* So, for now let's entertain ourselves with something easier and more entertaining.

Deva both emit sound and respond to sound. On one of my visits to Sydney, Australia, it was the Christmas season. Sydney is usually pretty warm in December, it being the Southern Hemisphere summer. Nevertheless, the cultural traditions from Britain and Europe persist with fake fur trees, tinsel and decorations of angels, snowmen and gnomes rugged up for the snow whilst shoppers are looking for that special summer gift for Christmas day and visitors from the other hemisphere complain that it doesn't *feel* like Christmas.

On one such warm day, I was in the Queen Victoria Building. Originally a market place, this beautifully restored edifice in downtown Sydney is now home to stylish shops and eateries. The two uppermost levels are both mezzanines that curve gracefully around an open central space that goes from the ground floor to an impressive Victorian dome in the roof. Beneath the dome stood a huge Christmas tree. It was bedecked with small white angels with smiling faces, pretty and child-like. They flapped their white wings, rising and lowering on hidden tracks. Human mimes and other costumed performers circulated through the building entertaining shoppers and tourists. At one end of the ground floor, in a large tiled space, the Sydney Graduate choir was singing Christmas carols. I sat down on a bench to rest my shop-weary feet and listen.

The singing was beautifully clear, layered and joyful, filling the large space above the singers. I became aware that there, above the choir something extraordinary and wonderful was happening. A great shaft of light, the circumference of the choir, was pouring both upwards and downwards in an exchange *of the light of the sound.* It was full of brilliant elemental lives, moving as birds do, in a swirling, spiralling mass. Sound and light are in fact two sides of the same thing. It is possible to hear the sound of light and to see the light of sound. Above the choir, I could sense a host of devic singers rejoicing, enhancing the human singing, both feeding it and receiving it. At the time, it was almost too powerful an experience for me.

Later I walked through the botanical gardens. Resting on the grass beside the wild flower meadow in the warmth of the sun, I could see in the etheric layers the effect of this beautiful singing upon the city as deva circulated it from the higher to the lower levels and back in an exquisite pranic dance.

If you can find a copy, there is some wonderful material in an old classic by Roland Hunt on deva, sound, colour and perfume, delightfully titled, *Fragrant and Radiant Healing Symphony.*

Words, Words, Words

Our spoken language can be a problem because immediately our words are thought, read or uttered they can create a limitation in our minds. More than that, words, like everything in our experience, involve deva.

My Italian-Australian friend, Biannca, once shared with me a lecture she had given on the role of elementals in human speech. She said that the vowels of human speech (those a, e, i, o, u sounds) are infused with astral plane *water* elementals. The consonants (sounds that are *not* vowels, like b, c, d, f, g, j, etc.) are infused with mental plane *fire* elementals. It is said that water and fire elementals don't get along so well with each other. In some respects, they are inherently antagonistic so when they clash a lot of "steam" or "fog" is created.

Isn't that what happens both within us and between ourselves and others when our mental and emotional passions clash? It happens too when we have a great idea (mental substance) but our emotions (astral substance) reacts with fear or overenthusiasm, clouding the original clarity of the idea with confusion and doubt or overestimating the effects that will come from it. Thus, a lot of "steam" or "fog" is created around us or between us.

When we humans use speech, we are forcing these two very different elemental types to get along. Maybe that is why great literature or oratory can be so uplifting. It succeeds in getting these fire and water elementals to dance together in a wonderful harmony.

Biannca pointed out that languages like Italian (and I would add the Polynesian languages, for example, Maori, Hawaiian and Samoan) have an emphasis on the vowels. Hence, these languages are excellent vehicles for expressing the water-based emotions. No wonder so many dramatic, emotion-filled operas are sung in Italian, and Maori are known for their oratory and make great opera singers. Languages like German and Russian however, have a greater predominance of consonants. They are languages of fiery passion.

So, when we speak, we create a song between the water elementals (the vowel sounds) and the fire elementals (the consonants) and then we give that energy to others when we coax, cajole, harangue, greet, jeer, criticize or praise. When we speak, we are using elementals that affect our listeners' subtle bodies, their emotions and their minds. This is one of the reasons we are urged by spiritual teachers to guard our speech with great care. Of course, the quality of what emanates from us must pass through our own subtle bodies en route to its target so whatever we dish out not only comes back to us via karma but travels through and effects our own substance on the way to its destination.

Sound as Healing

Sound carries us emotionally, lifts our spirits or plunges us into dread and despair. How different are the effects of a beautiful song from the sound of grief-drenched sobbing? I once watched a silent movie clip showing a view from the bottom of a man's trousers to his shoes as he was walking through autumn leaves. Then they re-played the clip with accompanying joyful music. Finally, it was replayed to a scary piece of music. The difference in our perception of the scene, caused simply by the kind of music, was astonishing. Yet, scientifically, it was only a waveform of air pressure pushing against tiny rods in our ears. Our *perception* of it, however, is the result of millions of years of evolution and experience.

Ultrasound is used by orthodox medicine to produce scans or pictures of what is going on inside organs and inventive alternative practitioners have created devices that send healing sound through our bodies to correct imbalances. Sounds that delight one person can have another covering their ears in distaste or even pain.

Our voices are vehicles of intention and feeling, and reflect our internal state. Author Stewart Pearce is a renowned Master of Voice and describes himself as a Sound Healer and Angel Whisperer. Stewart has experienced sound and light as one since early childhood. This is called Synaesthesia, meaning a cross-over of the senses. Stewart says his awareness means that he "uses sound holographically, and through the ever-increasing beams of light, perceives the multi-dimensional world and beings of light, such as the Devas and Angels". Light, perceived in this way, also means that Stewart sees colour, which helps to identify certain behaviours or states of energy.

Stewart has channelled a group of twelve Angelic Beings he describes as "Cosmic Guardians" for over thirty years, so he is surrounded in this work by the palpable angelic presence of these higher deva. He describes our voices as "the prisms through which our soul pours", particularly when we express from our signature note—*the song of our soul.*

Stewart teaches how to use our voice to heal psycho-physical wounds, changing old ways of thinking and feeling through what he describes as "the alchemy of sound, moving mortal disharmony into divine transcendence of unhelpful patterns of our feeling and thinking habits".

When we examine our personal relationship with the Deva via our physical, emotional and mental bodies such therapeutic possibilities will make more sense. Deva emit and use sound. Deva also respond to sound but to use sound to command deva is a potentially dangerous practice as we will see later on.

A group of people meditating deeply together can create a light and that light has sound.

A flash of unspoken anger produces a vibration that the highly sensitive can feel and "hear".

Everything vibrates and where there is vibration there is sound. It is sound that calls "reality" out of the void of potential to become a form of one sort or another, of one density or another. Everything that is, was or will be in the manifested universe has its own sound and accompanying light. Sound and light are like two sides of a page—the page does not exist without both sides. At these lower levels of density, in which we conduct our personal lives, sound and light give off colour that can inform us about their inherent quality. Our Universe is a cacophony or a symphony (depending on our perception of it), all the time. There's a pun here, because it is only our perception of *time* that leads to our experiencing sound as sequential!

Earth Sound

We have been talking about sound in a way that science would probably say is symbolic, not real, that is, it doesn't describe what is happening in the "real world". Yet, we are in an era when the findings of science are creeping ever closer to what has been claimed by the wise in various systems of philosophy for many thousands of years. The claim that the planet Earth has its own sound has recently gained traction as more sophisticated means of recording such things have been invented and used. In an article by Avi Selk, Spahr Webb, a seismologist at Columbia University, is quoted as saying "The Earth is ringing like a bell all the time". Our planet, say the scientists, is indeed humming, vibrating, stretching and compressing. Whether we are aware of it or not, severe earthquakes shake us up even if we are halfway across the world from where the quake occurs. The 2011 quake that hit Japan, is described by Webb as having "kept the globe ringing for a month" after the initial movement. On the other side of the planet the earth went up and down like a mattress with a kid on it, albeit slowly, a whole measurable centimetre.

Irrespective of earthquakes, the scientists say that Earth is sending out a hum that is actually getting clearer all the time. This hum or "song" has different frequencies and amplitudes. It is thought that the movement of oceans may be a major contributor as great volumes of water slosh against the sea floor. Slowly, science is beginning to build up a picture of the Earth, not only as a solid spheroidal mass spinning around in its regular journey around the sun. More and more, it appears as James Lovelock describes it in his paradigm-changing book, "Gaia". Lovelock's thesis is that we need to realise that the Earth is an organism—responsive, self-preserving and evolving. With ecologists and biologists also beginning to uncover more and more of the intricacy of interdependent relationships between all life-forms on our planet, we are getting closer to a scientific acceptance of the intelligence inherent in that intricacy—still a long way from a recognition of deva as we understand and experience them but an encouraging direction perhaps.

Where the Sound Originates

In the next two sections we'll recap what we've been learning from our framework in this chapter on sound.

Some Will or Intention may sound the *note* of what it wants to do or create—but it is deva that unpack that note into the *tunes* of Creation that the note contains. This process is happening everywhere, all the time. For example, when you decide (an act of Will or Intention) to go to the bookshelf to pick out a book to read, you don't need to individually command every cell, muscle, bone, tendon, etc. to move appropriately so they can carry out your intention, do you? No, because over the vast years of human evolution, the elemental intelligence in every part of your body (deva) has been evolved to do that for you.

The human kingdom is a kingdom of initiating Will. Deva is a kingdom of active, responsive Substance. Without deva, we don't *experience* anything because it's the response of deva (even at the very "primitive" level) that gifts us an interaction with matter or substance.

On its own, Intention or Will is powerless. It can only achieve a tangible result because something *responds* to it. What responds is deva. Deva is a generic term that covers the entire "kingdom" and like all kingdoms, it is hierarchical. The higher up the hierarchy a deva is, the greater the power and the greater the number of lesser deva and elementals a single deva commands and coordinates.

At the level of Creation (with a capital "C") whatever sent out the sound—Universal Will, Cosmic Being, God, call that whoever, whatever you like—it knows what it *intends* and deva knows *how* to respond, how to make that intention happen. Deva responds, picking up that sound and carrying it through a Void of Potential Substance, (also known as Unmanifested or Darkness of the Deep) so that it *forms* at the appropriate level of density. "Appropriate" means that the form matches the quality and force of the sound (Will or Intention) that was sent forth in the first place.

Simultaneous Creation

In the context of deva, we can describe the void this way: In that darkness of the void, deva respond to the sound or note. Sound is the "voice" or force of Will, of Intention or Purpose, the force that knows *what* it wants. Deva is the intelligent response that knows *how* to use the quality of that intention, to carve out or assemble the appropriate, matching response from the potentiality that is the void.

We've described this process of Creation as a series of events but actually, that's just our brain's way of needing to put things in understandable linear terms. The process all happens simultaneously in a waveform of sound and light moving through the unmanifested substance "hidden" in the void. The "further" that sound penetrates into the void, the greater the density of what is manifested or turned into form.

We'll imagine the void as a dark, invisible mass of creative clay. Will or Intention makes a sound—a note, a vibration or frequency that expresses its intention. That sound contains all the information deva needs to turn that sound (intention) into a "form", something manifest or visible. Let's say Will has the idea of a pyramid and that idea of the pyramid can be expressed as a sound. Deva picks up the sound and uses it to shape/cut/form/assemble a pyramid out of the void of potential. We can see that what is formed or manifested will match the strength and quality, the power, of the idea and the Will behind it. This is an important notion because if we think about it this way, we can see why some people are more proficient than others at creating what they want.

This principle of how deva respond to intention isn't just about manifested physical things. It's the same process for feelings and thoughts, which we will discuss later on.

Life in the Spaces

Deva described themselves as . . .

Those who dwell within the Earth, not imprisoned in soil or
stone as you might think, but existing in vaporous planes of light,
transport across a space between the solid and the real. For real
is that which is and "solid" just a name for a special point of
view. *(WE 1)*

Life is in the spaces. The vast space between the atoms, whether it is in our bodies or the vast spaces between the stars. It is here in these spaces and their correspondences on the more subtle planes that unformed Life resides. We have called it the "void of potential", the darkness from which "the Creator called forth the Light".

We can become conscious of the void. We use it all the time unconsciously. It is the well we dip into from which we draw an innate knowledge of what is and can be. This "space" is filled with intelligence. It *is* deva. By being aware of our own spaces within our seeming solidity we can find a universe alive with being, formed or unformed.

Letting Ideas Float

Physicists talk about subatomic particles that disappear and then reappear. Where do they disappear to and come back from? Perhaps they go to that "place" we are calling "the void" or *the field* (see Lynne McTaggart's book of the same name.)

Ours is an inside-out world of duality. The void of unmanifested potential is the "inside" of the visible manifested "outside". In truth the void (Darkness) and what comes of it (Light) are like two sides of a piece of paper. *Darkness and Light contain each other.* In *This World of Echoes*, there's an interesting statement:

The duality of your worlds is but an imitation, a reflection of the simultaneous Darkness and Lightness of Me. Your minds cannot but for an instant glimpse them as one. *(WE 3)*

Such are the apparent paradoxes we need to grasp or just accept. Our spiritual journey is full of paradox challenges. We make it harder for ourselves if we try to force our intellect to comprehend through analysis, which is what the intellect does best. It's easier to let these ideas float *above* or *outside* our intellect so that we come to *sense* and eventually comprehend them. We'll return to such heady challenges throughout our journey so if you don't "get it" now, let it go. If you are still struggling with these concepts at the end of the book, you may well find that if you come back again months or even years later it will make sense. I've often had to do that myself with metaphysical concepts that are difficult to grasp and other people assure me it's the same for them. On the second (or third) reading, it's no longer so new and we're not trying hard but also, the seeds were sown on our first reading and they have a way of sprouting as we go about life.

That's enough of brain-stretching metaphysics for now. Let's float off with something lighter—air.

Chapter Four

Air

Stillness and Breath

We talk about something being "as light as air". The qualities of "lightness", "floating" and "drifting" come to mind but some of these are qualities we also associate with water. According to William Wray's lovely book on Leonardo da Vinci, the maestro said, "The air moves like a river and carries the clouds with it; just like running water carries all things that float upon it."

Air feels to us more *unbounded*, less controllable or confined than the elements of water and earth. Physical air is a gas so its level of manifestation is just above the liquids.

Down here on the physical plane, air gives spaces between the solidities of the physical world, space that allows something higher, something life-giving to get through to us. It provides a space for the warmth and light of the sun to pass and gifts us the knowledge that there is "space" of a different kind within us where a higher illumination can reach our minds and hearts.

Not only is the air element light in weight, it is through the air (in the form of Earth's atmosphere) that light reaches us from the sun during the day and from the stars and moon at night. The moon—being a dead body—has no light of its own. It simply reflects to us the light of the sun that is hidden from us at night because it is lighting up the opposite side of the planet to where we are.

This function of air as a light bringer holds true in metaphysics. Air is symbolic of the plane of Buddhi, the plane of formless light and pure undistorted, impersonal love and intuition. We generally think of intuition as an advanced version of instinct or some sort of paranormal insight. It is used here in the esoterically correct sense as a much higher state of *illumination* wherein we experience a non-judgemental true state of Universal Oneness. We cannot *reason* our way to this state of true intuition, rather it is the gift of a higher insight that occurs when we have "done our work" on our personality self and shifted our consciousness, even if momentarily, to that higher level of soul and eventually to Buddhi. To live constantly at these levels is our current goal as human beings.

Meantime, Buddhi is a plane rarely reached by the consciousness of Earth humans as it is *above* what is aptly called abstract mind, where it is said our soul resides for the duration of our incarnations on Earth (see Fig 9, page 118 for the position of soul or "causal body"). As Buddhi is a plane of formless light, here again the qualities of air and light are intimately connected. An airy quality is not just about lightness of weight but light in the sense of "illuminating".

A Wilful Storm Deva

I grew up in a city noted for its wind. There were days when my older brother and I had to hold onto the railing beside the footpath to keep ourselves from blowing away as we toiled up the hills to school. I am not usually afraid of the wind though one day in Sydney it almost blew me off my feet as I tried to navigate between high buildings. I know others who find the wind discomforting to say the least. Not all the elementals are delightful little lights buzzing around the flowerbeds and truly, storm deva are hard to ignore.

Climate Change is clearly upon us. Of course, we need to take responsibility for our own attitudes and actions that have wreaked havoc with the beautiful harmonies the Earth has created over millions of years. We also need to understand that while clearly a planet is not a human being it is a *sentient* being with its own evolutionary agenda and the deva are its servants.

This was forcibly brought home to me one calm, idyllic evening off the coast of southern Italy. Our daughter-in-law's washing was dry and hanging from the lifelines that encircled the deck of the boat. Dinner was long over and the five of us were relaxing in a beautiful twilight that shone pools of pale gold on a glassy sea.

Despite the seeming tranquillity, I was inexplicably disconcerted. The dinghy was sitting like a contented duck off the stern yet I wanted to urge the men to haul it on board. I wanted to urge my daughter-in-law to bring that washing in. I held my silence and went downstairs. Something felt very wrong. The sound of relaxed conversation filtered down from above. I stood by the chart table, puzzled that what I felt inside seemed to have no external cause.

Suddenly out of the silence came a great roar. It sounded like a large boat bearing down on us. The Coastguard? There was no reason to suppose they had any interest in us. A moment later, the roaring engulfed us and the yacht pitched forward until it was stopped by the anchor chain. Shouts from the deck strove to be heard above the noise as chain and boat strained against a great force. The hatch over the master cabin opened and clothes began falling onto the bed as our daughter-in-law frantically pushed her washing down. My husband, Rick, leapt down the companionway steps, turned on the instruments then leapt back up to the deck.

We were being pushed away from the steep cliffs behind us but were easily within drifting distance of a rocky island to our starboard side. The men strained and struggled to get the anchor up while the wind pushed forty-one feet (12.5 metres) of yacht against the anchor chain. Night had descended rapidly. Our son told me later that on the nearby cliff top stood a statue of Jesus, his outstretched, cross-like arms lit dramatically by frequent flashes of lightning. When the anchor was freed from its hold on the bottom and the motor in control of our movement, the men took us away from both mainland and island into open waters where they traced large circles as the night wore on.

They knew of a marina within easy reach but the entrance was a narrow canal-like structure lined with very large concrete cones piled on top of each other to create an effective barrier against the sea. Given the strength of the wind, there was no way we should attempt that narrow channel in the dark. I curled up on the couch in the centre of the boat and slept as best I could until around 4.00 am.

There was no let-up in the ferocity of the storm. I sat up, centred myself and reached out to the storm deva. Its focus was intense and its power awesome. I asked if it would ease off a bit. The response was firm and unequivocal. It and its elementals had work to do. It would carry on unabated regardless of our discomfort, which was irrelevant as far as the storm deva was concerned.

I changed tack. "Could you tell me when it will be safe for us to go into the marina?"

The answer from the storm deva was remarkably precise and firm. "Ten o'clock," it said.

Shocked by such precision I wondered, "Can deva tell the time?"

Our son and his wife were sleeping as best they could in their cabin. Rick and co-captain Frank, were in the cockpit, keeping us away from shore as the storm continued to rage. I went back to sleep. Not once during the storm did I even poke my nose up top nor did I mention either my foreboding or the conversation with the storm deva to any of the others. It felt wiser to stay out of the way and see what unfolded. The morning was still windy but less so and it was sunny, judging from the light flooding the saloon. Eventually Rick poked his head down the companionway.

"We're going into the Marina," he said.

I turned and looked at my trusty little travel clock. It was 10.04 am.

The Power of Stillness

As with all who are part of the deva kingdom, smaller elemental lives are under the command and coordination of larger intelligences, most aptly called higher deva or angels. Similarly, the sylphs, nature spirits of the air, are responding to the greater command of higher deva whose energy governs the large, complex patterns of weather and they in turn are working with and interacting with other great deva lives that shape, change and evolve the body of the planet.

To know the true sound of something (including ourselves) we have to develop our internal "hearing". Ironically or paradoxically (or so it seems to us), to hear the *true* sound of great, powerful forces like wind we need to attune to the silence and stillness that produces them. The greater the effect, the greater the depth of centred stillness and silence (esoterically speaking) from which that effect comes.

The great deva come from a place of great stillness and containment that has a correspondingly powerful force when it manifests. Ours is a world of polarities so, the greater the stillness of consciousness, the greater the power it contains. Always at this lowest level of the great cosmic scheme, we are dealing with two sides of the same phenomenon or quality.

As incarnate human beings, and not terribly advanced ones at that, we can only penetrate a little way into this stillness and silence, but it is enough to give us a small taste, a tiny appreciation, of the power that lies in what is often referred to as "the uncreated". In a way, it is analogous to the still "eye" at the centre of an enormous hurricane or cyclone. It is as if that still "eye" holds the mighty force of the hurricane or cyclone together as it moves like a giant whirling wheel, a great chakra of energy, across the ocean and onto land. In the same way, the stillness of the interior life of the great storm deva unleashes from that very stillness, the great power of the storm.

It is the elemental servants of that deva life—the sylphs—that from the small internal stillness of themselves generate the gentle breezes that kiss our cheeks in welcome relief on a hot summer's day. Their larger counterparts can be seen or sensed riding before the storm clouds or working in concert, creating the cloud patterns that skid across the sky, streaking it with feather-like plumes or creating a carpet from textured tufts of cloud.

Learning to still ourselves internally and to appreciate the stillness at the heart of the mighty deva lords, teaches us fundamental and important things about the nature of our own higher selves, our journey back into the stillness of our original being. How do we do that? There are countless self-help books and philosophies aimed at leading us there. A good start is to look for every busy thought, every enticing emotion, every point of bodily tension and just let them slide off, leaving a calm centre. Then somewhere, with no effort, we may glimpse a feeling of "me-ness" beyond this temporary personality we are hiding behind yet grappling with every day. Our true Self is like a shy deer; don't approach or it will back off, even run away. Let it be and it will eventually drift in, even if only for a gentle, fleeting moment, more real and still than you ever imagined yet more elusive than a song long forgotten.

Airplanes

There are deva that accompany airplanes. Those that flank the large, long haul passenger jets are generally (in my experience) big and golden. Whether they accompany these aircraft as a matter of course or are called in by passengers like me or commanded by some higher deva authority, I have not thought to ask. They often work one each side of the plane and generally come in as the plane moves along the runway for take-off. Their presence is reassuring and beautiful and usually they hold a strong focus but I'm not past giving them a reminder of their duties if we encounter turbulence!

On one occasion, I was travelling not in a large jet but in a small, eighteen-seater twin propeller plane flying between the North and South Islands of New Zealand. I called in the deva of the air before we took off, requesting their assistance with the safe, steady flight of the plane through the air and smooth running of the engines.

I sensed the usual high presence of an overlighting air deva but it seemed somewhat distant. Then there was a second deva, small by comparison and to my surprise, "young". Goodness me, this deva was in training! It was not golden but a pale, pretty spring-green. Juvenile colours perhaps? It was like a teenager who had to be reminded of its duties now and then. It would wander off as we flew, doubtless attracted by something far more interesting than our capsule of metal labouring through the sky.

I couldn't really blame it for lapses in attention. It was a sunny day; the scenery below was gorgeous. A sparkling sea filled the hollows of the Earth where the folds and slopes of the land rose like sea serpents forming the Marlborough Sounds. Some of the land was shaved to the short green velvet of pasture. Other hills bore the scars of erosion or were covered with the spiky protrusions of pine plantations. A few hills were still clad in the soft protective carpet of indigenous forest, most of it regenerating and lacking the varied heights and densities of older forests.

I called the "young" deva back again several times, reminding it of its duties, especially when we came in to land. It seemed not entirely sure of this part of the procedure but it was accomplished with the skill of the pilots and I'm sure the young deva got a good lesson in a well-executed landing. I thanked it for its help and attention and it danced off into the blue, probably to re-join its larger counterpart or play with the sylphs in the clouds.

I wonder if lack of "trained" deva for small aircraft flights contributes to the frequency of accidents? So, when you fly in a small plane, call in the air deva, request a safety escort. Maybe you'll be contributing to their education. It could be that a large jet with its many, often hundreds, of passengers has a much more magnetic thought form for safety, a collective "prayer" or will, that attracts the greater beings of the air. Far more people are mentally and emotionally invested in the flight here, not only the passengers and the crew but their families as well.

In this, we have touched briefly on how our human inventions bring elemental lives together to create something with a new and specific purpose. We shall consider this aspect of our relationship with deva further in Chapter Ten.

Time Stealers

When communicating with deva, especially in such ancient places as the deserts or in mature forests, I can find myself transported as present and past merge into the reality of a continuous *now*.

In past times it was said that the faerie folk could steal humans away, entrapping them with a magical spell that allowed the faerie to capture their minds or whisk them away for years of human time. When they were returned, the world had changed and they had grown old without knowledge of time passing. Their human friends and family were long dead and gone.

It's true that being conscious of deva can take you out of human time, for what is time? It's the brain's perception of change. When consciousness is stilled and intellect suspended from its weaving, time is not experienced and on return to normal perception a gap in time *is* experienced because all the incremental changes that happened in between were not witnessed. The same sense of timelessness is experienced in deep meditation.

I'm not alone in this experience. Many times, when communing with deva, my travelling companions have also felt such a shift, a sense of missing chunks of time. When it's time to move on, with minds awed or mildly confused by the experience and hearts unwilling to return to "normal", we look at each other in wonder and whisper, "Well that was interesting!"

As we finish our communication with deva and re-embrace our human "present" the deva send us an acknowledgement. In Australia, a small willy whorl, a miniature tornado-like wind or a short unexpected wind in an otherwise still day was sent to signal they were releasing us to our normal reality.

When I was running one of my workshops on deva there were smiles and gentle laughter when a discussion of the deva we had each seen or sensed was concluded with a short swirling breeze that came out of an otherwise still day to encircle us.

This breeze of acknowledgement is noticeably different from the wind that is part of the normal interplay of elemental forces. At Kata Tjuta (the Olgas—see Chapter Two, page 53) for example, the wind did not dint the serenity of the land because it was such an integral part of the entire devic play yet I was constantly aware of its distinctive voice as it travelled the valleys and caressed the land. The sylphs, nature spirits of the air, have shaped those rocks over thousands of years. Tiny plants and flowers wobble with its breath or sit apparently silent in the stillness.

At the level that we humans normally describe as "physical", stillness is an illusion for plants are in constant motion, dividing their cells, growing, moving and sounding their notes, singing their tunes. Our interior silence however, enables us to meld into the land, to momentarily forget our own apparent solidity and lose our separateness from the world, from deva, from Life. It is no wonder that indigenous people, like the Australian Aboriginals, claim familiarity with beings that inhabit every part of their landscape, as alive and real to them as we are to each other.

When communicating or working with deva in New Zealand, my friends and I have noticed the unusual presence of large birds. Close to our destination or at the end of our work there is often a series of hawks sitting on fence posts watching our progress, or Kereru, a large native pigeon, crossing our path or dropping us a rare feather.

Chapter Five

Fire

Powering the Universe

Fire both powers form and destroys it, transforms, purifies and
transmutes. What you feel as vitality has fire at its base for fire,
in its many grades and guises, powers the Universe.
(Deva Servant of a Lord of Fire)

Fire is the driving energy of the physical universe. Though it fuels all
motion, fire is mostly hidden from our sight. It provides the energy
needed for both the building of form and the destruction of form.
Most of the time, it is an invisible presence in our lives. Until we light
a fire to warm ourselves, cook our food or light a candle, we don't see
it physically. Go within yourself and feel the tingling aliveness of your
body and you are touching it. When you see prana—the sparkles that
carry the vitality of the life force—shining in the air or feel it prickling
the palms of your hands you have recognised the presence of fire.

At the subtle level, fire is the most elusive of the elements for us
to grasp because it is so intrinsic to our lives. Esotericist, Helena
Roerich, wrote of the Fiery World in her classic books, as one that
most humans do not see or comprehend yet it holds so many keys
to our greater understanding of the nature of Life. Like all that sits
behind what most humans accept as "normal" it is merely a step
away, a slight shift in perception.

That buzzing electrical charge at the heart of every atom is part
of the fire of Life itself. It is Life's energetic signature that comes

forth from the Stillness to power every level of manifestation in our Universe. In the greater scheme of things, each human is just a spark of this great fiery Life.

All deva are *using* that inherent fire. They glow with its energy and in the larger, overlighting deva, there are visible fiery centres, the equivalent of our own chakras, from which the light and energy of their being radiates. On the Internet you may find graphic representations of such devic "chakra" centres in Dr Geo's digital book, *Angels of Canberra*.

The fire elementals, however, are composed entirely *of* this inherent fire. These elementals are unusual in that their effects seem to appear from nowhere. We feel we know where the elementals of physical water, air or earth reside although they may change in shape and appearance but they don't disappear or appear seemingly out of nowhere as fire does. The fire elementals appear when they are "ignited", when we strike a match, for example, releasing them into the visible world as a spark or flame or the glow of an electric lamp.

As Roerich teaches however, fire is all around us. We don't see the inherent nature of fire in all things until we shift our awareness to its all-pervading presence at the heart of everything. We may think it dormant but if we were able, we would see a fire that powers our Universe at every level, from the fizzing sparking minutiae of the atom to the marvellous firefly, the gargantuan galaxies and all the subtle levels beyond the physical. When we become aware of the Fire that fuels our Universe we glimpse, even if only for an instant, that everything is alive.

Grades of Fire

There are two things that I hope will become very clear as we journey through this book. First, is that what we generally think of as "matter" comes in many grades of density and second, that the type or quality of matter changes at each of these levels of density.

You will have noticed that I am also referring to "matter" as "substance" so that it is easier for us to grasp that the less dense a layer, the more subtle is the substance and not solid "matter" as we normally think of it. Go back to our illustration Building a House, Fig 2 on page 34 and you will see what I mean from the changes in the background shading and grainy texture.

Each of the symbolic "elements" we are looking at, are like this— they manifest via different grades of solidity, subtlety and quality. The Fire element is no exception. The nature and grades of Fire is a deeply esoteric or occult subject and way beyond the scope of this book to delve into in any depth. (Alice A. Bailey's *Treatise on Cosmic Fire* is an excellent source but, like Helen Roerich's work, is highly esoteric.) All that we need to know is that here too we are dealing with different grades of fire at different levels of subtlety. At the lowest level we can think of fiery energy as the fuel of our physical experience. It's the energy that drives all physical life, as we know it. In bodies, it's the energy of growth as well as destruction.

When the eventual breakdown and decay happens, any residual fire stored in the remaining matter is released to create a new cycle of growth elsewhere.

Earth Fire

The mineral kingdom was the first to manifest, that is, to take *form* on Earth. It forms the body of the planet, on which everything else can live. It began as liquid fire that eventually cooled and solidified into the Earth's crust; the layer of rock that forms a solid skin over the molten core of liquid fire. That fire has remained at the centre of our planet through long ages of ice. It has burst through in ages of reconstruction and change, building our mountains, continents, islands and the floor beneath the seas. When that central storehouse of fire is spent, it too will cool and solidify. The Earth will have run the course of this incarnation and its body will die just as all physical bodies eventually do.

The Being that has been using this planetary form, Earth, to express its life in the dense physical plane will still exist in the consciousness of its own higher bodies until it reincarnates in a new form. At a higher level of consciousness, our planetary Being is part of and subject to the more subtle levels of fire that are behind the consciousness of our Solar system, which is an entity in its own right. Above the Solar level, there is the far greater consciousness of the larger Cosmos, where the fire of Cosmic energy drives our Universe at levels of being and consciousness that we cannot comprehend from our small human perspective. Such large questions are not for us to pursue or speculate on here. It is only important that we realize that the Earth is as much a spiritual entity as we are, only on a much, much grander scale.

Worlds within Worlds

One of the things that studying deva (or metaphysics generally), teaches us, is that everything is part of something bigger. Each of us, as a human being, is like a cell (or an elemental) in a "body" we call the human kingdom. Humanity is one entity or Being. Similarly, all the elementals and deva are component parts of one deva being, called the deva kingdom. *Involution* then, is the apparent splitting of one Being into a multitude of parts as it descends into denser and denser planes of matter. It's a process of separation.

Evolution is the reuniting of those parts into a greater and greater unity but we all come back together with the *experience* of the journey. The prize we come back with is *consciousness*—a waking up, if you like, to a fuller awareness of who we are and the journey we are on.

What of the Being that is Planet Earth? It too is on this journey into separation and reuniting. The Earth too has Will or Purpose. This is what deva had to say of the role of the great deva in the creation of the Earth:

———✳———

See you here this planet, infused with fiery light, a liquid mass of meltedness. Do you think such fire has no purpose of its own? Nay, you cannot understand such creatures as these who can by the very stillness of their mind produce such turbulence as this from which the Earth was wrought . . .

From the stillness and control of the Creatures of Fire, the lands and the seas were wrought. Through such power as this, the thoughts of God could multiply. *(WE 1)*

We might want to think that everything is equal and it is, in that it springs from the same ultimate *source* we call Life, but Life *expresses* itself in ever increasing complexities from atoms to planets to solar systems to galaxies to Universes. The lowest reflects the highest and the highest is reflected in the lowest.

For example, if you have a dog, a cell in its body has a similar relationship to the whole dog as we individually have to the planetary Being. To the dog, you, its owner, are god-like. That's why it's devoted to you, or is learning how to be! Individually, each of us may only be a cell in the planetary life but collectively, as the human kingdom, we play a more important role, but probably not as important as we like to imagine.

Dragon Fire

The fire elementals inhabiting physical flame seem to come directly from the void and return to the void. We know their nature as both benign and destructive. They are known as *fire salamanders* on account of their salamander-like shape and movements. (Not to be confused with the amphibious animal called a fire salamander because it has flame-like markings on its body.)

In legend and mythology, we have represented and revealed the reptilian shape of fire elementals as dragons that can bring a great breath of fire from their bellies just as Earth shoots fire from its belly via volcanoes. The dragons of our stories reveal the ambivalence of our relationship with fire. They may be wholly destructive; killers of life and hoarders of the gold men desire for themselves. They are feared and sometimes respected and revered. Sometimes they are seen as wise and even as protectors. After all, they are ancient creatures, so surely, they have acquired much wisdom? In modern fantasy novels especially, the pinnacle of our relationship with this ancient creature of fire is when a human becomes their rider and the dragon becomes a partner in some great quest. The symbolism is obvious when we see the dragon of story as the mysterious, powerful fire that can destroy or aid us. We can command it if we respect its power and are careful of our relationship with this primal energy. To be a dragon rider is to have gained control of our own fiery nature; it's source, force and use.

Humans have good reason to fear physical fire. In recent years, we have seen the most awful power of fire in Australia, in the Mediterranean countries and in the USA. The Second World War saw man escalating the use of fire both on the ground and from the air. At the close of that war, firebombing brought conflagrations to German cities and nuclear bombs to two Japanese cities that rivalled the fiercest firestorms generated by nature. At all levels of existence, we treat fire carelessly at our peril and the danger goes deeper than just getting physically burned.

Our Human Fire

Like our planet, we are born with a certain measure of fiery energy and when that runs out, our physical form dies, just as our car stops when it runs out of fuel. It is said that the mental planes are characterized by the fire element. I think it is significant that now, as humanity develops its mental body, we have invented vehicles that rely on combustion, on the burning of fuel for propulsion. Perhaps we cannot find or wholly embrace energy that does not rely on this kind of fire until we move our consciousness to the higher levels of the mental plane, to abstract mind. At this level (the level of soul), we find "solar fire" and for our solar system, the sun is its source. We're talking here about a more subtle kind of fire and not to be confused with the physical fire of the sun. Symbolically though, it's interesting that we see the next stage of our energy use as involving solar power. Let's hope that's an indication we are beginning to look upward to the next stage of our development.

Perhaps the secrets of an even more subtle kind of energy may not be revealed to us until we are, in sufficient numbers, operating at a level of abstract mind, detached from the ego-driven personality. Research continues to explore the possibilities of tapping into safe, non-polluting and limitless sources of universal energy but without political and moral will, change cannot occur on any effective scale.

Mimicking the enormous fiery powers of the sun and the billions of other stars of the universe, nuclear power releases a fiery energy and is based on destruction, on the splitting of the atom. My personal opinion is that when the current limits of scientific thinking can be expanded into the more subtle realms and the stranglehold of economic profit is replaced by a more altruistic model, we will discover the secrets of universal energy that will revolutionize our lives and the consequences of our activity on the planet. This will not happen until the new generation of innovators are actively supported and not supressed by political and corporate interests as has happened in the past, a collection of which you will find in a fascinating volume, *Supressed Inventions and Other Discoveries*. (Look under O'Leary, Brian in the bibliography.)

The Fiery Nature of Will

At a subtler level, I think we can better understand the true nature of Will if we think about it as having a quality of Fire. Earlier we looked at how Will initiates action. It has Purpose, purpose that *wants*— to *be* something, to *do* something or *know* something—and it's the appropriate response of deva that gets Will what it wants. So, we quickly realize that the *strength* of Will or Purpose that is sent out into the void is going to determine the strength of deva response because it's the force and quality of the fire of Will that "gifts" deva the energy that is available for them to use in their response. Why? Because although down at this level of separation it seems to us that deva and the Will that command them are two separate things, the separation of the "One into the Many" is illusory. In truth, Will and deva are one, as everything is but in the *appearance* of it, the force, quality and focus of the Will that sends out the "I want" command, is also going to determine what *level* of deva responds to it.

We can immediately relate this to our own ability to achieve things in this world. When our will is weak or our purpose wavering, our results are going to reflect that. It doesn't take a lot of observation to realize that the people who tend to achieve a great deal, for good or otherwise, are highly focused individuals who have the power of a strong will and a clear purpose driving what they do. They have learned to harness a store of fiery energy sufficient to the task they have chosen, be it a mental, emotional or physical task. Actually, it's usually a dance between all these levels of density, though one may be dominant. Clearly, for physicist Stephen Hawking, it was the fire of the mental planes that dominated, whereas for a top athlete like Hussein Bolt, the physical is dominant but the fire also comes from mental and emotional focus. In both men, the fire of Will burned brightly indeed. For Oprah Winfrey, the strength and brilliance of her fiery will is evident at both the mental and heart level, with a compassion that is just as strong as the fiery will of mind.

At the very beginning of this book, we talked about the fiery light of faerie. It may be a tiny fire but collectively it accomplishes wonderful things. One faerie can look after a plant or two but a host of faeries can grow a stunningly beautiful, lively garden. The lesson for we humans is obvious. When we cooperate to fix our problems, we harness a huge amount of fiery energy through our *collective* Will. We can see the positive results in all the big social movements that improve people's health, education and living conditions. We can also see the negative results when selfish focus on power, for an individual or group, gives rise to a widening gap between rich and poor, oppression and war.

We can also begin to glimpse that the amount of fiery energy needed to achieve our human goals is miniscule when compared to the amount of fiery Will required to form and evolve a planet with the huge variety of life forms that Earth has, each form containing its own store of fiery energy and Will. More importantly perhaps, we can also begin to realize what a high level of Consciousness it takes to be a planet.

An Ancient Fire of the Land

A man I knew was heading for a new job in the centre of New Zealand's North Island. At a farewell gathering for him, I was most unexpectedly given a strong vision and sense of what was energetically influencing that area.

I saw a very ancient creature, a being of larval fire that was shaped like a huge slug and moving with a slow, heavy energy through a river of molten lava. It was a creature of the volcanic plateau where the man was going to live and work. There are active volcanoes on the plateau and plenty of volcanic activity under the big lake created by a huge eruption about 5,000 years ago.

To be shown an elemental of this region as one of fiery lava would hardly be surprising but in one of the most unexpected of my experiences with the deva kingdom, I realized this creature of molten lava no longer *belonged* here on Earth. It was a form that had been supplanted by later evolutions of fire elementals. At the same time, I realised that it was not for me to try to move this creature on to a higher path. It had been named by the Maori people who lived in the area and it was they who were holding it in their consciousness and keeping this ancient fire of a very ancient Earth here, against the tide of evolution. Because of this, only one of them could move this creature on.

A short time later, I related this experience to a woman who travelled frequently to that area. Through her and unbeknown to me, my tale reached a person of some spiritual standing in the tribe concerned. She confirmed that what I had been shown and told was correct and said it would be taken care of by the appropriate people.

This experience was a revelation to me. I had not thought, though it now appears logical enough, that a culture can, to a degree, hold parts of Earth's evolution back by clinging to past forms of elemental life within their collective psyche. This problem applies not just to "ethnic" groups but also to humanity as a whole. In the Ageless Wisdom tradition, this kind of outmoded collective thought form is called "ancient fire". It is past its "use-by date" as far as evolution is concerned because it holds us back or creates a barrier of resistance to a higher note that is trying to manifest through humanity on Earth. It's a problem we shall come across again when we look into our very personal relationship with deva.

The Urge to Purge

In the previous chapter on Air, I related my experience with the storm deva. Tales of such storms equally belong here in a discussion on fire.

In a storm, especially when thunder and lightning are involved, we are reminded of our relatively puny status as human beings as we witness these great, exhilarating forces of elemental life. I spent a chunk of my childhood in Western Samoa where tropical thunderstorms were a frequent occurrence. My mother would laugh and try to assure me we were quite safe but I'd dive under a bed or desk or into a cupboard anyway. As I grew older, fright turned to delight in the cleansing energy of lightning, thunder, rain and wind dancing fiercely together.

In Sydney, Australia, I experienced sheet lightning for the first time. I stood on my friend's roof garden as the lightning flashed in a multitude of brilliant silver sheets above the entire expanse of the harbour, releasing bursts of warm rain. It created the illusion that the sky was indeed made of solid sheets. In the midst of this spectacle, the Friday night fireworks were set off at the Harbour Bridge, close by the apartment. I laughed aloud as large bursts of multi-coloured man-made explosions added a childish imitation and a strange chaos to the cracking, flashing ceiling of sky.

An electrical storm is a wonderful display of the integrated effort of devic forces that cleanse and renew our world. Multiple deva lives participate in such storms—air, water, fire, and earth. The elementals are gathered and coordinated in an extraordinary display of dynamic, fiery purpose. Electrical charges build up and when they "fire" they release water clinging to particles in the clouds. The air is charged with electrical fire and sometimes the earth as well. Whatever it touches is charged with electrical energy and thus cleansed. Molecules are set dancing. Air is rearranged and water released from clouds. While damage might be sustained on the earth's surface, every part of the area is refreshed.

In an analogous situation, we also go through our own version of cleansing of electrical storm proportions when we meet emotional or mental crises that force us to rise to a new level of understanding. If we can resolve these storms of turmoil and confusion, we come out of it feeling cleansed and renewed. The subtle fire has done its work, burning off the dross of old habits.

Sometimes, houses or other buildings where atrocities have occurred are deliberately burned to the ground to purge the evil energy of the crime. Often in our history, "authorities" or mobs have tried to purge what is seen as dangerous or unacceptable by terrible physical burnings and wars. The tragedy is that a *spiritual* purification does not happen at the level of physical fire. It is a *natural* process of evolutionary progress at the subtle levels of a higher, unseen fire, whereby old, outworn "sheaths", that confine the layers of our subtle "bodies", burn off. We can go forward unencumbered by subtle substance that is no longer useful to us because we have finally shaken off habits, attitudes, beliefs and so on, that no longer match our new, slightly higher stage of consciousness.

Spirit and Fire

Our human intellect wants to categorize, pigeonhole and label as I have been doing here with the elements to show the differences in quality and function between them. Unfortunately, divisions like this can also block our path to understanding deva because their realm is an integrated, interacting dynamic driven by the constant songs of their being.

We can think of sound as the force that directs or commands creative action but it is fire that fuels its physical results. When our own fire dims too much we get sick and when the fire fails completely our physical body dies. Fire, in its different qualities and levels, is the fuel of our physical Universe. Stars are suns—balls of fire that will eventually run out of fuel. All physical bodies, be they suns or human beings, are temporary as the indwelling spirit must eventually leave that outer casing and move on.

Some years ago, an emissary of a "Fire Lord" showed me that when we see via the brain, that is, with our normal eyesight, we see only a slice of the Universe and it is a very narrow slice. When we become "conscious" or "aware", we begin to experience the life of the Universe in its greater fullness.

He used an analogy to illustrate his point. When we look up into the cold dark crispness of a night sky, we see the stars twinkling at us with a cool light yet they are actually fireballs, most of them many times larger than our sun. To see what they actually are, we have to put on a different perception, using a telescope or a spaceship to travel close enough to see their fiery physical bodies.

He went on to say:

———————✶———————

If you were to see the Universe as we see it, you would see fire everywhere. Everything would glow and fizz with fire. Some of the things you think are "inert" have a softer glow and when their fire is sufficiently extinguished, they fall apart. It is the fire in a thing that magnetizes and holds the lesser fires in its orbit. This is true of the subatomic world and a solar system.

There is also a message for us about our planet's purpose or fiery Will.

———————✶———————

You have not advanced enough yet, you race called "men", to know which fires of the physical realm are a result of Earth purging the old aspects of herself that space may be made for the flowering of her new and higher intent. *(WE II)*

The subtle fires of the Universe are within and around us to use with wisdom, as we need. The beautiful vitality of prana is our ally in bringing us a vital, healthy body. Prana dances out of the sun's rays, filtered by a perfected atmosphere around our planet to come to us in just the right measure for our health and wellbeing. What a dangerous game we play when we mess with that bubble of atmosphere surrounding and protecting our Earth from our fiery sun.

By regularly putting our awareness into our body and feeling the electric tingling aliveness that is there, we are told we can improve our health and immune system. In Chinese culture, this is the aim of Qigong. Advanced Raj Yogis and Qigong masters have proven time and again that such mastery is possible. When we feel that tingling aliveness, we remind ourselves that we are touching the faint edges of the great, intrinsic fire that powers the Universe.

Hidden Dangers

Clearly, physical fire can serve us, whether as a heat source for cooking or to keep us warm. The subtle fiery forces of the world are life-giving at all levels but here too danger lurks for the naive and undiscriminating.

"You're playing with fire" is a warning we give as a metaphor in many different situations but it is particularly apt here. There *are* dangers in dealing with deva inappropriately. As with any situation in life, it comes down to two things—the motive behind our intent and the depth of our understanding (or lack of it)—in regard to the forces we are dealing with.

Science begins with a deep curiosity about how the world of dense substance, form and phenomena works. The finding out is one thing to achieve but how we use what we have discovered raises a plethora of other issues. To split the atom is one thing, to use that knowledge to create a bomb that can wipe out millions of lives in a moment is another thing entirely.

The Purpose to which we direct our Will has three main pitfalls—power, pride and prejudice. When we examine our motivation for taking an action we do well to stop and consider if our motivation comes from any of these three dangerous "Ps". This is the crux of our current evolutionary journey, isn't it? Each of these three motivations is high in individualized self-interest. They can easily move us away from the narrow path of wise discernment and spiritual enlightenment. They can keep us in the thrall of matter, chained to the lower elementals that we are using—the physical and astral especially, whose thrust is involution, downward into matter.

Of course, to be here in a human body we have to operate at these levels but it's *how* we operate, whether our motives are entirely selfish or whether they serve to better the lives of others, be they close neighbours or a wider humanity, along with the living inhabitants of the kingdoms that share their world with us.

Our motives always have a quality of fiery energy because our will is their source, so our constant challenge is to learn to recognize what that quality is and how we are using it. To deliberately meddle with the fiery powers inherent in the subtle levels of the Universe is to court disaster if our own spiritual evolution is not sufficiently advanced. Our human ego is usually good at over-estimating where we stand in the great scheme of things. We can be unleashing forces we cannot control and the warning especially applies to deliberate attempts to use deva inappropriately. It is the quality of our motivation that unleashes a response from the appropriate deva. Fire of some kind is always involved no matter how miniscule. To live is indeed to "play with fire".

Chapter Six
The Multi-level Singing Universe

The Outside-Inside Worlds

We tend to think there is an outside world and an inside (subtle) world. Some people will tell you that only the outside world is real because we can physically see it, feel it, touch it, taste it, therefore we can agree on what it is like. They will tell you that the inside world is not like that; you cannot see it or touch it, and that everybody has different opinions about what it is like. On both these counts they say we cannot *prove* the inside world is even there, so it cannot be real, it must be a figment of our imagination or a result of brain anomaly. Such a view ignores the evidence of common and shared experiences of millions of human beings over many thousands of years. It also overlooks the fact that there is a huge variety of opinion about the nature of the outside, "real" world as well.

In the past, there was a lot of superstition about both the nature of the subtle worlds and the experiences people had of these worlds. In more recent times, we have learned to use our brains differently, to reason things through using what metaphysics calls the "concrete" or "rational" mind. We have developed what we call a "scientific" approach to things. The good thing is that we have lost many, if not all, of the astral superstitions of the past and in most parts of the outer world we no longer torture and kill people as witches or heretics who claim to know the inner, subtler worlds exist or merely believe they do.

The downside is that, in Western cultures at least, we have lost touch with or ignored the evidence that this is a multi-level Universe that goes far beyond these lowest levels we experience as physical. What we see as discrete, independent parts is actually a complex, interdependent whole, coordinated and influenced by a hierarchy of forces and levels of Being.

The Veil

Of course, the "outside" and the "inside" worlds are not separate from each other. They are part of a continuum of existence. They only *seem* to be separate because we are so used to experiencing Life in a particular and very narrow way and that narrow band of experience and perception is what we have defined as "reality". When we first begin to experience what I am calling the "inner" or "subtle" worlds they can seem so different that we think we have walked through a door or penetrated a barrier between them. Traditionally, this perceived barrier is known as a "veil". It's an apt description because it reminds us that the barrier is actually rather flimsy. The veil is both an illusion and a reality. It is an illusion because it is created by our beliefs and limited experience, yet it is real insofar as having substance of a different, subtler kind. When we become more practised at using our inner senses, we understand that there are not separate worlds but grades or states of substance so different levels of consciousness are needed to perceive or process them.

We can think of the outer life—what people usually call "reality"—as the top of an iceberg and the life of the inner world as the huge lump of ice beneath the water that we don't normally see unless the water is so incredibly clear someone can actually photograph it for us. Conditions have to be right for us to see or experience the inner worlds with any clarity. We have to be calm, clear of strong emotion, and receptive. We have to use our *inner* senses to see, hear or feel the vast existence *behind* outer appearance.

Building Subtle Structures of Reception

I like analogies. They don't *prove* anything but they are useful for helping us to understand something unfamiliar by comparing it to something familiar. So, let's look at it this way: transitions from one state of consciousness to another, from awareness of one kind of "world" or level of density to another, are like moving from solid ground at the bottom of the ocean up through the dense water, into the air, then higher and higher up through the atmosphere into space. To a sea creature, living deep down on the ocean floor, the earth beneath and the sea water around her is "the world". Above the sea is a totally alien world that the bottom-dwelling sea creature has never experienced and probably doesn't even know exists. To us, all these levels are understandable—earth, sea, air, space—all are part of one reality, one Universe. They are just different states or qualities of matter and we know that, as human beings, we can move from one to the other and still be "us".

The outer and inner worlds are like this in that they are different but interconnected states of being. We have to get into different kinds of protective clothing or vehicles to be at the bottom of the sea or in outer space. Similarly, to experience subtler worlds—finer levels of density or higher states of being—we have to be able to move into different levels of mind or states of consciousness and use different senses.

Just as we cannot stay at the bottom of the ocean or outer space without equipment or vehicles that enable us to deal with the forces in those environments, we cannot expand our consciousness much beyond "normal" without gradually building the subtle structures needed to both sense and process those finer levels. Every level or layer of the Universe is created and powered by forces of one kind or another. We need the appropriate equipment to deal with those forces.

In a delightful collection recounting his experiences with the deva kingdom the late R. Ogilvie Crombie (known as ROC) says in his book, *Encounters with Nature Spirits*, that his own subtle bodies were prepared for his experiences years before those experiences occurred.

It can take both patience and practice to learn to live in states of expanded awareness whereby our consciousness is not confined to only one or two layers or levels at a time. Some people are naturally more adept at this, the rest of us just have to keep working at it, *gently.*

Take Your Time—It's a Long Journey

We easily forget that our physical bodies are the result of millions of years of evolutionary development. I do not, by the way, see concepts of Divinity as incompatible with evolution. It's only in recent times that some major religions have adopted a very literal interpretation of their scriptures whereas it seems that in the past, societies were very much more comfortable with symbolism. Stories or creation mythologies were couched in terms that made vast periods of time more comprehensible to the ordinary populace. It's much easier to get a sense of the Creator's progress if we talk about "His" work taking place over a number of days, than over millions of years. It's the sequence rather than the time frame that's important.

"Involution" is how metaphysics describes the descent into matter. When the densest appropriate level of form is reached, the indwelling spirit or life "turns its gaze" upward again, back towards its point of origin, "God". New forms (or "bodies") are needed to express or house this now growing consciousness. We call this production of more and more appropriate, upwardly striving forms "evolution".

Getting to this point has taken millions of years of linear time. Linear time is what applies down here at this level of physical density. As we travel up through to layers of lesser density, we discover that linear time ceases to apply and eventually ceases to exist. It is replaced by a still point that enables a holographic time where all happenings are simultaneous, not sequential. *(WE I, II & III)*

Substance

Let's recap for a moment what we mean by "substance" in the context of understanding what deva (and their elementals) are and what they do. Metaphysics seeks to explain what lies behind or beyond the physics of the "real" world and what *causes* the physics of the real world. We've seen that in metaphysics, some words are used differently from the way we are used to using them. Light and sound, for example, don't just mean the light that we see with our eyes or the sound we hear with our ears. Similarly, "substance" does not mean only the solid, liquid or gaseous forms of matter we recognize in our 3-D reality.

We normally think of substance as something we can touch—the chair we sit on is composed of solid wooden substance. The drink in our glass is liquid substance and the air we breathe is a gaseous substance. These three states, solid, liquid and gas are the three densest forms of substance. We say they are "real" because we recognize them with our physical senses of sight and touch. Beyond these three grades of substance—solid, liquid and gas—are layers of subtler, less dense substance. Just as in our analogy of moving from the bottom of the sea to outer space we went through different densities of matter or substance, metaphysics says that substance does not stop at "air" or even "space". There are grades of substance that are finer and of a different quality than physical "space". Far from being empty, space is just another veil behind which another layer of more subtle substance exists.

Moving from the Outside In

We can visualize or understand these concepts using different frame-works. (Remember the elephant story on page 56?) Here's another way of describing or sensing our way into the subtle realms.

Imagine the physical Universe is one great mass. If we were entering from the subtlest level, we would notice that here it is composed of very, very fine substance; so fine, it is barely discernible. It emits a very high sound, a frequency that is matched or expressed by an equivalent quality of light. It is *knowable* but not visible. As we travel into it, we find that it is becoming more visible and the sound is getting lower. Within the substance, we can discern particles that are emitting both sound and light. Gradually the substance gets visually thicker and it is reverberating with lower, slower sounds or vibrations. At each level, the songs are of a different quality. There is a recognisable or signature tune within each level. The finer the level of substance, the faster, higher, finer, is the symphony of sound and light. The denser the level of substance, the slower and lower the songs are because *sound and light carry information about the quality of substance at each level.*

Every level may be knowable when we have developed the senses or sensors needed to pick them up but that doesn't mean we can describe what they are like to someone else. If our bottom-dwelling ocean creature was unexpectedly pulled up to the surface by fishers who then threw her back into the sea, how could she describe what the air is like to her fellow bottom dwellers? If we are to communicate our experiences of the more subtle levels of being fully and accurately to someone who has not experienced them, it is not words that we need. Telepathy would probably come closest.

Patterns and Planes

So, as our journey proceeds, we notice that there are sounds moving through the substance that are marshalling its particles into patterns or structures that form large bands. Then we begin to realize that within a band these structures have similar tunes. (Just as waltzes are recognisably waltzes and jazz is recognisably jazz and so on.) We can recognize a "family resemblance" in the substance within each band. These bands are what Metaphysicians call planes. Remember the diagrams of our house project and the oak tree deva (Fig 2, page 34 and Fig 4, page 35)? The higher levels were not as grainy (not as dense) as the lower ones. Each of those levels of graininess is a *plane of density and consciousness*.

As we travel further into this universe of substance, we notice that the particles are getting closer together so the bands or planes are becoming denser. The marshalling sound that is travelling through the substance and moving the particles into patterns is creating structures that are closer together the further into density we go. The sound travelling through the substance is of a lower pitch than it was when it travelled through the finer planes of this Universal mass. The sound is slowing down. Its waves are longer and flatter. The greater density is also cutting down the amount of visible light coming from the particles that make up the patterns. Eventually, we find ourselves in a zone that is so dense the sounds seem really slow and the light very dim. At last, we have arrived in the dense physical world of normal human reality.

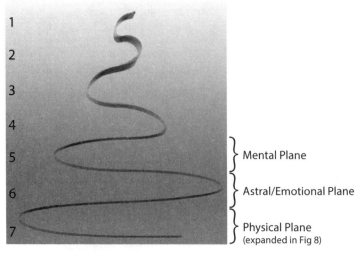

Figure 7 The Descent into Matter

Life at the Bottom

What are the songs that make up this bottom plane? (Plane number 7 in Fig 7 above.) Within each plane, we can distinguish seven subplanes— seven layers of density. That is, seven different kinds of substance. In Fig 8 below we can see what the entire bottom plane of Fig 7 (the dense physical plane) actually consists of.

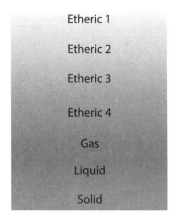

Figure 8 The Seven Subplanes of the Dense Physical Plane.
This is an expansion of what is in that bottom plane in Fig 7,
the plane that we think of as being our physical reality.

We recognize the bottom three quickly enough but what of the top four? For those people with etheric vision, the physical world that the rest of us see has a counterpart, a blueprint if you like, in etheric substance. What's more, it is said that energy can only become what we call a liquid, gas or solid physical reality if it first exists in the etheric. In other words, once the energetic impulse reaches the etheric subplanes it can (if that is its destiny) densify into gas, liquid, or solid. Where does the energetic impulse come from for this descent into this densest of all the planes? It comes from any *higher plane where the purpose or intention originates.*

Those etheric levels in our simple chart are where people physically see faeries, nature spirits and the etheric "bodies" of some of the overlighting deva.

If you want to see what is above the mental plane, take a peek ahead at Fig 9 on page 118.

I believe that one of the reasons sceptics or people who have not had any experience of the inner planes find it so difficult to accept that these realities *might* exist (let alone that they *do* exist) is this confusion about *where* they exist. As we have already seen, it is not a question that has an easy answer because we are trying to use the language and reference points of our physical senses and experience to describe things that are *not bound* to that physical level with its particular patterns of substance and the way it both appears and behaves.

We accept that water can exist in three different states—it can be solid in the form of ice, liquid in the form of water, and gaseous in the form of vapour as in steam and clouds. We know this mutable nature of water because it is part of our physical experience but if there was no water on our planet, so we had no knowledge or experience of it, how would we understand what it was like if someone from a watery planet tried to describe it to us?

If you landed on a planet totally devoid of water, how would you tell the inhabitants what water is, let alone how it feels, tastes and behaves? Which brings us to our fourth element.

Chapter Seven
Water

The Nature of Water

Water—too much or too little of it and we die. In the appropriate quantities, it enables us to live and thrive in this physical world that we refer to, with a very human myopia, as "ours". It is water that makes our planet look blue from outer space, whether as a vast expanse of ocean or as vapour in our atmosphere. Water is changeable, moody at times and is said to be the lower or physical out-picturing of the emotional (astral) plane (see Fig 7 on page 100). The correspondence is a helpful one. By observing the nature of water, we can learn a lot about the nature of emotions and out of that understanding, we can learn to master, utilize and live with our emotions and not allow them to cause harm in our lives or in the lives of others. We'll explore this connection between water and our emotions in greater detail in Part Two.

Like our emotions, large quantities of water out of control (or seemingly so to us), can be highly destructive. Water can flood land, destroy large trees and houses and drown strong beasts. In tsunami form, it can become a gigantic, fast moving wall that can sweep away whole towns, including substantial buildings and bridges. Yes, we all know water has the power to destroy us but it is essential to life on Earth—in every cell, not only in *our* bodies, but also in the cells of plants, trees and animals. Dehydration is said to be one of the most painful ways for us to die and access to fresh, clean water is one of the most pressing problems for much of humanity.

Water moves—as rain, rivers and seas—yet we talk of it as a passive, receptive element. That's because it seems to us that some force has to move it; forces like heat, cold, wind and gravity. There is a phenomenon we call "capillary action", which is thought to help the fluid to rise seemingly of its own accord. In addition, it is water passing out of the holes on the undersides of the leaves that "pulls" on the water within the tree's vessels, triggering sap to rise all the way from root to branch to leaf. For decades, scientists have accepted these two phenomena—capillary action and transpiration—as the reasons sap can rise up the trunks of even *very* tall trees. In his book, *The Hidden Life of Trees,* German forester Peter Wohlleben, casts doubt on these stock answers as adequate explanations. Apparently, neither these nor osmosis are sufficient to explain the rise of sap. So, at the time of writing this, the mystery of rising sap is not yet sufficiently scientifically explained. Devic intelligence within the trees has it figured out, even if we don't.

Water slips over what it cannot find a way through. If nothing contains it, it runs into cracks, seeps through gaps and soaks into anything that is even a little porous. Water finds its way between the solidities of the world. When water is not moved or refreshed in some way, it stagnates, as does our life when our emotions are "stuck" and turn sour.

Like the other elements we've discussed, water is infused with its own *elemental* intelligence hence we name these beings "elementals". Think of them as the intelligence of the raw essence of the element they infuse and we come close to realising their nature. They are usually described as the lower elementals and we are cautioned by metaphysicians not to conjure with this raw, elemental power. We'll look into why in Part Two.

Wetlands

One of the first water faeries or nature spirits I saw was in a wetland. The water moved very slowly through the reeds but there were open patches forming mini lakes or little streams. It was on one of these stream-like stretches I saw a cone-shaped water "spirit".

As we mentioned earlier, it's not really accurate to talk about beings of the deva kingdom as being either masculine or feminine, in the sense of gender as we understand it. Nevertheless, to me, this lovely water faery had a feminine energy and her cone-like etheric body was woven of pale grey-blue gossamer light. She spun along the surface of the water like a top, now and then opening her skirt-like cone releasing tiny, faery-like elementals. Their shining bodies and fast movements reminded me of dragonflies.

The cone faery and its smaller elementals energized the water as they skimmed over its surface. With nature spirit and elemental activity, there is a collective cooperation and service that characterizes them and what they do. This is hardly surprising given the structure of their kingdom. At this level, there's not much individualism.

Often a stream or river will have the cone-shaped water spirits with their collection of little faeries. Their function, like other transitional elementals that work with water, seems to be to energetically "aerate" the water. The size and energetic quality of the overlighting deva reflects the physical size of the waterway and the topography of the land.

On the surface, wetlands support the ecological dynamics of plants, fish, frogs, insects, waterfowl and other birds that live around the edges of the water. Time and again when observing healthy nature, we realize that on planet Earth, health and strength comes from diversity. It's a fact we often fail to heed and we ignore it at our peril.

Hidden Waterways

The great pressures and movements that exist underneath the Earth's surface create caverns and caves where crystals form and grow. Hidden in the dark are huge underground water systems that are as intricate and beautiful as those on the surface. They form reservoirs and feeders that nourish deep-rooting trees and provide a buffer in times of drought. They carry the waters of life to parts of the Earth we cannot normally see, just as within our bodies there are all manner of tubes, veins, arteries, intestines, etc., that circulate the fluids necessary to maintain us. These fluids primarily consist of water. The underground waterways of the Earth are, in a similar way, vital to the health of life both beneath and on its surface.

For our own "benefit", we have drained or otherwise destroyed wetlands over large areas, disregarding the fact that they are part of a greater system of fluid circulation that is both physical and energetic. It is often apparent when walking over an area of land, that there was once a major wetland system there. It still exists in the etheric blueprint for that area.

Similarly, with our subtle senses, we can often discern that the *physical* underground systems are still there, even though the surface wetland has gone. Deprived of their outlets and counterparts on the surface, often both the energetic and physical properties of these underground systems can no longer circulate as they were designed to do. The two were created to work in consort. They are in fact one system. When one is removed, the other has no balancing energy and the natural harmony is lost. This can cause energetic and physical stagnation of an entire area, sometimes adversely affecting the physical and emotional well-being of those who live where once a thriving swamp or wetland forest grew. In such places, it can feel as if the elemental life is very distressed.

A Wandering God

Parts of the beautiful riverbank where I walked were being bulldozed. Trees, shrubs and small plants were bowled over and submerged as machines destroyed and rebuilt the riverbanks. Large rocks were transported from two hundred kilometres away. With great rumblings, the rocks were tipped and manoeuvred to make a series of groins jutting out into the river. This "reconstruction" as the local authority described it, was part of flood control, designed to direct and contain the flow of the river at times of high rainfall and so prevent the flooding of houses near the river's edge as had happened in the past. One can certainly appreciate the need to protect people's homes when possible. We can also question the wisdom of where we put our buildings in the first place.

I knew that eventually these new rock groins, like older ones upstream, would be covered in weeds after soil lodged and built up between the boulders. The trees and vegetation would creep down from the banks and eventually it would all seem somewhat "natural" again. In the meantime, it was a hideous, destructive mess. Little creatures living on the fringes of land and water, naturally a place of abundant life, were buried under the gravel, or if they were lucky, washed down river to find another place to dwell. Herons that usually wandered the shallows to feed disappeared.

I consoled myself that it was only parts of the river bank that were affected and most of the lovely walking track was undisturbed. I wondered how the river deva felt about it. When I connected with the deva, I was mildly shocked to realize that I had automatically assumed the deva would be as uncomfortable about the disturbance and destruction as I was but I had wrongly projected my human feelings onto the deva. Instead, it was a cool aloof intelligence that told me:

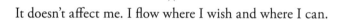

It doesn't affect me. I flow where I wish and where I can.

Of course! Rivers move over time, carving out wider and wider valleys and deltas. It is the nature of water to go where it can. A river deva is a wandering god indeed. I then asked about the ecology of the banks, whereupon the river deva told me I would have to ask the land deva about that, it had little to do with the river deva and thus I was dismissed.

It turns out I'm not the only one to experience overlighting river deva as cool or remote. In deva workshops I have held, others have reported similar impressions. In the absence of an appropriate science, such corroboration of experience is the closest thing we have to confirmation of the veracity of what we experience. Given that even with our physical senses, witnesses to the same events so often disagree as to what took place, I've been very encouraged by the reported similarity of what people experience with deva.

Reconstruction

Back on the riverbank, I turned my attention to the land deva. I found a complex arrangement of deva who were in charge of discrete sections of the riverbank and others who had a more encompassing role over larger areas. I realized the situation was more complicated than I had first supposed. I then chose a section of the river that was now unrecognisable, where curvaceous banks green with shrubs and small trees had been replaced by rock groins and gravel banks. In places the river was beginning to look more like a canal than the beautiful, naturally formed waterway it had been.

The land deva was resigned and told me:

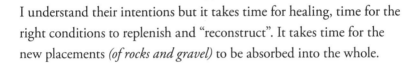

I understand their intentions but it takes time for healing, time for the right conditions to replenish and "reconstruct". It takes time for the new placements *(of rocks and gravel)* to be absorbed into the whole.

The deva "smiled" at the irony of her use of the word-energy "reconstruct". Deva give information telepathically as parcels of energy that our brain interprets in words; hence, I have used the term "word-energy".

I sent out the fleeting thought that members of the local Maori tribe had complained that having been brought from another part of the country, the rocks were foreign to the area and should be given a welcome ceremony to incorporate them into the local landscape. The deva assured me the rocks would eventually "be absorbed". Persisting, I asked if we humans could help, stopping short of asking specifically whether a ceremony was required. The deva responded:

Any sustained loving energy you send can be utilized. Energy is the food of the Universe.

I thought of how the Law of Attraction governs love, cohesion and integration. What the deva said made perfect sense.

Whether we choose to ritualize it or not, to hold a ceremony or just to take a moment or two to send love and gratitude to a place or a person, if our intent and feeling is pure, that is, it comes from our soul or higher self rather than our ego-personality, we are energetically contributing to the cohesion and integration of person or place. They can of course, deliberately choose not to receive our blessing.

Upon reflection, I believe that one of the reasons the landscape deva were so tolerant of the destruction was that a great deal of energy was put into the beautification of the riverbank by a band of locals called "Friends of the River". Over the years, these volunteers had planted thousands of trees and shrubs. The deva would have been well aware and appreciative of this human intention and resulting action that revitalized the riverbanks.

Change is key in the life of the physical universe. What we loosely call, "Spirit", is constantly evolving its modes of expression, so physical forms must also evolve to be more *adequate* instruments or housings for that ever-changing, evolving expression of Spirit.

As the Being that ensouls the Earth evolves, it too needs a more adequate physical vehicle, more refined, more suitable to the new energies of its being. It is always re-creating its body, the physical thing we call Earth, even though from our human timescale it seems that the planet is generally constant and stable. Actually, it is constantly changing, remodelling itself, growing new life forms, just as throughout our lifetime our own bodies change in shape, texture, suppleness, agility and strength, cells die and are replaced.

Watery "Mechanics"

Water plays on our emotions. The way it affects us depends not only on how the water is moving (or not) but on our particular emotional makeup. A shallow stream or river moving steadily over a bed of stones and small weirs can evoke a calm joy with its delightful sounds, its ripples and eddies catching the light as it bubbles and slips along its way.

Huge waterfalls can invoke awe, exhilaration and fear as the water roars and tumbles with a physical power that far exceeds ours. By contrast, a small waterfall has a more human scale. It can give us a feeling of dancing joy, its delicate sprays and bubbles sparkled by the sunlight.

When I first tried tuning into the deva of water I was puzzled. All of the deva life I met was not in the water but above it or moved between air and water. I thought there was something wrong with my ability or methods until I came across Geoffrey Hodson's book, *The Kingdom of the Gods*. Through this classic work on the deva kingdom, I was reassured and have subsequently come to understand the situation more fully. As you read through the various experiences I'm relating, you'll probably realize that these deva are either overlighting deva (as with the river) or a kind of intermediary deva that works with the water.

When water goes over a fall, it is interacting with air and is energized by that mixing. Aeration (the mixing of air with something else) is a key ingredient in the health of soil and water and the action of the nature spirits born of the appropriate elements is intrinsic to that process.

The Rock Water Serpent

On Uluru (Ayer's rock) in the central Australian desert, there is a unique and beautiful waterfall that seems to defy logic. It appears near the top of the totally barren orange rock and flows with a serpentine quality into large pools formed by the sensuous embrace of the smooth, curved rock. No wonder the local aboriginals say the spirit of this strange and beautiful waterfall is endowed with magical properties. Perhaps the same mysterious action that brings water up very tall trees is at work here too.

The deva of this waterfall is distinctive and strong, powerful and benign in a detached way. Like the river deva I told you about, such detachment can seem cool or aloof to our human thinking. Unlike other waterfalls, this one didn't have the same airy quality I had become used to. It rose out of the rock and without fountaining, returned to the rock, so it had a much earthier quality and a very ancient presence. It's a reminder that what is now desert was once covered in water and beneath the land underground streams and rivers may remain.

An Impressive Water Deva

Iguaçu Falls on the border of Argentina, Brazil and Paraguay, are amongst the biggest in the world, roaring with vitality and the power of huge volumes of moving water. Large clumps of grasses grow on precarious rock outcrops, puncturing the white falls with bright green. Their blades sway in the air currents and mist that arise from the water rushing down around them. Through wet season and dry, the falls and their large catchments enable an abundance of plant, bird and insect life. Thousands of butterflies flutter in the steamy tropical air or settle in groups on the white beaches at the falls' feet.

Personally, I find that when I'm standing before a large waterfall as opposed to a small, dainty one, it is the overlighting deva I am aware of, rather than the smaller transitional elementals that dance in and out of the tumbling water. I perceived the deva of Iguaçu to be a clear, shining and more masculine than feminine energy. It was enormously joyful and focused on its task, yet as all large deva are, it was acutely aware of every part of that which it oversees, reminiscent of the religious idea that "God is aware of even the falling of a sparrow".

We must be careful not to assume that the deva feels an attachment or sentimentality about those lives that it oversees, as we, in our humanness might. I have never met one that exhibits that *kind* of attachment. Love, yes but sentimental attachment or a sense of "ownership", no. The forms that a deva overlights come and go but the life that expresses itself *through* those forms endures. None know this better than the overlighting deva itself. We can say that at their own level they *are* the life that expresses through those lesser forms. In the same way, the cells of our bodies are constantly dying and being replaced, yet we still know ourselves both as "alive" and as "us" while our cells come and go. They too are simply conduits for a higher life—us. We, in turn, are a conduit for a still higher life, the Human Kingdom. "Down" here, the Universe seems divided and separated but that's just a result of our current experience, brain function and evolution. The higher we go into those finer and finer levels of being, the more unified things become, leading eventually, we are told, to fusion (see Fig 13 on page 250).

110

Rain

Nature spirits have a huge amount of fun, and none more so it seems to me, than those of rain. They dance the water from the sky in all manner of moods and music, from the Wagnerian symphonies of storms to the gentle drops of a light spring shower or the damp caress of misty rain.

Like their peers of the waterfalls, these dancing spirits of life are not beings of water so much as beings of the air, and we need to be clear that they are different from the simpler water elementals that infuse the individual drops of water. Once these nature spirits have loosed their cargo from the clouds, it is over to other parts of the deva kingdom to do what they will with the bounty. The shapes of leaves, the thickness of the canopy, the bumps and hollows, hills and valleys of the land, all determine where the tiny water elementals will find themselves.

In the vegetable kingdom, the energies of water and plants dance together, embracing and absorbing. No wonder rain in a garden or a wood feels so different to rain on a city street where it collects in drains and flows into pipes underground, usually ending up in rivers, streams and sea. How much more vitally energized our cities and towns would be if all our buildings had roof gardens, streets had mini forests and our city dwellings were built around courtyards of vegetation with fountains and places to sit and enjoy.

Nowhere is the delight of the rain spirits more palpable than in the lush excitement of a rainforest. Rainforests have evolved in consort with great quantities of water falling from the sky, filling the air between the plants and trees and soaking into the ground. Whether steamy or temperate, rainforests are bursting with life. Their music is as diverse as any symphony with millions of leaves acting as drums for the drops to sound on, while insects, birds and animals add their own layers of song.

In the earlier days of my journeys into the deva kingdom, I found that on a visit to such a place where deva life is so incredibly diverse and active, both my physical and subtle senses would often feel overwhelmed and I would get quite a headache. Sometimes, my brain (or my mind) would shut down completely for a couple of days afterward and during this time, I could not remember a thing about it. Then it would come back to me in exquisite detail, sight, smell and sensation.

Later I realized such shutdowns happened because the structures of my subtle senses, which we use to access these subtle realms, were newly opened and still forming. They were not used to the forces they were being subjected to. As we saw with R. Oglivie Crombie's account, with years of experience, practice and time, these structures were strengthened and appropriately modified (and still are). It is a process that happens gradually; one has to be patient and not force it. Remember it is as it is described, *subtle*.

Sea

Rachel Carson wrote a marvellous book called *The Sea Around Us*. Her language is a liquid and beguiling poetry of scientific report that gifts us a wondrous appreciation of what the sea is and does. The sea covers seven-tenths of the Earth's surface so it contributes significantly to our planet's blue wrap when seen from space. It controls our climate and weather patterns. It alternately covers and retreats from the lands in great cycles thousands of years long. It gifts us food, beauty and the energy of revitalizing ions where it meets the shore. We ignore, neglect and abuse it at our peril. As the great tsunamis of 2004 and 2011 showed us, when the earth shrugs and the sea flicks its mighty tail, our life on Earth and all that we have made, can disappear in minutes. Science tells us that life on Earth (as we currently define it) most likely first manifested in the sea. The sea gives life to form and can just as easily take form away.

Regrettably, I am not the best of sailors but I enjoy the sea and love its ever-changing moods and textures. Whether it be an expanse of ocean or a beach, the sea gifts us an endless variety of changing colours, patterns, movement and sound. Yet these are reflective of the forces that act upon water rather than something water *initiates* (in the sense that we understand that word). It is because of winds, gravity, the movement of the moon and subsequent tides that the sea moves. The receptive nature of water is a responsive mirror for these forces.

The sylphs of the air are agents of such forces, whipping sea into mountains and flags of spray. Where sea meets shore, they tumble the waves in concert with gravity, tide, stones, sand and the laws of motion. A seashore is deva's teamwork displayed.

Sea Deva Encounter

My friend Linda and I were visiting the Shetland Islands. They lie some 160 km (100 miles) off the north coast of mainland Britain, sandwiched between the North Sea and the North Atlantic. Shetland is a treeless landscape, beautiful in its openness and exposure to the changing light and cloud that sweep across the oceans. Grass, tussock, stone, cliff, shore and wide windswept moors are swathed in changing colours. On my first visit, dustings of snow created sheets of canvas for these plays of light, sharpened by the crisp, clear air of late winter.

The deva had called us from far away, like a siren. Maybe the sirens feared by sailors of old were in fact deva singing their tantalizing songs that were heard by people considered fey. Perhaps, as is the way in ages of superstition, the ethereal sea creatures were interpreted as beautiful but evil sea-maidens intent on luring humans to a shipwreck death. Maybe they were actually trying to warn sailors, rather than entice them into danger.

Linda and I were in a motel many miles away. We didn't know *what* it was that called; only the direction it called us from. Fortunately, Linda's local knowledge prevented us from getting lost in the confusing labyrinth of narrow, winding country roads. When we found our deva, "she" was an incredibly beautiful, enigmatic energy. It was in a lovely horseshoe bay. The water inshore assumed a deep turquoise where it lapped the steep cliffs, then merged to blue out in the bay. As the waves curled lazily onto a narrow sandy beach, all the colours blended to white.

Just as you cannot hold much water in your hand without it leaking out between your fingers, the sea deva could not be held to a single description of colour or shape. It spiralled and swirled in a dance that rose from sea to air and back again. Until then, I had not seen a sea deva that penetrated so deeply into the water. The movement was accompanied by a serene and rhythmical sound. The swirling, spiralling nature of this deva created the impression of an "eye", a centre about which moves a force, much as the force of a hurricane moves around a seemingly still "eye" or centre.

It was obvious that the deva's song, which was also its dance, was bringing energy from the air into the sea at that place. It was apparent that it did not stay only in the bay but moved farther out to sea in the course of its work, (though not very far out). I certainly got the sense that it was a localized energy serving the bay and close environs of the sea around that part of the coast.

Near the shore of any sea, there is an energetic exchange going on beyond the obvious ones of waves, tides and winds. Perhaps seen or not, known or not, these deva of bays and coves are responsible for the lifting and energizing effect attributed to negative ions that so many people report from being "down beside the sea". This is probably why ionizing machines never seem as effective to me as the energy of the sea shore itself. The chemical component is present but that essential, complex deva energy is missing.

It is at the edges or "the zone" where different eco-systems meet that life is usually most abundant—a seashore or riverbank. These are places where different kinds of deva are interacting and working together. In the forms that flow from deva activity and human life alike, diversity and cooperation is the key to abundance.

In the presence of such beings, time seems to disappear, which may support the suggestion that deva song caused ships to founder. Before we knew it, night was descending. We had to bid our beautiful new friend farewell and find our way back along those narrow, winding Shetland roads, our spirits buoyant and our hearts very thankful that we had heard and heeded the deva's call.

Macro and Micro

While the sea gives itself to wind and sun to create the marvellous array of effects that we see, it has its own great deva beings. As the years have gone by and experience has gradually added to experience, I have often found it easier to connect with the huge deva of whole systems and less easy to connect with the transitional beings. Perhaps it has to do with changes in resonance, just as we find ourselves moving into and out of resonance with certain people during the course of our lives.

I have found that the sea harbours great deva lives that channel the huge forces of the planet and those that reach us from across the solar system and beyond. If you find this a far-fetched concept, remember that the relative distances between planets and stars correspond to the relative distances between the atoms of our bodies. If we were able to experience being on a single atom of our physical body, we would find ourselves in a cosmos of atoms, each of them humming away in their own piece of space like suns in a great universe. Each of those atoms is subject to the forces within the cell, the "solar system" in which it lives—to the movement of the fluids, gases and solid structures. How blinkered it is to think that Earth, along with we tiny human beings who inhabit it, is not also subject to the forces and their qualities, of the larger system in which *it* lives.

Large Sea Deva

There are overlighting deva of seas and oceans. Like the Shetland bay deva, they may be associated with a smaller area of the sea but subject to a higher deva who oversees larger bodies of water. These larger, overlighting deva appear to be focused in the air just *above* the sea, but they are also *in* the sea in that their consciousness "holds" the sea beneath it. Of course, they have in some respects the heavy quality of a large body of water. The few I have met have seemed quite "serious" but I don't assume they all are. I have a lot more work to do in respect of these deva before making that generalization. While there may be general qualities in common between deva of similar function, I have found that they can feel as individual as human personalities do.

So far, it has seemed to me that the shape these large sea deva take and the nature of their activity, differs somewhat from their counterparts on land. Their energy "bodies" seem more spread and flattened out than those of overlighting land deva, hugging closer to the sea, whereas the "head" or "top" of a large land deva is usually quite high above the land they oversee. The deva of a large area of sea is holding in consciousness a great mass of substance that moves ponderously. As we saw, the localized bay deva of Shetland was, by contrast, working a small area and was every bit as shapely and full of movement as a similar-sized land deva.

A large sea deva holds its energy regardless of what else is going on above the surface of the water. It is dealing with great currents that flow even at the deepest levels of the sea. These are part of a huge system of ocean currents that circle the planet. Even a force five hurricane or cyclone is only affecting a relatively narrow layer of ocean near the surface, despite its huge impact on air, land and sea surfaces. In the deep, deep ocean, the sea is "doing its own thing". A great sea deva is also interacting with the large "outside" forces—the pull of the moon and the spin of the Earth. We must remember too, that the sea is contained by land below and around it and the shape of that land also affects where and how it can move in response to these forces.

The Joy of Deva

Great hosts of deva life travel with tremendous speed across the oceans on the summons of rightful song. They are not deva of wind and weather but part of a great layer of Light beings that are agents for upliftment and change for *all* life on Earth. They mediate between the kingdoms and act as transmitters of light from the Buddhic plane—well above the normal level of human consciousness—to the planes below (i.e., the mental, astral and physical, see Fig 9 on page 118). Sound and light are their vehicles and their expression. Their wings are joy and their numbers countless. I have most often encountered these Light beings from the extremities of a land, like the northern and southernmost tips of New Zealand, though I have also been aware of them whilst standing on a seashore.

I put my question, "Where does deva joy come from?" to a high deva that had invited me to ask questions. I have included "his" answer here because it captures the feeling of these wonderful Light beings that traverse the oceans, singing their joy across its surface.

In the joy of creation, we celebrate. At every level we contact purpose, whether the purpose is that of a higher deva or of a being with independent thought, like you, a human being. Our joy is in the joining of your purpose with our knowing. There is the light of knowing and the sound of Being. When these two are united, creation happens. Creation is testament to there being no separation. In truth indeed all is unity, all is One. Simple, isn't it?

Purpose or Being just is. It cries out that it is and its cry finds us in the darkness of our knowing and ignites our light. When Love is part of the purpose, love is manifest in our light. Being and knowing reach for each other and the result is Love. I say again, the sound of Being ignites the light of our knowing. It repeats and repeats at every instant in every plane, dimension and realm, creation on-going, demonstrating the oneness of I and Am.

Of course, we higher deva have Being and Purpose. We have evolved through the marriage of Creation. Our light and sound are inseparable from each other though to you it may seem we are more one than the other. We are both the servants and the instigators of creation. We serve that which is higher than us and we instigate the next stage of the purpose shared. Only in the minds of humankind are there separations and distinctions required for so-called understanding but your understanding is merely a stepping stone for revelation and realisation and one day you too must marry the sound and the light that is you.

Layers of Consciousness and Perception

We're beginning to see how multi-level our Universe is, so let's lay out a map of the levels of our physical universe as understood in Ageless Wisdom and some cultural traditions. Though the labels and details may differ from one teaching to another, the main idea of a hierarchy of consciousness and different densities of substance remains.

Fig 9 below shows us where we are in relation to the hierarchy of consciousness and form that composes in our physical universe.

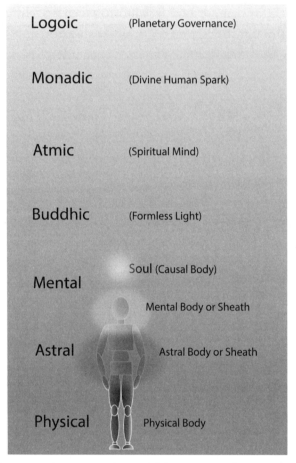

Figure 9 The Seven Planes of the Cosmic Physical Plane
(Adapted from Ageless Wisdom Teaching and the works of Alice A. Bailey)

This schema helps us to get a sense of proportion, an indication of our place as personality-based humans in the greater scheme of things. It clearly shows us how far we still have to go in our journey to higher consciousness. Our normal thought processes originate from our mental body and our emotions from our astral body. You'll also notice that the matter of the planes gets denser as we go further down.

Clouds

I love clouds. They are changeable, exciting and beautiful. They are one of the things I most look forward to when travelling by plane. Flying up through towers of cumulus exhilarates me. Flying over the South China Sea, I once witnessed a parade of popcorn clouds shining a beautiful clear yellow and below them, the sea was washed with umber shadows and silvered ellipses of light. The vast formations that create landscapes in the sky can feed my inner child's delight for days afterwards.

Although clouds ride in the air, subject to the forces of the air deva, I have placed them here because they are primarily water vapour (or ice) clumped together. They sit at one of those transition points where form moves from one state to another. It is in such transitions that life *happens* and clouds demonstrate so graphically to us that life is change, a constant state of creation. Clouds are a transition point where water turns from liquid to vapour and back to liquid again. They leave moisture on the skin as we pass through them or droplets on a plane window.

Clouds are herded and shaped by the sylphs of the air but they move en masse like the sea. Time-lapse photography shows how they roll and tumble like waves, are pulled into feathery sprays by drafts of wind and glide across the sky like a tide. Their watery composition reflects the light of atmosphere and sun and sometimes they form surreal "lands" every bit as complex in shape and size as terra firma itself.

On a journey from Wellington, New Zealand's capital at the base of the North Island, to the South Island's West Coast, the planes often fly over the beautiful Marlborough Sounds. The views are spectacular. On one particular day, the snowy tops of the southern mountains poked up out of a great land of cloud. This cloud land had its own bays and inlets that mimicked the bays and inlets of the Sounds beneath. On the other side of the plane, to the Northwest, the cloud plain had an abrupt edge and beyond it the Tasman Sea shone gold and blue, turning orange in the distant horizon. From this one small plane, I could see water in three layers—cloud, snow and sea.

I was mindful too that beneath the surface of the sea there is another land most of us never see. Its mountains rise under layers of deep water that form a darker landscape. Where sufficient light can reach, plants and animals that look like plants, cover the slopes and flats. Here too the world darkens or lightens as clouds above reveal or obstruct the sun. Here too, water finds the cracks in the land and fills them up. Its currents are the rivers and streams of the sea that scour and etch this under-land. In this one short plane ride, I was reminded that water gives life to our world on all three lower levels as solid, liquid and gas—ice, water and vapour.

These layers of sky, cloud, land, sea and the layers beneath the sea remind us of the many corresponding layers of the "inner planes" or "subtle layers" of our universe. For example, water is the lower correspondence or out-picturing of the astral plane, the plane of desire and emotion, which we will meet in the next chapter. In its turn, the astral plane is the lower correspondence or out-picturing of the Buddhic plane of formless light and so on, up and up. The notion to grasp here is that the higher levels are the originating sources of the lower levels so their qualities are *reflected* in (and distorted by) the lower levels.

Airy Shepherds

The energetic sylphs are the airy shepherds that herd the water elementals in the vapour to form what we know as clouds, from flat silvery sheets to towering cumulus. The sylphs do their shaping under the direction of larger deva who wield the great energetic forces that create what we call "weather". It is an extraordinarily complex inter-action and feedback of energies—of land, sea and sky. As always, the mediating work is carried out by the transitional nature spirits, in this case we're calling them sylphs, but the larger patterns are controlled by the intelligence of their coordinating deva who in turn respond to and interact with great planetary deva. It is helpful in this context to think of a force as the energy inherent in a large group of elemental lives that is harnessed and manipulated by the intelligence of organising deva. Similarly, the myriad elementals of our body's cells are maintained in a dynamic order by a larger organising intelligence that enables them to function as a living system—our own body elemental.

Deva do not act aimlessly. There is joy and purpose in what they do, whether it is bringing a seed from ripening to its fruition as a fully-grown tree or herding the clouds together for a rain party.

It is no wonder that many indigenous peoples could predict the weather and not only from practised observation. Deva talk to those who are prepared to listen and willing to learn the meaning of their song; a language beyond intellect, a communication that speaks directly from deva to the human heart. We may judge the ancient rain dances and other appeals to the nature spirits as primitive and superstitious. What we need to do in the twenty-first century is remove fear, superstition and cultural ignorance so that from deva we can better *understand* how our world works, to cooperate rather than interfere, perhaps to learn what action is appropriate and when. There are some wonderful pioneers who have brought this field to our attention in ways that are appropriate for us today. Their work forms the foundation upon which others can proceed and exchange information. The question is not whether we are capable but whether we have the wisdom to understand our interdependence with deva and to know the limits of our wisdom.

Ancient Water Elementals

Of course, there is deva life *in* water. In my home country, New Zealand, elemental beings known in the Maori language as "taniwha", frequent rivers and underground places. Volcanic taniwha (Western tradition would probably call them "dragons") inhabit the molten flows deep and not so deep, in the earth.

Our relationship with the elemental beings is more entangled than we realize. Now and then, it's reported by our New Zealand news media that a taniwha is being blamed for an inexplicable frequency of vehicle crashes on a seemingly innocuous piece of road. Farfetched as it may sound to a "scientific" Western mind, these explanations should not be so lightly dismissed.

In his book, *Nature Spirits and Elemental Beings*, Slovenian Marko Pogačnik, describes how our buildings, for example, may be placed over what was an outlet for an elemental being. They are bound to that piece of land and no amount of exorcism can extract them. All exorcism does is cause them terrible distress. Building a road over an outlet of powerful elemental force can have equally disruptive and distressing consequences for both humans and the elemental. Sometimes, the elemental can be "transferred" elsewhere but the situation can be more complicated in different ways. If the elemental entity is quite large and deeply embedded in the land beneath, shifting them may not be practical. In one old house I had experience of, no amount of help, requests or "assistance" from even experienced workers in this field were able to solve the being's discomfort and its energy continued to remain a problem in one exterior corner of the room.

Also, in the past, in a form of "black magic", people who wanted to curse the land or otherwise hinder their enemies, attracted very negative elementals, embedding them in an area. The tie between humans and the elementals of the land can be so strong that the elemental can be held back, unable to evolve or return to its "parent" deva because the psyche of the humans are holding it, binding it to that place.

Amidst the assault on traditional cultures, the old thought forms and emotional attachments to the elementals can imprison both parties binding them to an out-grown mode of being even though over time, these old thought forms would have eventually been replaced without external interference. So, unfortunately, when an elemental life that needs to be free to move to its next level of evolution, is held back by the continuing hold of a human group or powerful individuals, it is only that group or a powerful member of that group that can release the elemental. Why? Because deva that are bound by human will can often only be freed through the relinquishment of that will.

Attraction and Repulsion

Without moisture, even the rocks eventually crumble, yet water also wears rock away and fire destroys water in its liquid form. Such happenings demonstrate at a physical level the Universal Law of Attraction and Repulsion. We are all familiar with attraction. It's the love glue that binds friends, families and nations. It brings the bee to the flower and keeps the planets in their orbits. But this is a world of polarities and attraction is only one side of this Law. Without repulsion—one thing being repelled by or "pushed away" from another—there would be no movement. What we call "creation" would not exist. Everything would be stuck together. Only by the action of attraction *and* repulsion can anything *happen*.

What we see as "Life" happens in the movement that results from this fundamental Law. Atoms are drawn together by attraction and then their relationship falls apart, breaks down (dies) when they are repulsed by each other. Not only is water essential on its own, and as a carrier of nourishment and cleansing, but along with other liquids it glues the particles of the physical world together just as our emotional life is the glue that attracts and binds people together.

Wet sand sticks together, dry sand blows away in the wind. When the cold of autumn causes the cells at the base of the stalk to close the passages between leaf and branch, the leaf dries out, the water in its cells evaporates and the leaf can no longer be sustained. Released, it floats to the ground to rot and thus feed another cycle of "life and death". What became a leaf through attraction disintegrates into reusable matter through repulsion and then through attraction its matter is reused by soil and plant. The more familiar we become with the deva kingdom the more we experience its constant and complex movement.

This world we experience is one of duality where everything contains its opposite. It is only when we can raise our consciousness beyond this level of duality that we experience the peace, the stillness from which all this movement arises.

Fluidity

The quality of fluidity is a wondrous thing. The water elementals transform their substance into solidity as ice or snow, submit to the heat of the fire elementals and melt back into water, then do so again, vaporize and so submit to the air elementals. Here the nature spirits of the air—the sylphs and their higher counterparts—shape them into clouds, making of the sky a sea as serene or as turbulent as the ocean itself. Take a moment to contemplate the wondrous nature of the Being behind this world of fluid phenomena.

Somewhere, up there in the planes beyond our reach, is a deva whose intelligence reaches "down", extending itself into denser and denser, slower and slower rates of its vibrational pattern. Here on the solid Earth plane, its *quality* pervades our world as ice, snow, streams, rivers, oceans, rain, emotions, feelings, joy, and the sublime ecstasy of formless light and on up to planes we can, at present, know nothing of, though they are right beside us.

How differently we see the world when we recognize this high and beautiful intelligence in the water around us and within us. What a difference it makes to our respect for this life-giving element that in temperate lands we have so little regard for because there *seems* to be plenty of it.

Our emotions are said to have a watery quality so what is the relationship between deva and our emotions? Where, on our scheme of the planes of density do we find our emotions? If you've not come across this idea that our emotions have density or substance of some kind, I suggest it's time for a break and the taking of a deep breath . . .

Part Two

Who's Singing
Your Song?

Chapter Eight
Emotion

Human vs Deva Evolution

The deva kingdom is said to be on a parallel evolution to ours though at the higher levels it is ahead of our human kingdom. There are also differences in what triggers or spurs that evolution. Deva evolve through joy. Humans apparently drew the short straw in the evolutionary stakes so we learn the hard way, through pain. That's why we usually find we learn the most from our mistakes and hard times. Apparently, for us, it can take a number of positive experiences to outweigh the impact of a negative one.

According to researcher Rima Laibow (and many others), it seems we are indeed hard-wired to pay more attention to the painful episodes in life than to the positive ones. Of course, there are humans who seem to have conquered this tendency and are able to stay in a positive emotional and mental state pretty much no matter what.

That deva evolve through joy explains why the higher we are able to make our contact in the kingdom, the greater the joy we experience. Sometimes, though rarely, we encounter nature spirits who, even though they are on the upward journey, have a pretty negative attitude towards humans.

Mostly though (in my experience), contact with deva, especially the nature spirits and their higher counterparts, is joyful. They gift us a genuine drug-free "high" that leaves us with a lasting, heartwarming imprint.

Our Own Cosmos

Imagine you could go within the spaces of your skin, to see your body as a collection of cells. What if you could zoom closer to see each molecule as a collection of buzzing energy we call "atoms"? What if you could see your body *only* as these energies—a vast organization of energy and light? Imagine yourself inside those spaces between your atoms and experience your body as a vast cosmos. It's a cosmos full of knowing, full of intelligence that knows how to do what you, its "god", asks of it. Here in the spaces of this vast cosmos of sparking atoms is where you will find deva. It starts with your knowing, is sensed with feeling and may or may not be confirmed with sight.

You are not just your physical body though, are you? You also have an emotional "body" that cannot be seen in the way your physical body can be seen but it can be felt and its effects, its responses and reactions can override the smooth running of your physical body.

You have a mental body too, without which you would not be reading this book. It is subtler still and you probably can't see it either but it is experienced as thoughts and its effects are felt.

The Sea of Deva

Both inside and outside, we live in a sea of deva that surrounds us as water surrounds a fish. We are so *in* it that most of us are not aware of it. The deva kingdom infuses *all* substance and because of our lack of awareness, we do not realize that such substance surrounds us in multiple levels of density. Here, "subtle" and "subtler" means it's less dense than solid and that for us, it is accessed as different levels of consciousness.

A heaving body of ocean, a liquid, flowing river, moving, changeable clouds, they're all expressions of an elemental life we call "water". The same element sloshes, flows and gurgles within our physical body. Its higher counterparts form the subtle "waters" of our astral/emotional body. In Chapter Seven, we acknowledged how water affects us emotionally. When the water elementals interact with the rocks of a streambed or fall as rain, their song stimulates our own watery astral elementals, delighting us with its musical tumbling and soothing us with the gentle patter of rain or, as a raging sea or a flooding river, instilling us with fear. Water is also traditionally used as a symbol and metaphor for our emotions, for obvious reasons.

Like our emotions, water is a changeable fluid. When it is cold enough, water freezes into crystalline forms of snowflakes and ice. When our emotions "freeze", we become emotionally cold, uncaring and unresponsive to the needs of others. Toxins can be created by emotional turbulence that triggers the release of chemicals that flood our physical body. Whether in sadness or joy, when we experience strong emotions, we can cry spontaneous, watery tears that help to remove those toxins from our bodies. As well as being a receptacle of emotions then, water is also a natural cleanser. Water can have a quality of clarity and stillness just as our emotions do when we are calm or meditating deeply but physical water can also become stagnant. Tears can wash our emotions clean, getting them out of the body whereas harbouring them can lead to an unhealthy negative accumulation or to a stagnant emotional life.

Our Own Subtle "Water"

If there is intelligent deva life in every atom of physical matter, what of the more subtle layers that make up the vehicle you, as a human person-ality inhabit? What of your emotions? Does your emotional body have matter or substance? Of course! You may not normally see it with your physical eyes but yes; it is composed of substance that is finer than solid, liquid, gas or etheric (see Fig 8 on page 100 for those layers). So, the substance of your emotional body (sometimes called a "sheath") is above the etheric plane. You'll find it in Fig 9 on page 118 where it is called by its usual name, the "astral body". It may be less dense but it's no less *real* than the physical matter you can see with your eyes.

To the trained eye, the emotional body *is* visible, changing colour and form in a heartbeat. It spreads outward or contracts, flares, sparks, floats, soothes, expressing pain or pleasure. While not all of us can see it, we can usually *feel* it or *sense* it via our own or other people's emotions. Yes, our emotional body *is matter*, emotional/astral matter and what is infused into every "piece of matter" at every level of density? Deva—a kingdom of responsive intelligence that at each level of being has its own quality. The qualities of fluidity, changeability, seeping into things, flooding, thirsting, crystallizing, becoming solid or evaporating into "thin air", these are all characteristics of both water elementals and the astral elementals that constitute our subtle emotional body. Unruly little devils at times aren't they, causing problems whether we're two or eighty-two. Now there's an evolutionary challenge; how do we get those emotional/astral elementals under control?

Astral Body Dangers

Our inability to master our astral elementals causes us to be wildly enthusiastic or totally despairing. When our life is a constant drama, we are allowing our astral elementals to run the show. Addictions to drugs, including tobacco and alcohol are also astral body problems, often attempts to supress the fear, sadness and other unresolved emotional issues of our ego-personality.

When people regularly take mind- and emotion-altering drugs like marijuana, cocaine, methamphetamines etc., they can easily damage their subtle bodies, creating a shattered appearance like shards of broken glass that is clearly visible to those with etheric vision. Like a tree suffering the effects of acid pollution, the song of life can no longer sound through the structure of the person's subtle bodies, and eventually their mental, emotional and physical life is severely crippled or falls apart, a state that can be very difficult to mend. Even a cannabis addiction (a drug often declared "safe" for adults but potentially disastrous for the young) can inflict this kind of damage. Earlier addictions often emerge later in life as unpredictable, often vicious or violent reactions from the person's astral elementals, reactions that are way out of proportion to the situation that triggered them.

From nature spirits up, the world of deva, particularly the higher deva is incredibly joyful and deeply rewarding. It is rich and full, alive and healthy. If young people were taught to connect with the *higher* Life behind the outer appearance of things, they'd never need drugs to get "high" because Life itself can provide all the excitement, mystery, wonder and fulfilment they crave. Perhaps they would realize the beautiful responsibility they have for their own evolution and for their contribution to the evolution of everything else on the Earth.

Withholding the nourishing "waters" of love from a child stunts its growth, in extreme cases, its physical growth, cognitive and motor abilities, and in lesser cases its ability to relate to others in a healthy way. The documentary series *Why Am I* is particularly interesting on this topic. An impaired emotional life can have consequences not just for ourselves but also for those around us.

When our physical body dies, our consciousness withdraws into our astral body or sheath. This is the basis of the phenomena of ghosts and hauntings. These are beings whose consciousness is still stuck in the astral plane or who have left a very powerful imprint on the astral field that surrounds the collective we call humanity. Cremating a person's physical remains as soon as possible after death not only helps rid the planet of the diseases that the body may have died of but also destroys the astral sheath. This allows the person's surviving consciousness to make a quicker retreat to the mental body and from there back to the causal body or casing of what we call the soul, in the plane of higher, abstract mind. You can see where that is in Fig 9 on page 118.

A Warning Tale

Maybe you've heard the story of *The Sorcerer's Apprentice,* made into a famous cartoon by Walt Disney? The lazy apprentice is supposed to be cleaning the floor while his master is away but he consults the Sorcerer's big book of spells and conjures brooms to fetch buckets of water to do the job for him. He does not have the knowledge or skill of his master and unwittingly unleashes elemental powers that he cannot control. Like the hapless apprentice, we meddle with the lower elementals at our peril and in doing so cross the line from cooperation with nature to the dangerous magic of our lower nature. At this level, the elementals are on the path of *involution*. By deliberately trying to harness them, we are bringing our own consciousness back down into a denser material level that we have already evolved out of or are trying to.

Today, deliberately manipulating the lower level elementals is what we call "black magic". We can see then why it is so important to keep our consciousness at a higher level while still aiding those that genuinely need our assistance.

A similar principle applies in ordinary life too. Social workers, psychologists, doctors, nurses, healers and all such helpers need to keep their minds clear and their consciousness high to do their work effectively. They need compassion of course, because compassion is of a higher order than sympathy, which while it may identify with the sufferer, doesn't actually heal or help them find the most appropriate or wise solution.

Where Does Healing Happen?

Joe (whose farm harboured the Quarry creature), said that a problem has to be healed at the level at which it occurred. He says that what we don't heal on this plane is left on this plane for us to sort out when we reincarnate or for others to do it on our behalf, if they can. Why? Because, in this case, the problem is in the substance of the plane or sub-plane where it happened. It is the energetic state of the elemental life involved that needs to be transformed, transmuted or trans-figured respectively, depending whether it occurs on the physical, astral or mental level. As we saw with the fire salamander that was being "held" in the land when it really needed to move on, humans can create problems for deva. We can call upon those in higher planes to assist but if Joe is correct, there may still need to be a responsive being on the plane where the problem exists to enable the healing to take effect. Note, however, that healing is the *release* of a condition and the release happens because it is being dealt with or seen *from* a higher level of consciousness.

So, an important thing to realize here is that when humanity succeeds in raising its spiritual consciousness, it has a ripple effect and healing occurs automatically in the relevant planes. What's more, the effect of one person's enlightenment on the collective energy is multiplied many times when it is joined by the enlightenment of even one other person. This is true whether we are talking about achieving one stage of our enlightenment process or the whole package. In other words, the collective effect is greater than the individual effect. This is why the motives and qualities of our leaders are so important.

The Plane of Desire

The elementals of emotion are the intelligence of desire. They *want*. That is the nature of their being and the quality of the plane of density they inhabit. The astral-emotional plane *is* the plane of *desire*. The quality of the plane and the kind of deva infused into the matter of that plane are one and the same. No energy, therefore no matter or substance of any kind is intrinsically "bad". It's how it is used and where its power is directed that makes it "good" or "bad" according to the effects it produces.

In human terms, what is desire? It is reaching for something we think we do not already possess or that we want more of. The thing we desire can be an experience, an attribute or some kind of knowledge, ability or skill. Or it can be a material object like a new fashion item, a restaurant meal or tickets to a sports event—there are millions of possibilities. It could also be something like wanting "your" team to win or your child to "do well".

Furthermore, as Eckhart Tolle points out in, *A New Earth*, the ego-personality *identifies* with *objects* of desire. This means that if these things we identify with—physical objects, opinions, someone else's affection for us, our concepts and beliefs etc.—are threatened, we can feel our entire identity is threatened and react accordingly.

We project onto objects (or sports teams) qualities that we want, and that is why we desire them. In the case of sports teams, we want them to win so we can feel that we, as their supporters or part of their "tribe", are also winners and thereby "prove" a measure of superiority over the opposing tribe. Desires keep us in a constant state of emotional disturbance. Will I get it? What if I don't get it? Someone else has it, so why can't I have it?

Why do we so identify with the elementals of a plane that we allow them to overwhelm us? First, in our evolutionary journey, it was the physical plane elementals that drove us and for some people that's still the main motivator of their lives. More and more, it is the astral plane elementals of desire that drive most of humanity. In the future, it will be primarily the mental plane elementals we identify with and that will be the focus of our kingdom. It is a matter of resonance. What we resonate with "sticks" to us. We lose ourselves in it, as we do in a piece of music, a dance, a movie or a sport's fixture or the person we are besotted with. We lose ourselves in that field we are most aware of, that which we pay most attention to.

The Quality of Desire

It's not that we have a powerful astral/emotional body that can override even our physical body and sense of reason that causes so much strife for us (and our world) but how we direct that powerful intelligence. Our desire can be selfish. We can want more "stuff" just for us. Our desire can trample on the needs of others if we let it, making us blind to injustice and filling us with greed. It can lead to our thinking, "As long as I'm alright, as long as I get what I want (whether I need it or not), everything's okay. I don't care if other people suffer, that's their problem, not mine. They should just be as clever as I am or work as hard as I do." At the level of societies and nations, this is a disastrous attitude for all of us.

On the other hand, our desire can be selfless and compassionate. "It's okay for me to live comfortably but we'll all be so much happier, healthier and safer if everybody has what they need. If I have been blessed with opportunity to earn more than most, I can share it around a bit more. Not everybody can be a chief. If we were all 'chiefs' the food wouldn't get grown, there'd be no one to drive it to the store or put it on the supermarket shelves for any of us to buy. Oh my gosh, I'd have to grow my own food!"

Desire and Distortion

Humanity, as a kingdom, has a *collective* emotional body. History shows us that when societies experience an ever-widening gap between the rich and the poor, the crime rate soars, social and psychological problems abound, health systems are stretched and jails bulge with prisoners. When the emotional body of human societies is healthy and equality reigns in all areas, including health, education and wealth, crime rates go down, everybody's welfare improves, productivity rises, people are happier, healthier, more productive and we all benefit.

Why? *Desire is a distortion of Love.* Love is responsible for the Law of Attraction and Repulsion mentioned earlier. (Or the other way around, take your pick.) If you take a look at Fig 10 overleaf, you'll see that the waveform is distorted more and more by the density of substance as it moves down through the levels or planes of manifestation. This is why we find it so difficult to appreciate the vast gap in the quality of consciousness between our normal reality and the reality that exists in the planes above our normal human perception. Desire is a distortion because it is filtered or twisted by the lower levels of density it has passed through to reach "down here" to our very dense physical level of human being.

Now, remember how we pictured the song of Creation as producing a dance from Oneness to separation and back to oneness (Fig 5 on page 59 and Fig 6 on page 61). Fig 10 overleaf helps us understand the dynamic of our journey into density and why our world is a dualistic distortion.

You can see that the further we go into denser and denser substance the further we get from that central point from which Intention or Purpose originated. That point of origin is often called the Stillpoint. Buddhism teaches that we should strive to live by what it calls the "Middle Way", which is the same concept. When we are able to stay as close as possible to that central, Stillpoint or Middle Way, we are not distorting a higher ideal or intention by ego-personality tendencies of control, ambition, self-interest, selfishness and so on. In other words, we are living effectively but harmlessly.

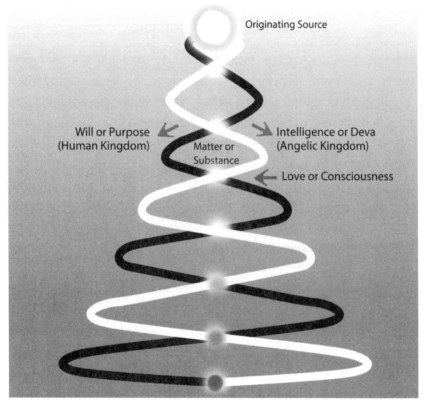

Originating Source

Will or Purpose
(Human Kingdom)

Intelligence or Deva
(Angelic Kingdom)

Matter or
Substance

Love or Consciousness

Figure 10 Double Waveform Descending through
the Seven Planes of the Cosmic Physical Plane

We can also see in Fig 10 that this distortion of the journey into matter creates the duality we take for granted, giving us two polarities to our journey through every plane. At the bottom level those polarities are physical, like day versus night, black versus white. At the astral level (the second band up), it gives us polarities like happy versus sad, calm versus stressed.

A Ladder for the Astral Elementals

Every attribute, characteristic or tool we have available to us can be used to evolve us, or to keep us where we are or even send us backwards. Take that divine impulse to love, for example. At the level of soul, it is inclusive, non-judging and unconditional. Bring that note down to the world of the personality and it can be distorted into possessiveness: "You're mine, only mine!" or conditionally, "I'd love you if only you would _____" and judgementally, "If you were worthy of my love you wouldn't have _____."

What role are our astral elementals playing in these everyday distortions of the divine attribute of Love, turning it into something that is almost devoid of its soul qualities? Well, they are blameless. After all, they can only *respond* to the force and quality of our intention. In this respect, *we* are *their* gods if we but realized it.

By having physical bodies that are predominantly water and subtle bodies of astral substance, we help those classes of elementals to evolve through our own evolution. As we master our emotions, we are turning them away from the path of separation and *descent* into denser matter and onto the long path of *ascent* back to Oneness. In this sense, their evolution and ours are not so much separate as interdependent. As part of the original Oneness, we and the elementals we use, are in this great journey together.

What does it mean to master our emotions? In moving our emotions out of the ego-personality's grip and into the domain of a higher impulse, we turn callousness into sympathy, then sympathy into compassion. Similarly, we turn anger into acceptance and from there into understanding and forgiveness. In these processes, we are moving our responses up through the astral plane to lighter, less dense levels thus transmuting our own astral elementals. We are bringing them under the command and impulse of the higher aspect of ourselves and at the same time, we are transforming our personality by infusing it with these higher qualities. Thus, we have not just a horizontal polarity (of distortion within a plane) but also a vertical Spirit-Matter polarity.

It is also important to realize that our astral elementals also respond to the dictates of our mind because our thoughts can impact on our emotions, especially if we tend to identify with our mind rather than our emotions. Is any of this mastery easy? Heck, no! If you think it's easy because you already have it sussed (as opposed to just being emotionally uncaring), you've probably already done the hard yards some other lifetime.

The Astral Sea

The Astral elementals can carry us on their oceans of emotion, oceans that easily drown out any small voice of reason that rises up against them. Since our astral body is composed of them, it's a body that is responsive and watery. At the least, it ruffles in a breeze of feeling. At worst, it becomes a tsunami of rage, grief, fear or uncontrolled enthusiasm and greed for that which is desired. It's easy to see why philosophies like Buddhism stress the need for detachment from these swings and seesaws that come from attachment to our desires.

We register these elementals as a mass rather than as individually identifiable beings because our astral body does have a singular identity just as we have a single identifiable physical elemental that commands the smaller elementals of the organs and cells. The effect of the astral body is visceral, affecting the lower chakras, particularly the solar plexus (just above the navel). Its effects seep with a flooding or crawling sensation through the watery tissues of our body via the action of chemical messengers.

As we have seen, the astral elementals are most associated with our need to feel loved, to give and receive acceptance and belonging at a level that reassures us with its presence or frightens us with its apparent lack. When we define ourselves by our desires and emotions we are trapped in the distortions or delusions of the astral/emotional plane.

What is it with these astral/emotional elementals? Why are our emotions so difficult to master? Why do we so often not even realize we *need* to master them? Why is it so easy to feel pulled down by the astral elementals?

Remember all those attributes of water? Water is the lower corre-spondence or "out-picturing" of the astral plane so, like water, the very nature of astral elementals sweeps us away as floodwaters can sweep cars, houses, people and animals along on its currents. It is the nature of emotion. Like water, the astral/emotional elementals need something to contain and direct them and that something is whoever is capable of using them, in this case, us.

Whatever we identify with rules us, dominates our experience and determines our choices, which in turn leads to more experiences of the same sort. Only by recognising our attachment can we be freed of it with diligent practice. This is why spiritual paths always have an emphasis on discipline and routines like regular meditation, or prayer or simply checking ourselves regularly to make sure we are staying centred and present.

Astral Fog

At this point, we probably need to remind ourselves what we mean by a "plane". A plane is a band of matter or substance that has its own pattern, qualities or characteristics. What we are describing of the plane is true of its deva life as well. Remember deva are *infused into substance at every level of density* of our solar system. A plane has its own degrees of density and the planes of the physical universe unfold from the least dense at the top to the densest at the bottom.

Because this intelligence in matter that we call deva is either coming into dense matter (involving) or evolving to less and less dense forms of matter, the deva at the bottom of a band or plane of matter are going to be of a different quality from those at the top. It's like that with the astral elementals. At the lower levels of the astral plane, the elementals are a murky lot, while at the top (known as the "higher astral") they're a lot clearer and lighter. Movies and books often depict the lowest astral elementals as dark, shadowy beings, like the entities that attack the murderer in the movie, *Ghost*, or the Dark Riders in *The Lord of the Rings*. We even talk of people who are morose or deeply depressed as being in a "dark mood" or having a "black dog" on their back, or being under a dark cloud, because actually, they are.

So, the lower astral elementals are cloudy-looking beings. Our *untamed* emotions gather so many lower elementals that their effects are substantive. They can be seen as well as felt.

———————✳———————

Human emotion generates fogs so thick they are as effective in blocking your spiritual sight as physical fogs are in blocking your view of the world around you. Can you see then, how both the individual and the mass of humanity, perpetuates its own blindness?

You see then, that when your personality is taken over by the higher intent, you automatically cease to add to the emotional fog and misplaced loves of the world and with practice of staying your life in this state of higher intent, you destroy the residue of these grey clouds of murky ego purpose and help those about you by the clarity of your own intent. *(WE II)*

I notice that when someone clears a problem of the emotional body through a sudden insight or a healing of some kind, they suddenly appear clearer to me. I had literally been seeing them through a veil of lower astral matter. This emotional fog not only affects us individually, it affects humanity as a kingdom and consequently it affects the Earth too.

Battle Grounds

Our bloodthirsty human history has left its mark on many sites around the world, sites where the lower astral elementals have had quite a time. Having travelled a good deal, I've visited a number of famous battlefields, in the UK, Europe and the Middle East. In my home country, New Zealand, we lived for a long time on the coast where a large island sits offshore. A bloody battle took place there between the resident Maori tribe and invading warriors from another, led by their fierce chief. Even though a century had passed, the strange astral fog of both the battle and the deceased could often be seen. Slowly, over the years, a number of us, independently and often unknown to each other, worked to help these poor creatures to move on "into the light".

The big battle sites, like El Alamein in Egypt and Gallipoli in Turkey have been visited by thousands of people over the years and it's obvious that much work of this sort has already been done. It doesn't take away the impact when we stand on sites of such terrible slaughter, realising what has taken place there yet these places can be remarkably free of the astral fog of unquiet dead, though there is often a lingering sadness in the land. Perhaps just by visiting such sites and acknowledging the events in a compassionate way we help to heal the hurts of the past.

In the *Bhagavad-Gita*, a famous text from India, our own battle to overcome, to master our emotional body, to bring all its elementals under higher control is told through the main character, Arjuna. The opposing army is made up of the demons of his lower self—his astral/ emotional elementals. We must all face this battle and eventually win, if we are to master that plane and not be driven by it. Our aim is to move our focus so that our consciousness rests instead on the higher, mental plane. Eventually we must free ourselves even from the mental plane and centre ourselves in the higher realm of the Buddhic plane, and so on, up and up, into even higher and higher states of being that are currently way beyond our average comprehension.

Most of us are still tossed about by physical and emotional storms as we struggle to learn how to rule these bodies, and not be ruled by them. In Robert Redford's movie, *The Legend of Baggar Vance,* we are given a modern version of the *Bhagavad-Gita*. The story centres on a game of golf, but if you are not a golfing fan, don't be put off by that, it's a great watch, especially if you open your mind to the metaphors.

Desire and Aspiration

Desires can keep us out of alignment with the core of our being for there is always something else to desire and the getting does not satisfy us if it comes from our ego, not our higher being. Desire keeps us trying to live in a future that has not yet arrived, whether that's five minutes or five years away. If we are living in anticipation of a future event or obsessed by the past, we are not living consciously in the present and when we are not consciously *present*, our higher self cannot command our attention and infuse our lives, yet the consciousness of most of Earth's humanity rests down here on this astral plane of desire.

Aspiration is a different kind of desire. It is aspiration that has us reaching for higher meaning, seeking spiritual enlightenment, things of the soul and beyond. It is also aspiration when we seek excellence for its own sake, to do and be the best we can. Here we are calling upon the *higher* astral elementals to respond to our intent. They are not as dark and murky as their lower, less evolved brethren. There's a trap though, because aspiration, like everything that originates at a higher level can be distorted by our personality into ideological or religious fanaticism.

How vigilant we have to be with our intentions and the motives that drive those intentions! The quality of our intent attracts an equivalent quality of deva life. It's the lowering of our once-high intention to the lower strata of desire that engages those murky astral elementals and adds to the fog of emotional garbage that wraps itself in subtle layers around us, and around the subtle layers of the whole world.

Evolving Our Elementals

Unless we're primarily motivated by our body's most basic instincts—sex, hunger and so on, we have more or less overcome the drives of the *physical body* but by then, we've developed the next level up—the astral body and its emotions of anger, frustration, joy, laughter . . . Try as we may, often we can't control these sorts of elementals. They seem to have an agenda all their own. Even when we're "grown up", they can sweep us away on an overwhelming tide and give us one heck of a ride, keeping us addicted to drama of one sort or another. They can wreck our friendships, release unpleasant chemicals all through our bodies and make water pour uncontrollably from our eyes.

But what happens when we've got control of those emotional elementals? Our digestive parts can work in happy peace, we feel *lovely* and *loved*. We stop being hurt or incapacitated by the opinions of others, by what they say, whether it's nasty, kind, true or not. There's a dancing joy in our step, in our solar plexus, heart and mind and a smile on our face.

But put a big crowd of humans together who *don't* have control of these emotional elementals and all hell can break loose. Bad things can happen; violence, cruelty, tempers can flare and again we forget we were all One to begin with. The same crowd of humans, when motivated by higher promptings of kindness can get that mass of highly contagious astral emotional elementals to work together to help out, solve problems make other people happy and improve everybody's well-being.

By engaging in the same old emotional dramas and distortions, anxieties, fears and so on, we are both gathering new elementals of that lower astral nature to us and strengthening the ones we are already using. When we refuse to get involved in the dramas of life (our own or other people's), we are taking power over our astral elementals *because then they are no longer driving us.* By mastering our emotions and raising them to the qualities of soul love instead of ego-personality desire, we bring these elementals under the command of our higher self or soul (also known as our Solar Angel). Thus, *we evolve them* into something higher. Every step up the ladder of spiritual evolution we take we are *at the same time* evolving the elementals we are using into their higher form.

The astral plane of desire and emotion does not follow the same rules or conjure the same experience for us that the more solid physical plane of our bodily sensations does. Over the long evolution of the emotional body, we have become familiar with this "new" plane of experience, this finer, more subtle level of matter with its very different set of elementals, who have a very different kind of intelligence to the physical body ones. Unlike the deva and elementals of nature, we don't recognize emotions as elemental entities separate from us because we experience them as if they *are* us.

We have learned that if we lose an arm or a leg, we are still us, yet most of us are so identified with our emotions that we cannot see that we are not our sadness, our desire or our anger. We are something else besides and were all our emotions to disappear *we* would still *be*.

As with all our experience in the 3-D physical world, we are prisoners of a fixed perception. What is the nature of that perceptual prison? It's "matter", which seen from a different perspective is simply a spark of energy playing games with other sparks of energy to form patterns that in their largest expression we understand as "planes" or levels of being. We are locked into using only the lowest, densest of those planes and when we step out of that prison, we enter a very different set of realities.

The Astral Illusion

Yet, we need our emotional elementals. Without them, we cannot develop their higher qualities of empathy, compassion or inclusive love. Without them, a form of psychopathy rules. Emotional elementals have their lower and higher purposes. Think greed versus fair sharing, meanness versus generosity. Our emotional elementals bring us desire, for better or worse. We simply have to decide who is boss and to which use we will put them. That's our challenge and our job as human beings. How we govern our own elementals affects every other kingdom on the planet as we all dance together for good or ill.

When we get a higher impulse, one that is unselfish, inclusive, compassionate, serves the greater good and so on, we have two choices. We can distort it with our own personality-ego self-interest or bring it into our everyday reality in a way that accurately *reflects* its higher nature. A piece recorded in one of my journals put it this way:

———✶———

The receptive emotional body of humankind feels the pull of a vast sea of elementals who move mindlessly, without direction. Where there is no direction there is no way out. Your job as human is to gather and uplift these forces, to draw this water to the sun where its illusion will evaporate and thus elevated, it sparkles the air with joy.

Does the ocean not get colder with its greater depth? And does it not get warmer the closer to the light? Such is the illusion of emotional tides.

The waters of emotion must be purified if they are not to poison the smaller, human life. Would you drink of a poisoned well and expect your body to thrive? When you recognize the waters of your life for what they are, emotional elementals swirling leaderless inside, you can uplift them, like lost children in search of love. Where are they to find it except in you where they reside?

Fear is the darkest of these beings. It blocks the brightness of the sun and can reside anywhere—in your heart, in your mind, deep in your past but reaching forth to strangle your present. Seek it, chase it and it may hide elsewhere. Let it be, sit quietly to observe and it shall reveal itself.

Powerful it may seem but it is in fact a shy animal that must be coaxed out with gentleness and reassurance. Like you it is afraid of non-existence, not realising there is no such thing, only transformation.

Nothing dies, it just becomes something else and the only alchemist of your life is you.

The Truth about the Astral Plane

So great is the problem of "out of control" human emotion, it causes wars, creates fogs around humanity and kills the health and joy of the Earth with greed. Yet mastered and raised, the astral elementals become great allies in our spiritual journey. Whatever it is we want, that *desire* is composed of astral substance. Clearing and overcoming the sway of the astral plane in favour of a higher level of under-standing and Being helps all of us.

Herein lies a clue to the truth about the astral plane. We are told in some of the metaphysical texts that the way we see and experience the astral plane is an illusion born of that distortion of our journey into dense matter. If we were to see it as it truly is, we would know it as a plane of beautiful light. It's the paradox of our spiritual journey that as our consciousness rises, the duality we perceived before, dissolves and the dark illusions of duality dissolve with it, to be replaced by an all-pervading Light for which we are ever-searching.

———————✶———————

The delusion of mankind is a murk so deep it puts a band of smoke about the Earth so thick the angels barely find their way. But every time a human opens up their flower of Truth and looks with honest heart upon themselves, a shaft is cleared, a way is found, and Light upon the human ground pours down and there upon the Earth is found the shining clarity of heaven. *(WE II)*

Chapter Nine
Thought

From Feeling to Mind

The paradigm of this book is that there is nothing we do, feel or think without involving some level of the deva kingdom. The intelligence required to move our physical body is deva, responding to our command, whether we are conscious of issuing a "command" or not. It is automatic to us, a skill perfected over millions of years of evolution and until something goes wrong, like a stroke, for example, we don't even have to consciously command our body to move.

Our emotions, as we've discussed at length, are proving hard to bring under control. Even politicians, supposedly leaders of our nations, succumb to fighting in the chambers of government, verbally or even physically, hurling insults or fists at each other like wayward children in kindergarten. Yes, in humans the astral/emotional elementals have found a wonderful playground. When our sense of self comes largely from our identification with our emotions, we give these elementals free reign. Perhaps when we can remember that they are inherent in a form of matter or substance that we are *using*, we can more easily learn to use that matter wisely.

Now what about our thoughts? Thoughts might trigger a reaction from our emotional body and our physical body but they are obviously not our emotions. Thought exists in the plane above desire or emotions and it is here we meet the elementals of the mental plane—the intelligence of thought, of reason, of science and "concrete knowledge" of the apparently "solid", "real" world of our sense perception. If you've got thus far in this book, you're well used to using this class of deva because we use them when we read. Just as we can sense our emotional body or sheath, we can learn to sense our mental body. I feel it bulging mostly about my head but it expands above my head too. Clearly, there are differences in quality between your emotions and your thoughts and only a little contemplation shows they are very different beasties. The nature of mental elementals is as fiery as the astral elementals are watery.

The Fire of Mind

We saw how closely our emotions resemble the qualities of water, so how does our mental activity resemble the qualities of fire? In popular literature and comics, we often represent an idea as a light bulb switching on above a person's head. It's an apt representation of thought as both electrical and illuminating. A thought can be a bolt seemingly out of nowhere that illuminates a problem or answers a question. It's a fast, sharp, fiery, electrical connection. Of course, our thought processes can be a slower current too—an explorer finding a way through a labyrinth of pathways.

Thought elementals can prove just as unruly as emotional ones though in different ways. Our thoughts can fire-off seemingly at random; spark, then go out or become "lost in space". According to Barbara Strauch in *The Secret Life of the Grown Up Brain,* this is especially true when we're past forty-five. They can be as scattered and difficult to herd as flies in a kitchen. Thoughts can come so thick and fast they can dam up, causing headaches and confusion. Furthermore, their song can be heavy or light, depressing us or uplifting us. Once again, as with the astral elementals, it requires focused will to get these elementals working for us productively.

We actually jump about a good deal between emotion and thought because most of us haven't fully mastered either. Eckhart Tolle sees the emotions as the body's response to the mind. Certainly, thought and emotion affect our physical body, as we've seen. It's a three-way interchange between these three different kinds and levels of elementals. Until we learn to master them all, rather than *identify* with them, we think we *are* our body, our emotions or our thoughts when actually they are choices we are making.

The Quality of Thought

Though our current science does not generally recognize it, both emotion and thought are as much substance or matter as anything else we call "physical". However, they are each different *qualities* or types of substance, finer, subtler than what we conventionally consider "matter" (see Fig 9 on page 118). Deva is the intelligence infused into that substance that causes it to *respond*. Our human will is the *choice* component of our lives. When we identify so strongly with our emotions in particular, we can feel that we have no choice and often declare, "Well, it's just how I feel!" Our will is also the *knowing what* we want. It is our will that chooses what we will think, what we will feel, what our reaction will be. It's the *quality* of that choice that determines what nature and level of deva life responds. Why?

As we saw with the astral plane, there's a gradual change in the quality of elemental response within a plane from the bottom of that plane to the top. These differences in grades or layers within a plane are called subplanes. A petty thought, say of jealousy (which clearly has a strong emotional component) or gossip, has a very different quality than a thought of generosity, a no-strings detached type of giving or sharing. Choosing differently harnesses different elementals to serve us or elevates the elementals we are using to a higher state of being by our choice to master our baser emotions and thoughts.

In our first encounters with the mental plane, we find the elementals of concrete or "rational" mental substance. They make up the first four layers of the mental plane and at the higher levels are the substance of which our intellect is constructed. (You can peek ahead to Fig 11 on page 154 to see what that schema looks like.) What a comfort these elementals are to those who identify so strongly with them that they make their lives here. They bring humans the smug comfort of knowing that *this* is reality because this is fact, reliable, palpable fact. Surely it must be because it's *rational*, isn't it? This is where concrete science rules the human mind, where we can look down upon the masses that live by their emotions or dismiss those who know reality as less defined or less solid, as airy-faery thinkers out of touch with the "real world".

At every level of deva that human beings use, we can be tricked into thinking that only here is *reality* and what is beyond that level is mere fantasy. Why is that? The level we identify with *is* effectively our reality because the level above or beyond it cannot be accessed *in the same way*. If we haven't opened a finer, subtler set of sensors, or to put it another way, have not engaged with or learned to use a higher level of deva, we cannot *experience* that higher, more subtle level.

The concrete or rational mind would say that thoughts are the product of electrical currents travelling along the neural pathways of our brain, analogous to the way wires carry electricity to our houses. Consequently, such a point of view implies that without the brain, there is no thought. In Norman Doidge's fascinating account, *The Brain That Changes Itself*, that position is beginning to look rather tenuous as we discover people who function at a normal level with large chunks of their brains missing or severely damaged. With advances in electronics, we are finding ways for people in an apparently vegetative state to communicate whereas it was previously supposed they were unaware of themselves or their environment. Alzheimer's is a disease that creates physical cobweb-like structures in the brain, yet Barbara Strauch reports that autopsies have shown some people have had high mental function even up until their physical death yet autopsy showed they had advanced Alzheimer's. Somehow, these people have found a way around the physical disability of the disease. They are functioning from a level of *consciousness* that is overriding the brain's limitations.

There is no doubt that we *use* the physical matter of our brain as an essential tool in thinking, emoting and running our physical body but I think that as the concrete sciences come to realize that consciousness, not the brain, is ultimately in charge, we will make great leaps forward both in science and evolution.

Generally, our thoughts seem to be very programmable. Here we find our beliefs and when *they* team up with our emotions, they can be very "concrete" indeed. How does this fixity of thinking start and why does it seem to fly in the face of the mental elementals' ability to zip, dart and discover new territories?

Early Programming

As a species, we are born early, so our big brain can make it through the birth canal undamaged. Consequently, we spend the first years of our lives building the neural pathways and connections in our brain that we need to function as fully circuited Earth humans. It seems at this stage in our evolutionary journey our brain is the major physical instrument we use to deal with the planes of matter in which we find ourselves and to help us mediate between "us" and what we perceive as "not us".

In *The Biology of Belief,* pioneering cellular biologist, Bruce Lipton explains how we are biologically hard-wired by the messages we receive from our environment during the first six or seven years of life. It is known that we begin our incarnation as a human baby with predominantly slow brainwaves known as "delta". As we grow through the first years of life, our predominant brainwaves speed up to "theta". Being in a theta brainwave state makes us very susceptible to suggestion. This means that the stimuli pouring into us from our environment, including the words, moods, emotions and instructions from the significant people around us (e.g., parents) are taken on board by our huge subconscious "mind". In other words, these environmental stimuli form an automatic programme to our advantage or detriment, physically, emotionally and mentally.

In the framework of this book, we could say that this kind of programming allocates the *quality* of the elementals we have at our disposal. Alternatively, we can see it as an *automatic programming of the elementals we are using.* The quality of elementals that our parents, caregivers and siblings are using are imposed on us via the emotions, thoughts and speech of those "significant others" in our lives during those early years. So, we are to whatever degree, programmed by their level of operating in the world.

Metaphysics would say that it's not quite that simplistic, that we come into a life with an incarnational history that predisposes us to perceive what comes to us from our environment with our own bias. We may have a twin sibling who is exposed to the same environmental input as we are but who responds very differently because they've had a very different incarnational history, incurred different karma etc. What is karma? Simply speaking, it's the playing out of cause and effect over many lifetimes. What we do, feel and think individually and collectively causes effects in "the field" and "the field" has no option but to respond. It is more accurate to describe it in this context as "our" field. If we don't learn and change from our experiences, we just get more of the same. As Bruce Lipton points out, the subconscious is a neutral database. What's in it is neither good nor bad, it just *is*. In this sense, karma, as the effect of an earlier cause, is a consequence not a judgment. Programming notwithstanding, we are not, as we might like to think, a total tabular rasa at birth. We can't blame it *all* on our parents.

Since so much subconscious programming occurs in early childhood however, it is clearly in our collective interest to provide help, resources and training for parents before their children are even born. While politicians may claim it shows as a great cost to the economy, the outcomes down the track are enormously beneficial (and ultimately economically quantifiable) resulting in a healthier, smarter, happier, more emotionally and mentally stable populous. Some of the major findings of one the world's longest running studies of the long-term effects of both genetic and environmental input in childhood, commonly referred to as The Dunedin Study, clearly demonstrates how positive input can even override apparent genetic predispositions to extreme violence. The findings are presented for mass consumption in the four part documentary series *Why Am I?: The Science of Us*, mentioned earlier.

"But what about consciousness?" we may ask. "How does it fit into this idea of early programming?"

We don't yet know if brainwave states equate to levels of consciousness but for me and anyone else working in the field of esoteric philosophy or metaphysics it is obvious that consciousness is using the brain as its instrument, not the other way around. We'll come back to this question of consciousness later.

The Ordering Brain

There is a strong ordering aspect or tendency to the human brain (especially the so-called "left brain") that causes it to look for patterns and categories. It's the part that needs to "make sense" of our experiences *by* ordering and categorising. It's the aspect of being human that enables us to build machines and structures, not just physical structures but organisational ones, like bureaucracies, philosophies and business systems. The "left" or linear side of our brain doesn't like things that don't fit the order it has imposed upon life. To those addicted to this orderly view of the universe, the suggestion that it may not actually describe the true or complete nature of reality can be literally unthinkable.

Our tendency to contain experience within a known structure and order can actually prevent us from even *having* certain experiences. If our senses present us with data that doesn't fit because it has no precedents, our brain may not even recognize or record the experience because it cannot make sense of it. Sometimes it will choose something that approximates it that seems to make sense even though it may be misleading or inaccurate.

We may be doing this when we see faces on deva or elementals. They may actually be either shape-shifting to mimic us or we are imposing a face on what we see of them because that's how our brain tries to make sense of something that *can communicate directly* with us. Rather than saying, "Okay, there's this beautiful pale green light talking to me," our brain reasons, "It's talking to me, it must have a face to be doing that." In his informative book, *Nature Spirits and Elemental Beings*,

Marko Pogačnik illustrates the elementals he deals with by using graceful, squiggly lines that for him express how he experiences them. The shapes describe the movements of deva I've talked of in this book.

The Subconscious Advantage

Our programming means we are using the same elementals in the same way time after time. We have turned our decision-making over to them because we are not making any conscious new choices as to how we will think, feel or behave. So, our seemingly vast and powerful subconscious feels like a gigantic hurdle when we're battling to overcome ingrained, learned responses and beliefs about both the world and ourselves. What's more, we may be almost wholly unaware that they are probably programmes, not necessarily "truths". Yet, without those elementals taking care of automatic responses for us, we wouldn't be able to function as we do. We couldn't drive a car pretty much automatically, while talking with our passenger or listening to the radio. We wouldn't even be able to walk without attending to every part of the movement and balance required. These basic physical skills have been developed over millions of years since the very beginning of our descent into Earth matter. So, bless your automatic subconscious and its obedient elementals, be grateful and then learn how to function at a higher level.

In this regard, a healthy "right-brain" function is helpful. It cares less about order, than about experience. It likes to go beyond the separateness that our journey into individuality has imposed on our view of reality to experience the interrelated oneness of everything. When neuroscientist Jill Bolte Taylor experienced a massive left-brain stroke, her experience became almost exclusively right-brained. In *My Stroke of Insight,* she gives a very vivid description of how different reality is without that left-brain filter. Although the "right" and "left" sides of our brain dance together, for many of us, depending on both predisposition and enculturation one or other "side" may dominate.

With good meditation training, we can control the influence of a bossy left-brain without totally losing direction by wafting off entirely into the right-brain view. We can find that middle pathway between the two hemispheres of our brain. Then, by mindfully raising our attention to the higher levels of the mental plane, above concrete reasoning, we can move as close to the soul as our personal development enables us. By tapping into this higher level of consciousness—our higher self—it's so much easier to overcome early subconscious childhood programming with different responses.

Unless we are in a totally still, meditative state, we are thinking and feeling pretty much all the time. Only by operating from a higher point of consciousness, can we avoid the automatic responses of our subconscious programming and change the legacy of ancestral patterns written into the substance of our physical, emotional and mental "DNA".

Where Are Our Thoughts?

Get a better sense of the plane of our thoughts (the mental plane) and where it sits in the bigger scheme of things with Fig 11 below.

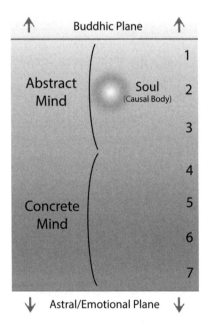

Figure 11 The Seven Subplanes of the Mental Plane. This is an expansion of the third plane from the bottom in Fig 9 on page 118.

The bottom section is where our normal, personal mental life takes place. It's called "concrete" or "rational". It's where we learn to reason things through, so it's the most comfortable place to be if you're after the "real", factual world because it is the elementals in the substance of these planes that will convince us of the legitimacy of that view.

We may think we have found our way to the pinnacle of achievement, the human intellect. We want to believe that here, we're done with the occasional takeover by our physical body with its drives of hunger, sex, activity and rest, and we're definitely done with the tumults, illusions and unpredictability of the emotional plane. Actually, we've just embarked on the next great stage of the human journey and even this plane has its own pitfalls and illusions. As with every stage however, it contains a gift and the prize of mastering the mental plane is *discrimination*.

Helpful Imagination

Thought elementals can entice us to run off on tangents, confuse us with a multitude of options or carry us off into imagination. Imagination often gets a bad rap from the "logic-based", concrete/rational thinkers as if imagination is a childish pursuit that has no higher value. Yet imagination is one of the greatest allies we have in ascending to the next, higher state of consciousness. It can be both a seeking for a new reality and a rehearsal for a new state of being. Albert Einstein said of it: "Imagination is everything. It is the preview of life's coming attractions."

Creative people use imagination to bring something new into our lives, be it the invention of a machine, a work of art or a new way to approach an old problem.

We've talked about the concrete rational thinking that takes place in the lower four levels of the mental plane, so what of the upper three levels? In those top layers, we find the substance of abstract or higher mind. At its best, imagination reaches into those abstract layers. Our soul body or higher self resides here and this is the source of highest possible inspiration for most of us. It's also our source of true intuition as opposed to psychic phenomena (astral) and instinct (a hangover from our animal ancestry).

The Distortion Challenge

When we're blessed with a soul-sourced inspiration, our challenge is how to bring it into form with the least amount of distortion. For example, how can we provide housing for those who cannot earn enough to afford market rents or house purchase prices? How can we accomplish this laudable goal without distorting it with games of personal or political power and financial gain on the part of providers? How can we also do it in such a way that the recipients have a vested personal interest in the outcome so that they will value their new home rather than take it for granted and treat it with disrespect and worse, ending up in the same disadvantaged position they started from? The organisation, Habitat for Humanity seems to manage this feat as do others springing up around the world.

What if we could motivate the gangs found in so many countries to turn their considerable manpower and experience into schemes like Habitat instead of investing in drug addiction, violence and filling our prisons with inmates? The parties involved all need something that is essential for our on-going spiritual journey. It's simply described as "good character" and spiritual texts often emphasize its importance. It is the moral foundation for our climb up the evolutionary ladder while we are in a human body. Good character is the foundation for creating good in the world. Good character isn't weak however; it doesn't mean we put up with other people's bad behaviour or tyranny of any sort, at any level.

The higher inspiration of abstract mind can help us overcome the selfish motivations of those astral elements in the lower subplanes of desire. When we experience the light of high ideals, it illuminates rather than creates astral fog. Those elementals of abstract mind can shine a brighter, wider light on our lives and our kingdom as a whole because they are inherently *of* the light. Always, however, the challenge is to be aware of the distortions that can result from bringing those ideals down into physical form at one level or another.

Lessons from the Parking "Angels"

In recent years I have noticed that all kinds of people who may or may not be interested in "spirituality" talk about how they "order" parking spaces for their cars when driving to the shops or attending an event. Maybe you do it yourself. First, figure out approximately (or precisely) where you want the parking space to be and then *know* in a very decisive way that it will be there for you. It's a process characterized by detachment and a wild desire or desperate, needy wanting will ruin it.

Feeling and stating your intention to the universe, the parking "angels", your higher self or whatever you choose to call it, then *knowing without question* the parking space will manifest when and where you need it are the key ingredients. What's more, you don't confuse the energy of your will with doubts or desires. This is an art you have mastered and the deva respond to that mastery, as they must. One of the reasons it works so well for people is that they have been specific in what they want. Your message is clear. That is to say, your mental and emotional intent is clear, not cluttered up with anxiety, desperation or worry of any kind.

What is really going on here?

When our consciousness rises to a higher level, we can literally and figuratively *see* more. By analogy, when we're in a canoe on a winding river, we cannot see what's around the next bend. When we fly above the same river in a helicopter however, we *can* see what's around the next bend in the river. The ability to "see from above" is what happens in psychic phenomena. It's the ability, random or deliberate, to move out of linear time to one degree or another. Obviously, this is a complex subject so we cannot delve too deeply here.

Thought operates at a higher level of consciousness than emotion, so it gives us a greater "view" of the landscape of life. It is using a higher level of deva who operate at the plane of mind, so we are resonating in a different layer of the sea of deva. I think the combination of our clear intent, our unwavering *knowing* that we'll get a parking space and the fact that we don't allow ourselves to fall into the lower astral state of emotion, all work together towards the outcome our will is choosing. What seems to be magical or the work of angels is simply a right use of our abilities and the appropriate response of the active intelligence of the elementals of the mental plane.

The Power of Focus

The focus we use in ensuring our parking space is the kind of detached focus that makes for successful business people. Metaphysics calls it "one-pointed focus". Clarity of intent is the key, followed by sustained application of one's energy to bring that intent into some level of physical result. In Alice A. Bailey's *Letters on Occult Meditation*, it says of the captains of industry, finance and business that "Supreme concentrated attention to the matter in hand makes them what they are, and in many respects they attain greater results than many a student of meditation." Why? They have all those astral and mental elementals under control to get what they *intend*. So, when those highly successful people change the *motive* of their intent, for social good instead of personal gain, great social improvements will be swiftly achieved. The only "magic" involved here is that of Life itself and how it works at this level.

The lesson from the parking "angels" is quite simple. Work on your manifestation mastery with detachment but leave it up to deva to fulfil your intention in *their* way. When you order a parking space you don't dictate to them which car will have to move and when, for it to happen do you? No, you take care of the "What" part (the purpose or what you want done) then you sit back and let the elementals take care of the "how". Your consciousness is in command and the deva kingdom responds.

We can get so good at feeling out the "field" that we may sense that actually, there is no parking place where we want one right now but there is one just a street away or if we go around the block once, we will time it right because another space is going to come available then. This is plain ordinary old psychism, a step up (perhaps) from instinct. It's not a very high achievement at all really and we use it far more often than we realize. Sometimes it's the "hunch" that isn't a desirous guess but a "sixth" sense. It's like going up in that helicopter as opposed to paddling the canoe down the winding river. When we do this successfully, it's because we've read the field correctly. Similarly, when we are very familiar with an environment, we pick up subtle clues that others don't notice. We are resonating with the devic life that we are familiar with. We may also, subconsciously, be communicating with that devic field, which responds to our inquiry and intent.

Parking may sound like a simplistic example but in mastering the art of ordering a park, you'll be on your way to discovering how to work consciously with deva in a detached and mindful way. You'll be discovering how to bring the astral and mental elementals you are using under your conscious command naturally, without "spells" or other such practices.

Eventually, when we live consciously from our abstract mind or higher consciousness, we automatically bring these elementals under the control of our soul, that is, under our own Solar Angel or higher self. When we master our elementals with the consciousness of our higher self, it is a transmuting and transfiguring process for them and raises the energetic resonance not only of our own subtle bodies but also of humanity as a kingdom. I'd like to say I've got this under control but like everything, knowing how doesn't always make the habit easy to acquire or transfer to other situations of habit.

Distaste for Hierarchies

I know that some people will balk at the hierarchical model on which this book is based. They think it is the enemy of equality. Nevertheless, we are all at different stages of our personal journey through the human kingdom. The hierarchy is one of experience and realization, not of one's intrinsic value. We are equal in the sacredness of our *being* and we're all learning different things in different lifetimes.

We don't judge an older child as being superior to their younger siblings, we rightly recognize they have just learned more because they started earlier. Even people with little interest in metaphysics or religion will describe someone as an, "old soul" and we understand what they mean.

Occasionally we meet someone who seems to stand "head and shoulders" above the rest of us. Such people have dignity without arrogance, poise without snobbery, kindness and good judgement. Such people are not weak. They are iron-strong but compassionate, wise and thoughtful but joyful too. They have mastered their elementals and come under the direction of the higher aspect of themselves, their soul or higher self. Their consciousness "rests" at a higher level than the consciousness of most of humanity. Imagine what the human kingdom will be like when we have all evolved to that lofty state of being! As we can see by another look at Fig 9 on page 118, even such evolved humans still have a good deal further to go but the nature of those higher levels are beyond the scope of both this book and its author.

Ancient Fires

Thoughts are powerful, as so many self-help books and motivational experts tell us. Our thought elementals can affect the emotional and mental elementals of those around us. When we use our mental elementals to introduce a new idea, the elementals that other people are using and *identifying* with, may rebel.

Our thoughts generally take place in the lower levels of the fiery mental plane, in the region we call "concrete" or "rational" mind. Like our emotions, they become habitual responses. Our thought forms, beliefs and opinions about the nature of reality, what should and should not happen, can be found here, though many of these beliefs may be emotion-based as well. Our groups, be they a family, tribe, organisation, religion, or nation, all reflect the thought forms and emotions we hold as members of these groups. Metaphysically, this collective thinking that's been held by an individual or a group for a long time, is called "Ancient Fire". It's an appropriate name given the fiery nature of the plane of mind and its elementals. When someone comes along that wants to challenge these accepted forms, they can receive the full force of the group's resistance. Sometimes, those judged to be a threat to the strongly held thought forms of the group or some powerful authority, have been literally burned to death to "purge" the group of this perceived threat to the supremacy of its existing thought forms.

The resistance of Ancient Fires can prevent new and better ways of doing things as people, businesses and governments protect their perceived self-interest. As we see in the book, *Suppressed Inventions and Other Discoveries*, many a pioneering thinker or reformer has been unable to succeed because of the greater sway of the old thought forms at that time. Nevertheless, what seemed like failure, an idea attempting birth before its time, may still lay seeds in the collective consciousness that sprout at a more opportune time when someone else turns up with a similar idea or invention.

There is a personal challenge for all of us in this concept of Ancient Fires. A quote from composer and philosopher, John Cage is apposite here. He said, "I can't understand why people are frightened of new ideas. I'm frightened of the old ones."

Dealing with our own "Ancient Fires" of the mind is just as big a challenge as getting control of our emotional/desire elementals. We often need to ditch some long-held thought forms or beliefs if we are to move on to a higher level of understanding and consciousness. In *The Lord of the Rings*, the Balrog (whether Tolkien intended it or not) is the personification of the Ancient Fire that does not want to be replaced by a more advanced order of thinking and being. Not only is the creature *made* of fire, it is the spawn of an ancient, earlier "Lord" (Melkor), who was bent upon distorting all that the Creator (Illuvatar) intended for Middle Earth. In a metaphor for our battle with our own personality with its physical, astral and mental bodies, Gandalf describes how he plunged into the deep waters (astral matter), all the while battling his "enemy" before the battle took him to the mountaintop where he finally defeated and "threw down" the Balrog. In metaphysics, the "mountaintop" symbolizes the highpoint just *above* the soul, where the three levels of our personality—physical, astral and mental—are overcome. When Gandalf defeats this ancient fire, he is no longer "Grey" (like astral fog and lower mental plane illusions), he has ascended into the Light and become Gandalf, the White.

Mental Plane Illusion and Pitfalls

Just as the astral plane has its illusions, so too does the mental plane. Of course, these illusions have a different quality. For instance, ideals, originally lofty, can quickly be distorted into an idealism that becomes narrow and blind to the bigger picture.

If we look at Fig 10 on page 136 again, we can clearly see the distortion from the still-point to the outer extremes of the waveform as it makes its way into density. It's the distortion at every level that creates the illusions at every level. You may find that the illusions of each plane are sometimes given different names: **Maya** for the physical plane, **Glamour** for the astral plane and **Illusion** for the mental plane. Whatever it's level or label, the illusion is our inability to see the *true quality* of the substance of that plane. Again, we can see why spiritual teachings, especially those from the East, emphasize the importance of maintaining a still centre, walking the middle path, learning to align with our higher being, *detached* from the vast swings of emotion or thought forms which distort both our true nature and the true nature and source of the substance we are using.

We also need to remember that we don't always develop evenly. So, someone who has a highly developed intellect may not have developed empathy to other people's struggles and shortcomings, and their unbalanced achievements in the mental plane result in a sense of superiority over those who do not live their lives here. We may be faced with another lifetime that forces that missing learning upon us. While detachment is a necessary part of our upward spiritual journey, it is detachment from *identification* with the substance of each plane (physical, emotional or mental) not a disregard for the suffering of others.

How do we overcome mental plane illusions? The same way we got this far. We habitually raise our consciousness to a higher level until it actually rests there rather than just occasionally operates from there. Meantime, our physical, astral and mental elementals are the ladder we must use to make that climb, defeating our own Balrogs on the way.

Personal Songs of the Mental Plane

When the time comes that most humans have mastered the astral plane of desire and are primarily operating from their mental bodies, the fogs of the astral plane will have pretty much disappeared but as humanity falls prey to the illusions of the mental plane, what will we produce? Perhaps we can get some clues from listening to the noise of our thoughts.

If you could describe the sound of your thoughts, what would it be? A cacophony? A jangle of notes? Or is it a tune that begins gently as if finding its way and then gains confidence and surety as it places notes harmoniously and coherently together into a clear, vibrant song? If the mental elementals are the notes, we are the composers, picking out those of the right pitch, tone and vibrancy. Or perhaps you want your thoughts marching, orderly aligned and steady? It's your choice, after all.

There are so many variables that go into our choices and predilections for how and what we think, we would be here for hundreds more pages if we tried to explore those variables any more than we have already. We can however, quietly watch and listen to our thought processes to discover their qualities and behaviour. Are they leading us or are we leading them? You may find that some kinds of thinking tire you quickly whereas others are less demanding. Which ones trigger reaction from your emotional elementals? Do those reactions feel good or uncomfortable?

Posing and answering such questions can tell us a lot about how we are creating the quality of our lives, how we are using our own elementals, where we might want to make changes and why. We get a sense of what kind of song our life is singing both generally and in different situations. Realizing what enables us to create a song that is harmonious, feels good and uplifting and it helps us figure out how to eliminate the unnecessary or downright uncomfortable choices we're making.

"Ancient fires" is a salutary lesson for all of us. At every stage of our lives we are called upon to discern what we should keep and what we should let go, be it a habit of thought, an emotion, an attachment, a relationship, a belief or material belongings. The problem is that by *identifying* with something, we literally continue to give it energy, life and form. We can, if we are not wise in our choices, prevent positive, evolutionary change in our environment and ourselves.

Into the Abstract

Remember, the higher up a plane we go, the greater the light we find shining on the activity that characterizes that plane. At the top of the mental plane, we come to a Light that seems quite different in quality to the concrete, logical, reasoning elemental life we found at the bottom. It's up here in the higher reaches of the mental plane that we find our soul unfolding like the petals of a lotus in its own "body" made of a substance finer than any we've encountered so far in our journey with our own personal elementals. Here in higher or abstract mind, our hitherto sense of individual identity merges with the light and substance of Angelic Love. It comes from our own soul (our Solar Angel) and from the other souls whose causal bodies sit in that plane beside us. Here we find ourselves just a reach away from the Buddhist's Nirvana, the plane of Formless Light, the "Raincloud of knowable things" where we will not just use deva but *unite* with them for the next big phase of our journey.

Here in the highest layers of the mental plane, the fire of thought has become an illumination brighter than any we have met along the way, a light that sings a quality of love we've not encountered before. Here, the hells of the world dissolve into compassion and acceptance that makes forgiveness at once possible and inevitable.

From our vantage point in "ordinary" life, this feels like the home our spirit has longed for but as we approach, we see there is yet more beyond—greater light, deeper knowing. We have reached the top of the third plane of our physical universe. It's where we have aspired to reach but it's not the top, not even half way but it's way far enough to contemplate and aspire to for now and we can thank the deva kingdom for giving us the ladder to get us here.

From here on, it's a whole new experience.

> "There comes a time when the mind takes a higher plane of knowledge but can never prove how it got there."
> **Albert Einstein**

Chapter Ten

Deva We Create

Organizations

From birth to death, we dance between proving ourselves as individuals and the necessity and desire of interacting and cooperating with others. In cooperating, over time, we often go from a state of "me" to "we" or "us". We form groups to get things done for play, service or self-interest.

Everywhere humans form organizations. They can be small or very large, created for every purpose dreamable. Gradually such groups may cohere and just as atoms become molecules and molecules become cells and cells become bodies, each creating a higher, more complex elemental life, so humans grouping together, create something new. When the human group reaches a point of coherence in its purpose, activity and life, the combination of committed human will and the deva intelligence it has harnessed, creates a new *entity*. This applies whether the new creation is a criminal gang, a church, a business, a nation or whatever. We begin to speak of the organization as an entity with its own character and we treat it as something with its own identity even though our contact with it may be via individual human beings.

We dance with these creative energies every day in everything we do. Our houses, schools and workplaces become something more than we who created them through the force and quality of our choices—our collective will that harnesses the deva intelligence in the substance available to us.

Is it misleading to say that we create such deva? Perhaps it's more accurate to say that when we reach a certain quality of intent and the organizational skills to carry it out, we co-opt many many kinds of elementals together and this automatically calls in a higher deva to help coordinate their activity according to the on-going *quality of our intent.* That higher deva is operating at a higher level of consciousness than the elementals.

How can we understand deva as having consciousness? As I understand it, the elementals are not self-conscious but when we reach the level of nature spirits, we find a level of self-consciousness because they demonstrate it to us in their communication. The higher up we go in the kingdom the greater the consciousness we encounter. Deva (both lesser and higher "angels") have levels of consciousness that can command vast numbers of elemental lives, just as we have evolved to command (more or less) the countless elemental intelligences within every cell of our bodies, though that command has mostly been relegated to our subconscious, enabling us to attend to higher things, like emotion and thought. Eventually, emotion too will be under our automatic, subconscious control.

Airport Deva

I'd not given the implications of this collective activity any thought until one day when I was sitting, people watching, at Heathrow Airport (London, England). Secure in the knowledge that I had hours to wait with no pressure to be anywhere but where I already was, my mind was relaxed. My elementals were near still as a watchful cat when they brought to my attention, awareness of a very large deva. With growing astonishment, I realized it was the overlighting deva of the airport itself, a supreme overlighting intelligence. Heathrow Airport is one of the busiest, most organized places on Earth, in the human world that is. Its deva sits high in the sky above the airport, and its extent, like huge arms or wings, covers and infuses the entire complex. The deva is energetically aware of every airplane coming and going, even from quite a long way off and is aware of the minds of the pilots. It holds in its consciousness, the exquisite timings, the movement of people, goods, vehicles; all of it.

What a wondrous being this Heathrow Airport deva is! Truly, the quality of an organization's deva is testament to the clarity, commitment and above all, the quality of intent of the human beings who are behind the great decisions that created it. I was awestruck at the power and majesty of this being, "created" by collective human effort yet surpassing them and becoming something so much more. The quality of its intelligence was exquisite.

We don't need to think much about the organizations with which we deal every day to realize that each has its own recognisable quality, its own signature, its own devic energy and light (or lack of it). I noticed in particular (and with other airports since), that the deva holds the Air Controllers in its consciousness, and that safety is its key intent. I don't want to distract an airport deva from such an important job so I just send it love and the warmth of my appreciation, marvel at its capabilities, and leave it to its complex work.

Electronic Mischief

There are other deva that are also relatively new to our planet, like the electronic deva that overlight computers and the elementals within. As anyone who uses a personal computer or laptop knows, these elementals can seem very capricious at times. Even when we understand how to use the programmes that run them and there is no apparent fault with the hardware, they can behave like sulking children or prima donnas, working smoothly one minute and refusing to play the next. Sometimes, "capricious" seems too kind a descriptor. I enjoy computers, and am no technophobe but there have been times when I have despaired at their apparent inconsistencies, especially for something supposedly built to function entirely on "logic".

It's not just our hands that mould the products we create; it's also our emotions and thoughts. I think the creators of one piece of electronic equipment I purchased (at no small expense) must have harnessed a group of mischievous imps when they invented this particular device.

It was before external hard drives came on the market and I needed something to hold large graphic files that were too big for a CD. Five times, I had to return the unit to have it replaced by another. On the failure of the sixth unit I gave up in disgust and woefully said farewell not only to the expensive device but its expensive storage discs as well.

The main elemental seemed to have a developmental problem. It was incompletely formed. It did not have the coherence of say, a car or truck elemental, and it was struggling to coordinate its components. Every time I tried to communicate with it, I met with a scattered, relatively low-level intelligence that didn't seem able to stay put within the physical equipment, a little like that deva-in-training in Chapter Four that accompanied the small plane.

This electronic elemental was also struggling to work with the other equipment it was connected to—printers, a scanner, keyboard, mouse and the main processing unit (my computer). Each of these pieces came from different companies and it appeared that was part of the problem.

The mindset and intent that goes into the substance of a machine comes from the person or team that designed it plus those that manufactured it. Unfortunately, even if all the hardware had come from one company, the design and manufacture would most likely still have come from a number of independent designers and suppliers of both the system and its components. A potpourri of design ideas and qualities of input contributed to the final collection of products. Unlike a planet, we humans are not so practised at manifesting very complex, interdependent systems.

This poor electronic elemental was confused and struggling with a mish-mash of parts that were not part of a coherent design and manufacturing purpose or programme. It was as if the physical structure of the machine was somehow incompatible with the elemental.

A very young child, building with blocks or drawing a picture of themselves, clearly hasn't mastered the skill of accurately building a replica of a house with their blocks or a very "realistic" picture with their pencil. Their observation and coordination are inadequate for the task. When we try to invent new technologies whose idea we sense but incompletely and without appropriate background practice, we are no better off than young children. No wonder we cobble elementals together that frequently "walk off the job" or are just plain unreliable. Our will is wobbly, our plan inadequate and our intention unclear. Most importantly, we do not have the inter-connectedness of the deva kingdom to realize the ramifications of our actions until it is too late, if we even care what those consequences are.

Intentional Design

Much of Steve Jobs' success with Apple was due to his dedication to product excellence. He placed a very high value on the wise use of mental elementals, on our ability to think. He understood the role of the *quality of intention,* especially in regard to design. Today, it's fashionable in both government and industry to talk a good deal about "the process" in a way that implies that concentrating on the *process* of what we are doing will yield the results we want. In *The Lost Interview,* Steve Jobs, talking of product deterioration when very successful companies shift from a focus on product quality to production processes, strongly disagreed with this "process" approach. He argued that the intention should focus on the end *quality of the product* a company wanted to produce. He argued that we cannot produce good products without an understanding of good design and the *craftsmanship* required to turn a great idea into an excellent physical object or "product". The same applies to all of us when thinking up solutions to life's challenges and bringing those solutions into *form.*

I was told many years ago that there are computer systems engineers or trouble-shooters, working with highly complex systems, who, when called in to fix an obscure problem, do not *do* anything until they have sat, often for quite long periods, tuning into the machines. Whether this is true today, I don't know, but consciously or not, they are working with the electronic deva. Also, I have met first-class mechanics of factory machinery that insist effective problem solving is 80% thinking and 20% action.

That kind of thinking is akin to meditation. It's not a forcing but an allowing, letting the mind explore from the secure basis of familiarity with the ABC of what the machine does and how. Whether we are mechanics, artists, musicians or engineers, we use a similar process but we only get there after a "training period", practising our scales, learning how the machine works, practising with our pencils and paints, studying (often for years) the knowledge and skills of our trade. We learn to command the elementals within the materials and machines and only when we have this level of mastery can we respond adequately to the promptings of inspiration. Only then can we breathe in the light of higher deva to produce a "masterpiece". What is a masterpiece? It's a piece whose component elemental intelligence we have mastered or coordinated to a high degree of competence. Our high intention and the created result as music, art, machinery or product match each other in vision and quality. The distortion (see Fig 10 on page 136) that occurs as we manifest our idea into form is minimal.

Pressure to bring out new products and a public demanding cheaper goods, inevitably lead to things that don't work, break easily and so on. We are not using deva well by churning out mountains of low quality, easily breakable goods that by and large we didn't need anyway. Not only are we misusing the elementals but destroying oceans, lands and air with the resultant rubbish and pollution. Ironically, it is the deva of these wild places that have evolved, not from our desire and will but through the long, long evolution of the Will of planet Earth, that are so dreadfully impacted by the results of so many of our ill-considered inventions.

The Internet

The deva of the Internet is like nothing else I have found in the deva realm. Its sound is unique and "alien". While there is one supreme Internet deva holding the entire system in its being, it has a number of top "lieutenants" if by analogy I can call them that.

These lieutenants are very close to their leader in skill and sit very near below "him" or rather "It". Together they hold in their intelligence a system that has a frequency or resonance unlike anything else on Earth that I've come across. Even the grids of electrical power systems across the globe don't come near to the nature of this buzzing complex of deva life that generates such a peculiar sound and incredible light that fizzes with energy. Astrologers may say it has a very Uranian energy. Uranus is said to be the planet which, for us Earthlings, holds a futuristic note. Its influence is sudden and unexpected often having an alien, innovative or "out of left field" quality to it. It has the sense of the new, exciting or revolutionary about it. When Uranus creates new relationships with its planetary brothers, watch the sparks or lightning bolts of ingenuity fly.

Deva of Commerce

I only became acquainted with these beings in 2006. They have a surprising lightness to them but that is really a comment on my expectations of what they would be like. I wondered why I thought they might be heavier, less jocular than I found them. Perhaps it's because I have tended to think of commerce as being a serious, and culturally, a predominantly masculine domain but my brief communion with these deva has given me quite a different appreciation of the quality at the centre of this vital human activity.

They showed me that at its heart, commerce is not actually about making money. It is about the communication of people and goods—the flow from one to the other—person, place, thing. In English these days, we use the word "business" instead of "commerce", thus emphasizing the *activity* of commerce. We are in "business" and it's a serious bus(y)ness we engage in, or so we think.

But commerce, I learned from these deva, is about creating clear channels through which words, information, ideas, services and goods flow. Its affinity to the Internet is clear in this context. Both commerce and Internet are about moving things along channels of communication but the quality of the two is very different. The commerce deva have a more earthy feel to them, probably because of their long involvement with the bartering, exchanging, "commercial" activity of human beings, which until recently in our history was very much a face to face activity and is still, mostly, a physical exchange of goods and services.

Behind both commerce and Internet is a joining of Intelligence and Will binding us all into a consciousness of unity. The deva of commerce, to me, have a great friendliness to them, a sense of "business as play" and an eagerness to be of service, qualities which again I confess, surprised me.

Four years later, I again contacted the deva of commerce with questions about the financial difficulties being experienced by many countries and individuals.

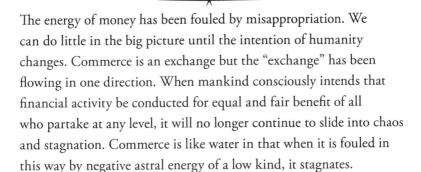

The energy of money has been fouled by misappropriation. We can do little in the big picture until the intention of humanity changes. Commerce is an exchange but the "exchange" has been flowing in one direction. When mankind consciously intends that financial activity be conducted for equal and fair benefit of all who partake at any level, it will no longer continue to slide into chaos and stagnation. Commerce is like water in that when it is fouled in this way by negative astral energy of a low kind, it stagnates.

When I asked how we as individuals could weather these difficult financial times, the deva said:

If your intention is to improve and sustain others in some way, you will succeed. If your thought is for your own need, you will not succeed. [Then, once your intention is pure . . .] Put your request of need to us and have faith that your needs will be met.

How, is not your problem, it is ours. Give us your need and intention clearly. Give it to us in joy and trust and you will be surprised what will happen. We are experts at how!

Creative Interaction

What I had not realized is that deva of commerce are part of the great deva of Communication. I find these deva particularly intriguing because they are active where different entities end or begin. They are deva who mediate *between* individuals or interest groups. The "place" where systems meet is a zone of maximum intelligent deva activity—a zone of intense creativity.

Think about art for a minute. What do artists do? They take different materials and put them together with a particular intention in mind to create a picture, a sculpture, whatever. An artist is forcing very different elementals to work together using their own elementals of the mental body and often their emotional/desire elementals as vehicles for their artistic intention. Remember, deva respond to the quality of our *will* or *intention*. It is the simple elemental intelligence within the various materials the artist decides to use that knows how to combine (or not) with the other materials. Add to this the interaction with our own desire and thought elementals and it's a dynamic song. Similarly, the activity at the meeting point between people involved in commerce is a very dynamic dance and again it is the intention of each of the participants that determines how the deva respond.

Communication is an exchange—of ideas, feelings and actions. The potential for disharmony is huge. If the participants have very different intentions and their respective elementals are running the person instead of being run by the person, anything can happen from a mild disagreement to an angry confrontation to an unbalanced transaction that leaves one party feeling powerful and triumphant and the other beaten and victimized.

———————✗———————

If each participant is in control of themselves and the intentions of both are for fairness of exchange then the outcome will be peaceful, equitable and beneficial.

"Commune" means to be *with* someone or something, to share another's experience or being. When we commune with nature, we are observing and absorbing as much of what is around us as we can. We are trying to be one with nature. Being "one with" the other party is the original characteristic of "communication". In that edge zone between things however, it can become highly charged, a clash of elemental forces, especially in a human activity like commerce.

Zones—Interactive Edges

At the edge of every identifiable system, there is a zone. A system can be a cell or seashore, an elephant or jungle. The zone is where life moves up a notch and creation is faster and bolder. It's an unseen incubator where Will, in its widest sense, meets and elicits the response of different kinds of deva.

In ecology the zone is where sea meets shore, river meets land, mountain meets plain. The zone is the change place where nature experiments, where mangroves develop, desert becomes oasis, where beaches enable the proliferation of shellfish, bird life, grasses and insects.

According to Bruce Lipton, in a cell, the zone is the membrane. It's here that all its "technological advances" take place, where it figures out how to feed, ingest, expel waste, move and so on. In this tiniest of zones, the new happens and the rest of the cell follows its lead.

"The zone" is where Will and Intelligence are at their most creative, cooperative best, where deva sing with expert coordination and seemingly inert matter proves it is alive. Overlighting deva sing in the zones, like our lovely Shetland sea deva or the river and landscape angels we met earlier. They are getting all the parts of a system to interact and work harmoniously. Such a place hums with deva song. It is their activity in the zones that makes the Earth shine with the light of healthy, vigorous life, just as we do when we are healthy, happy and in harmony with all that surrounds us.

When we are reaching for mastery in the plane of thought, the zone is the edge where reason stops and inspiration begins, where the past transforms into the future. Those who change the world are at ease in the zone. They're the inventors, the visionaries, the creators in all fields of endeavour, who lead with the courage of the imagination and intrepid explorer.

Traditional thinking will tell you it's the brain that is your creative "machine" but the brain is simply the receptor of impression and stimulus, a programmable storage device and the clearing house for instructions. Observe instead what is happening, for example, where your physical body field meets your emotional field. That's where the push comes from—the trigger to laugh or cry, be vengeful or rejoice. Author, Stephen Covey, said our life is determined in that split second between stimulus and response, in other words, in how we manage the zone.

Managing Our Elemental Zones

The zone where your astral/emotional field meets your mental field is where sparks can fly, where an idea triggers excitement or thought stimulates an emotional response. Higher still is the zone where concrete reason is met by abstract mind. Here intuition from the realm of soul or higher self, plants inspiration and is received as a subtle realization or a blinding "Ah hah!"

At each such zone different kinds of deva meet, the higher either stimulating or meeting resistance from the lower but always prompting or seeking a response. The zone is not a quiet place for a complacent elemental. The force of emotions triggers responses in the physical body. The force of mental stimulation evokes responses in the emotional body and the force of the higher mind subtly moulds and changes the rational or lower concrete mind.

So, it goes on, up and up, for our existence does not end at the abstract mind and at each level, deva are involved. At each level our will, be it as simple as wanting to move a hand, as complicated as baking a cake or as complex as finding the answer to a quantum physics puzzle, elicits a response from the deva of each appropriate level.

The zone can also be called the "danger zone". Humans are creatures of habit. It's easier to live with habit than reinvent our lives every day. Habits make for comfortable elementals. They can respond the same way each time. That guy Jack, he always riles us, so if our astral elementals receive a new command, "We will *no longer* lose our cool when Jack's around", what are they going to do? You know that struggle? Those astral elementals are about to bust out and react to Jack but we have a new ruling from a (slightly) higher Will. The zone becomes a war zone with our thought elementals insisting we keep calm and our astral elementals trying to do what they've always done when Jack's around.

We live in a symphony of energies and forces. The edge zones are where the power of a theme multiplies—like when three straight lines form a triangle or people group together to achieve a goal. The power of edge zones connecting is what evokes the effectiveness of group effort and unity. So, here's the crunch: *the process of unifying in an effort to evolve, calls in a higher order of deva that can coordinate the lower elementals.*

When we are able to override those lower astral elementals that want to get even at the sight of Jack, we have achieved a step towards self-mastery. Self-mastery is actually mastery of those elementals. Our Self is not our emotions, that is, it is not our emotional/astral elementals. Our Self is not our physical body *or* its elementals. Our Self is in part our will but it is more than just our will. It is what occurs when our will and those elementals dance together to produce that magical marriage we call "consciousness".

So, every "body" or "system" be it the organs of your physical body, or the feelings of your astral body, has an edge zone. The "defining edge" of your thoughts is a zone, so is the edge of your personality, which we define here as the sum total of your physical, emotional and mental bodies.

Every organization—from the bond between couples to the group that studies together, to a business, a bureaucracy or a nation—each has an edge; a zone that interacts with everything around it that it defines as *not it*. The devic life, the intelligence that inhabits each of these seemingly separate "things" are coming up against the deva life in the other "thing" and behind them is a will of one sort or another at one level or another. Everything we do is a song and dance of will and intelligence that creates some kind of consciousness. Phew! There's a lot of busyness going on out there, in here, everywhere. No wonder we need to withdraw regularly to sleep.

From Void to Form

There is a place of course where everything "sleeps". We've touched on it already. It's given many names: "the void", "the darkness", "the waters of the deep". Science, from what I've read, has dubbed it "the field" because scientists need to invent new names when they discover something that's been around forever but feel they need to "prove" (in a way that's acceptable to scientific method) that it's there. They also, I have noticed, can get pretty cantankerous at the suggestion that their discovery is recognized by "unscientific methods" under a different guise. That's okay; it's just their mental elementals guarding their territory. All that's needed is a more synthetic view.

We can think of the void as the "void of potential". A void is empty, right? Well this void *appears* to be empty but the tricky thing about The Void is that it's *full* of everything that can possibly be. It's all sitting there in potential, waiting to come into form, to manifest, to go from being a possibility to an actuality, from the *idea* of being a tree to actually turning up in the world as a seed which grows into a physical tree.

Sound too far-fetched? Quantum physics talks about particles appearing out of the field. As we saw in Chapter Three, Creation stories (including the Judaic-Christian traditions) talk of the void too, either as a void or darkness. So no, this idea of manifestation coming from the dark void is not a New Age concept. It's as ancient as humanity's ability to think about Creation and to perceive it because it *can* be perceived or known in some way. We can theorize about it but we can also *connect* with it.

Our Mediating Zones

We've already mentioned chakras. They are centres of energy that sit between our physical body and our etheric body, which is the blueprint for our physical body. Chakras are quintessential edge zones that *mediate* between a finer substance (our etheric body) that most people cannot see (though many can) and our physical body. The chakras pull energy *into* the physical body via the major glands—pineal, pituitary, thymus and so on. Traditionally there are seven major chakras—at the base of the spine (root), in the abdomen (sacral), around the area of the stomach (solar plexus), the heart, the throat, between the eyebrows (ajna), and just above the head (the crown). In addition, there are dozens of "lesser" chakras in various parts of the body. Another biologist, Lyall Watson reported in his influential book, *Supernature,* that chakras are part of an energy matrix that showed up in Kirlian photography and matched the map of acupuncture points.

Our chakras are traditionally depicted as "wheels of fire". For a long time, I was doubtful about their existence as we often are if we have no direct "evidence" for something. When I became able to sense and then see them in the etheric, I saw them more as fountains of light pouring from a dark vortex than as "wheels of fire". I realized that while the chakra looked from an angle like a spiralling fountain, when viewed from the top or "face on" (and probably with better etheric vision than I possess) it would indeed appear to be a "wheel of fire".

In our body, chakras are the link—the conduit or gateway—between the subtle and the densely formed. In their turn our chakras are influenced by more subtle forces like emotions and thoughts, which are forces originating on the astral and mental planes. One of the principles taught in Esoteric Healing is that there are also higher chakras that interface between the astral and physical body and again there are chakras between the mental and the astral body. We can even more plainly see then, how the patterns, habits and strength of our feelings and thoughts can influence our lives and physical health.

In her wonderfully accessible book, with the delightful title *Punk Science,* Dr Manjir Samanta-Laughton takes the role of chakras to a cosmic level.

Conscious Creation

When we invent something, we often do it by experimentation. The elementals have to respond to our changes of mind, our muddling as well as our clear thinking. When it all "comes together" for us and our design is well executed and efficient, the result is a thing of elegant efficiency, be it a car, a motorbike, a store or whatever. The intelligence of deva has been well used and we can say that the end product has integrity.

Fine human designers intuitively know how to marshal the elementals of their thought forms into coherent, well-functioning systems. They are skilled at using focused will to serve the purpose of their design with clarity and care and the result is a thing of beauty as well as functionality. It is no wonder that people who love machines get so enthusiastic about them. They are appreciating the skill of the creative process and the triumph of the marriage of human purpose with deva, the form builders. Sports cars and vintage planes like the "deadly saviour", the Spitfire of WWII, are rightly held in great reverence by their appreciators.

When we design from a higher consciousness, we open the door to the true creative power that sits right beside us in the spaces between the buzzing particles of energy we call "matter". When the clever, intelligent people of the world make the qualities inherent in Universal Love a key ingredient in their endeavours, it raises the game for the rest of humanity too. How? Whenever people use the systems, services or products that flow from creative minds they are interacting with the *qualities* that went into those creations, whether it is a health system, an office, a supermarket and the products inside it, a computer, a car, train or light bulb. The quality is held in the design and substance of the thing, in the elementals of matter and in the overlighting deva that holds the totality in its intelligence.

When we are able to consult and cooperate with higher deva of nature upon whom our new idea will impact, and cooperate with them in our designing, we will do more than avoid the kinds of disasters our industrial and technical ages have wrought upon the Earth. We will also create something entirely wonderful in ways we cannot yet imagine.

The universe is a feedback system. The parts are interdependent. When we are the initiators, the deva cannot give back a quality we leave out of our Will or purpose. When our purpose changes, we call upon a different level and quality of deva to respond and/or evolve the deva we are using.

Here's what Steve Jobs also had to say about the importance of quality:

> ". . . the way we're gonna ratchet up our species is to take the best and spread it around everybody so that everybody grows up with better things and starts to understand the subtlety of these better things."

Of course, the attitude of quality has to be applied not just in the design of products but also in the commercial and service attitudes and ethics of a company. When the original Will that goes into the formation of an organization or even a country, is imbued with noble qualities, if those leading or working within the organization don't support those qualities, they will eventually divert the original purpose. It is terrifying how quickly the noble principles upon which a nation or an organization was founded can be hijacked by the negative intent of self-interest.

How We and Deva Create a Building

Remember back in Chapter One we saw in Fig 2, page 34, that building ourselves a new house is an example of how we and deva create a new song together? Since then, using our explanatory framework of metaphysics, we've seen how we and deva are unceasingly interacting in the differing layers of density that comprise our Physical Universe. Remember too that each of those layers has its own characteristic consciousness. You may at this point, want to flick back to Fig 9 on page 118, as a reminder of what those layers are.

Architectural Designer, Diana Polkinghorne, aptly demonstrates how our Metaphysical framework can be applied to understand what happens in a very practical situation. Fig 12 overleaf, which Diana has created, shows how a building project, whether it's a new building, or an alteration to an existing structure, comes into physical being.

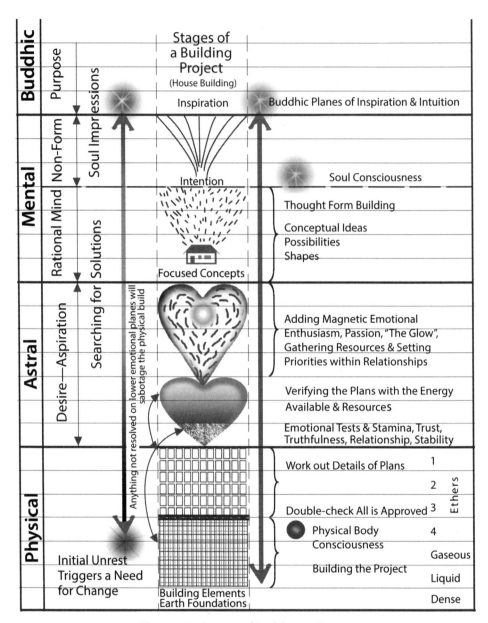

Figure 12 Stages of Building a Project:

From Need for Change—Searching for Inspiration—to Building

(Reproduced with permission of Diana Polkinghorne)

DEVA WE CREATE

Over many years, Diana has consciously applied this relationship of the building process to the schema of the planes, each with their seven subplanes or grades of substance. This enables her to understand and improve both the process and the outcome for everyone involved—herself as designer, her clients, officials, suppliers and the builders engaged in the physical process of manifesting the desired outcome, which of course is the building itself. A building is so much more than a physical structure. It needs to fulfil many functions— safety, utility, ease of use, a pleasing aesthetic and be "fit for purpose" whether it's a home, an office, a restaurant, a factory or whatever. Diana points out that things do not always happen in order and slide up and down the "scale" as the project unfolds.

One of the most important things we can realize from studying this figure is how our *mastery* of the elementals infused into each of these levels of matter determines whether the outcome matches our original intention or how much distortion it suffers from as it works its way down those planes. Our intention may lie at the highest point we can currently connect to (as in this example) or it may be based at a point further down. What do we actually mean by *intention*? Often, we mean the end result in the dense physical world. It might be a solid structure but it could be a behavioural outcome or an action that we want. It may be a feeling that we want to have. It may be that we want to convince someone else of the validity of our idea. So, let's be a bit more specific about what we mean by "intention" here and wherever else we've used that term in this book.

We're talking about a *motive* that carries with it a certain kind of *energy*. When we think about intention this way, we realize how much the outcome is going to depend on where the source of our intention or *energetic motive* lies. Does it come from the highest point we can contact—from our soul, inspired perhaps by its connection to the Buddhic plane? Or does it originate in the area of concrete reason, home of the intellect? Or is it actually sprouting from a subconscious desire low in the astral plane? We can see from Fig 12 that until we get down into the layers of "rational mind", our soul-sourced intention doesn't have form or imagery, as we understand it. Remember too that even if our intention, our *energetic motivation*, comes from our soul, we still have the challenge of bringing it down into form (rational mind, desire and aspiration and a physical outcome). *The closer we can hold to the quality of energy of that original high point of motivation, the more the lower outcome will be infused with the energy of its higher source.*

Diana's figure shows us how we need to understand both where our intention comes from and what influences can sabotage it on its way into a dense physical reality. We can quickly see how this process that we engage in every day in whatever we are doing uses matter or substance of varying kinds and how we use that substance at any level will affect the outcome because deva are the *builders* of form. It's easy to see that unless we call upon the qualities of our soul consciousness when we set our intention, we can't possibly bring those qualities into the mental, emotional or physical consciousness of our lives or into the world at large. A high energetic motive or intention is going to engage a higher level of deva and, applied to the process all the way down the planes, it will serve to elevate the lower elementals and uplift the entire system. This is why so many spiritual texts and genuine teachers remind us to guard our thoughts and examine our feelings or emotions in the light of our higher, soul-infused inspirations and ideas.

According to Laws

How both dangerous and benign our power has already proved to be in the world!

Now here's an interesting thought, it is said that humans are merely the *elementals* in the throat chakra of planet Earth. We are not as much in charge as we think. We might give the planet a sore throat or worse, with our filthy pollution, our wars, environmental destruction and the astral fog we create with our out-of-control emotions. The planet has its own methods of self-healing however, so we better figure out how to cooperate with the Being that is Earth/Gaia or find ourselves purged with a planetary version of antibiotic.

How do the higher deva that we use in our human activity "become"? Does the questing of humanity create them or are they already there and are simply called into service by our desire and purpose? If we take the view that they are emanations or expressions of divine principles then the latter is true. We simply call them out into service as we evolve. One that comes readily to mind is the deva of Heathrow airport and those that accompany our large planes.

It seems from our human standpoint, that overlighting deva come into being out of the collective activity of particular types of elementals. It is not quite that simple. The "field" or void of potential, already contains an idea, say "commerce". It's not commerce as we know it but the outcome of a fundamental creative *Law* that governs the activity that characterizes commerce. In the metaphysics of Ageless Wisdom, these Laws are described as the Law of Economy, the Law of Attraction and Repulsion, the Law of Synthesis and so on. The deva and their elementals are responding to the Law under which they serve. We can think of such Laws as forces or flows of energy that determine how the different aspects of Creation balance. They are the higher, subtler causal laws that play out in different expressions at all levels of our physical universe.

When our intention pulls an idea out of the "field" or "void", it is automatically infused with a matching level of intelligence in substance—physical, astral, mental, abstract, etc.—intelligence that acts according to the appropriate Law.

What's Our Job?

Whether we can see it or not, there are deva and elemental lives responding to the commands we send them from the astral/emotional plane, the mental plane or from higher levels of our spiritual consciousness. When the astral and mental elementals aren't obeying us, they are under the control of their own Lunar Lords. These beings are responsible for driving the elementals downward into denser and denser matter. They are part of the great *involutionary* forces that have resulted in the material creation we call our physical universe, including our solar system and its planets. We too, in the earlier stages of our human journey, have been on this downward path into matter, learning over countless ages to use these dense materials. You can hear an echo in this of the religious idea of the "fall". There came a point where we could go no further into density and our direction turned towards the light of our origins, to the subtler, less dense planes from which we descended.

Our job is to "rescue" the astral and mental elementals we use, in the sense that by getting them under our control we bring them into our own *evolutionary* journey, away from the *separation* of matter towards the *unity* and eventual return to Oneness of spirit. No wonder we evolve through our difficulties rather than our joys, at least while we are incarnating as human personalities. Our use of physical, astral and the lower, concrete mental elementals is constantly pulling us backwards to a denser consciousness while the thrust of our soul's journey is in the opposite direction—*a return to greater and greater unity through mastery of the substance we are using.*

By our *choice* of thoughts, our feelings and our actions, we attract deva and their elementals, marshal them and direct them. For the elementals we are using, we are the "gods" and they our servants.

Not Ours to Control

The multitudes of nature elementals follow higher purposes than ours. They carry out the planetary Will that decided solid earth and rocks, sea, air and rain would be a good idea. They do the bidding of the Purpose behind the creation of the elemental songs that built the atmosphere around the Earth; the bubble of air that enables all of us to breathe and thus to live in these miracles of creation we call the human body. Such grand, planetary symphonies are under the control of high deva, so mighty in their consciousness we recognize them as Angels or gods.

If we could see it truly, we would experience the world as a complex web of moving energies, of light, sound and colour, above and around and through us. We each have our own field of intelligent matter of which we are the overseer. When we really know ourselves to be the creators of our own lives, we cast our intention and our focus into the abyss of possibilities and without investment in the outcome know that deva will respond in ways, forms and opportunities we did not imagine could be ours. The intelligence of deva will come up with not one but several answers to our intentions because they must, because our previously learned skills automatically call them out when we *rightly* set our intention—our energetic motive—and send it into that field of possibility.

Most of us are not that good at our job. We've not been at it as long as the deva of nature and we're still learning to command our own physical, emotional and mental elementals and through them, all the trillions of energy particles that compose our various bodies.

It's obvious that compared with the deva and elementals of the plant kingdom we're amateurs in this form-building business. They have spent many millions of years evolving the forms they inhabit yet we treat them with appalling ignorance and arrogance. So, let's leave behind humanity's erratic efforts for a while and take a journey of joy and relief from all this heady thinking, and return to the deva of nature.

Part Three

Symphonies

Chapter Eleven
For the Love of Trees

Besotted

I'm passionate about trees. Hence, much of this next part of our journey with deva is about trees and forests. Trees are the most complex structures of the plant kingdom and most closely approximate individualization of any member of that wonderful kingdom. They are not self-aware or individualized *in the same way* that human beings are, but the larger, older trees especially, do develop what we may perceive or interpret as something *approximating* a unique identity and sense of self.

Humans love to project their own experience of themselves and their perceptions onto others. In doing so we often make erroneous assumptions about the nature of other creatures. We anthropomorphize, that is, we project human characteristics onto what is not human.

At the other extreme, we do not recognize the animate, intelligent life that exists in members of other kingdoms that share this planet with us. This kind of separated thinking leads to arrogance and abuses of those other kingdoms and of course, our environment in general. Either approach can mean we miss out on the deep connected joy that comes from realizing (as best we can) the true nature of life on Earth.

One of the problems we run into is language. The words we use have been formulated to express our own experience of living. When we try to describe our experience to others, we have to use the words we already have as a starting point to lead us to a closer approximation

of the reality we perceive. In the end, the only accurate way to understand the other kingdoms in nature is through direct experience and
contact. The best tool we have, in fact the *necessary* tool, is detached,
impersonal Love. Without a genuine love for other life forms, we
cannot begin to understand or cherish them.

It's generally easier for us to notice the deva of nature than any
other kind. They evolved here long before us. This beautiful garden
in space is their creation. It's their response to imperatives we are too
puny to comprehend.

Archetypal Architects

Over two thousand years ago, Plato, a philosopher of ancient Greece,
taught that there are archetypal "ideas" from which things in our
world emanate. In deva too there is a hierarchy from higher to lower—
from idea to form. The idea or blueprint or design of "oak tree" for
example, is held by an advanced deva (Fig 4 on page 35). It holds the
intelligence, plans the blueprint for every oak tree that ever was or
ever will be and modifies that blueprint to evolve the form through
time. This evolution happens through the deva's relationship with the
elemental lives infused into the body of the tree and as a response to
the changing state of the environment around it and devic purpose.
The song is always being sung. The essence may not change but the
notes may vary a little as it responds to the bigger song of which it is
just a tune.

An individual oak tree is a wonderfully complex thing that begins
with a small seed; an acorn that contains all the material and design
instructions needed to transform it into a shoot then into a seedling,
a sapling and eventually into a mighty oak. From the "DNA" within
this little seed comes a complex, living structure with millions of cells
and systems that support not only the life of the oak but also the life
within the surrounding soil, forest, air and the wider environment.
What a wondrous intelligence it is that knows how to do all this!

The oak tree has its primary elemental or nature spirit, spawn of
the oak tree deva, an elemental that oversees the unfolding of that

individual oak's potential according to the blueprint provided by its originating deva. It's no different really from us having a human blueprint from which, according to religion and metaphysics, we come into body. We incarnate from a higher point—a soul or higher self, which in turn comes from a still higher point of origination. It's interesting to note that Buddhism does not generally recognize the Western idea of "soul" because the aim of the Buddhist is to reach Nirvana, which is the plane of Buddhi and that is the next plane up from where the causal body of the soul resides. (See Fig 9 on page 118.)

The seeming paradox is that creation happens from the top-down and from the bottom-up simultaneously. The higher Will, be it a human soul or the oak tree deva, is singing the intelligence within every tiny whirling bundle of energy we call *matter* into the world of physical form, to create out of substance something that expresses that Will or Purpose. So, here's an important metaphysical concept.

Evolution is the continual experiment of putting together forms that are better and better able to express the growing mastery of the indwelling spirit. (Be that "spirit" the archetype of a tree or the spark of a human being.)

So, when we connect with the elemental intelligence of a tree or a bed of flowers, we are only connecting with one level of the deva kingdom. Above that elemental is the deva of the tree species, which holds the particular design of that particular kind of oak tree and above that again is a deva of "oak tree" and above that, a deva of "tree". We call these layers of higher deva "overlighting" deva because they are a linking, umbrella-like intelligence that *coordinates* the activities of the lesser deva and elementals in its chain of command. These higher deva (also known as "angels") are the *architects* of the multitude of physical forms—the individual trees themselves that bless the Earth with the function and beauty of their lives.

Just what is it that nature spirits of the trees do? They are of a higher order than the lower elemental life of the trees' cell systems and they feed the energy of life through those physical structures inhabited by the many lesser, smaller elemental intelligence.

That's the analysis but what's the relationship between the nature spirit and the overlighting deva or angel like? I'd love to be able to tell you I found out via some glorious revelation on a beautiful day when the world was bursting with spring unfolding its lush green leaves to the sun in showers of light. Actually, the learning came through death.

What Is Death?

While taking one of my favourite walks, I came across a dead bird. It cannot have been more than a day or two out of the egg. The wind had been strong during the previous days so I guess that it, or the entire nest, was blown out of the tree. Farther along the track, an old cottonwood had also lost a large limb.

I manoeuvred the little bird onto a large leaf and carried it back to the house thinking I would find time to draw it the following day. I also photographed it. That was a sensible choice as the next morning, less than twenty-four hours after I found it, the internal organs were turning to mush, eating through the paper I had laid it on. The smell it emitted was pretty strong by now and not in the least bit pleasant. I deposited the wee bird amongst the dead leaves under shrubs where the microbes could do their job and this small assemblage of featherless flesh be dismantled and recycled.

"From dust to dust", says the Christian bible and certainly that is the appearance of it, but stepping further back we can see the process of physical death as "from void to void". The physical form is sung from the uncreated potential and when that lifetime of manifestation is over the *idea* of it withdraws from the substance of it. Its song ceases to penetrate the lower dense planes and all the elementals lose their organizer. The body's coherence is gone, leaving those elements and elementals free to be organized into a different song. In the case of that little bird, it would become nutrients for the shrubs growing above it.

Has the idea of the bird departed too? No, it is still there, where it always was, in the dark spaces of the void, an integral part of the One Life that sits in the void as a potential, apparently individual life, until another singing of the deva's song calls it out. The song will gather, via two parental birds, the appropriate matter with its infused elemental intelligence to manifest as a new bird of that species.

The deva of that species is constantly singing. Its song is a design that organizes, assembles and enlivens the collection of matter as surely as an architect designs a house, specifies the materials, organizes the builder and thus "creates" the house through the agency of those who are physically bringing her or his plans into form.

From a metaphysical perspective, death occurs when the spirit that has been "enlivening" a physical body leaves that body. This may *seem* to be a choice, as if a deliberate decision has been taken by that indwelling spirit to depart and with its departure, the organizing life force that has governed the physical body's activities departs. The body breaks down and eventually disintegrates. Or it may be that through accident or illness the body is so damaged that no amount of Will on the part of the indwelling spirit can continue to animate the body.

When it comes to human beings, death raises many questions for us, questions about what causes the ensouling spirit to turn away from its task of enlivening and living through the body. Does it really choose to leave or is it a "victim" of disease? Is it acting out karma, the law of cause and effect? Or has it simply achieved what it intended to achieve in that lifetime?

Such questions have occupied sages and scientists and filled books since humans gained the ability to ponder such questions. It is a fascinating subject that swirls around questions such as, "What is the nature of that indwelling spirit? Is the physical subservient to that spirit? What control does a spiritual Master have over the timing and process we call death? What about death in the other kingdoms of nature, when an animal dies, when a plant dies?"

The Death of Trees

A lovely artist friend called Carol had taken Linda (of the Shetland sea deva encounter), and me for a walk. On our returning, we came to a row of large macrocarpa tree stumps (aka Monterey Cypress). Without being conscious of what I was doing, I left the other two and walked along the row. About half way along, I woke up to where I was and realized the others had not followed me. I looked back. They were just standing where I left them, watching. Carol waved me on.

"Go on, do your thing!" she called.

Obviously, the trees were not newly felled. The tops of the stumps were silvered grey from the sun yet they exuded a disturbing distress like the writhing of an animal or person in pain. I didn't rationalize or think, I just intuited what to do and called on the overlighting deva of the macrocarpa trees. It descended in a large misty column reminiscent of a tree trunk. Then I coaxed the elementals that were trapped in anguish in the roots and stumps to return to their overlighting deva. Wraithlike, they rose into the descending column of the deva. When it was done and the poor tortured elementals were reabsorbed, I walked back. Carol and Linda were just standing, watching and smiling.

Why did the deva not withdraw its elementals at the time the trees were cut down? Eventually I pieced the answer together but only after several other brushes with the death of trees.

Another Rescue

In the town where we lived for many years was a river. It gathered the mountain streams, ran down through the foothills then wound its way past the town to the sea. Along its edges ran a public walkway. In spring, white arum lilies graced the banks outside the house fences that bordered the walkway. In summer, large beds of nasturtiums tumbled across the riverbank and open areas. Their green, water-lily-like leaves were punctuated with bursts of colour where the flowers poked up their heads. Along the track were some large, huggable cottonwoods rising from a wonderful profusion of mixed greens and flowers of many kinds. Two cottonwoods had grown up so closely together that at one point they had formed protrusions towards each other that touched in an arboreal kiss. Naturally, I dubbed them the Kissing Trees.

After we left that town I revisited whenever I could. One year as I came along one of the entryways to the river track, I felt a sense of unease that increased to dread. I quickly discovered why. A command had come from bureaucracy that only trees native to New Zealand were allowed to grow there now. The beautiful mixture of native and exotic species was gone. The tall cottonwoods were just squat stumps and the beautiful beds of tumbling nasturtiums, lilies and other flowers were no more. I'm all for preserving our native forests but this was not an area large enough to be a significant contributor to such a programme. There were already large native forest reserves within ten or fifteen minutes' walk up the hill behind the town. To destroy this wonderful celebration of nature seemed to me puritanical in the extreme. There are few flowers in New Zealand's native forests and those are mostly small and seldom seen. This walk had been a delight to the eye and the senses and full of joyful deva life.

Some while earlier, on the other side of the river, my friend Grace and I had come across many young pine trees that had been roughly cut down, their trunks left strewn about. Grace shivered in discomfort at their palpable distress and we immediately set about calling down their deva and gently moving the tree elementals back to their originating deva.

It doesn't have to be done in this brutal way when we *have* to prune or cut down trees.

A Kinder Way

When my husband and I came across a newly cut grove of young pine trees along this same river track, I was surprised that there was no anguish. In fact, the overlighting deva had descended to the centre of the grove and the elementals were peacefully moving from the stumps to the larger deva. When new native trees and bushes were planted between the stumps they grew with speed and before long a joyous little forest of indigenous species was growing tall and strong in place of the pines.

In the first two instances I've related to you, why were the trees so terribly distressed? It puzzled me that the overlighting deva had not retrieved its elementals until I realized it must have been a sudden happening with no warning. Perhaps the violence of the energy emitted by those who cut down the trees created a barrier that kept the elementals in shock and unable to leave. We know from accounts that when people die in traumatic circumstances they can be caught in the astral plane for some time, unable to reconcile themselves to the sudden, unexpected and maybe violent death. There's a most interesting book about this by Helen Greaves called *Testimony of Light* that was brought to my attention by a Dutch Naturopath who had lost her young child to the Nazis during World War II.

Why was this second little pine forest by the river so different from the one Grace and I discovered? This second little forest was on private land that bordered the river track. It was part of a large property that was primarily covered in native trees and shrubs. It's likely the pines had been planted as a small timber investment. When making inquiries, I learned that the current owners were keen conservationists so perhaps they were *mindful* of what they were doing. Their intention was not to create destruction for its own sake but to replace the exotic young pines with indigenous trees that would be an *extension* of the many native trees already on their land. They employed a professional, experienced gardener who clearly understood the physical needs of the new plantings as the new trees and bushes grew with healthy vigour. It's my guess that the young pines were well warned of their coming demize and that the attitude of gratitude and respect allowed for their natural and easy passage back to the overlighting deva.

The Importance of Roots

In my account about the row of macrocarpa trees, I said there were only stumps left. They had weathered to a lovely silvery grey and had obviously been there for quite a long time yet the elementals of each tree were somehow trapped within the roots of those short stumps. In the little pine forest where the higher deva was absorbing the elementals back into itself, it was reaching down into the ground under and into the root structure. I just accepted this as natural and didn't give it any more thought until I read Peter Wohlleben's book when I was in the middle of writing this one. He points out that there is growing evidence to suggest that the root system of a tree acts like a "brain" that stores experiences and plays a major role in communication between trees. It's not surprising then that the tree's elemental life retreats into the roots when the upper part of the tree is destroyed and not just because it's the only part left.

Because of my experience with this kind of elemental distress, I warn bushes or trees that I am about to prune, to withdraw their energy into the roots until I've finished the job. I also explain why I need to prune them and wait until I feel they have indeed withdrawn before I begin. They respond quickly and it only takes a minute or two before I can get on with the job. For something more major or for the complete destruction of a tree, I recommend giving them twenty-four hours' notice. When we do that, interesting things can happen.

Preparing Trees for Death

When friends Debbie and Pat were about to build their new house on a steeply sloping hillside, they had to remove a fifteen-year-old Norfolk pine that grew smack in the middle of where the house had to go. Norfolk pines mature into very tall trees with large root systems and the piece of land was too steep and too small to even contemplate constructing the house around it. I asked to be allowed to prepare the tree before the arborist came to cut it down.

Debbie joined me, clearly unsure what to expect. I asked her to approach the tree from the higher side, holding her hands up with her palms towards the trunk.

"Slowly," I said, "see if you can feel any change as you get closer."

Nothing, another step, nothing, and then nearly at the trunk a look of surprise crept over her face. A few inches closer, almost touching the bark, an excited grin transformed Debbie's face. "I can feel it! It's tingling, it's alive! Oh!"

The realization that this living tree was soon to be killed dawned on her face.

"It's okay," I said, "close your eyes and we'll explain what's going to happen. Send it your gratitude for how beautifully it has grown. Thank it for holding the ground with its roots. Appreciate it."

The tree's energy expanded in response, touching our human hearts like a caress.

"Now we'll explain in our minds how the house needs to be built here. I'm going to call in the Norfolk Pine deva now and ask it to retrieve its elemental from this tree before the man comes to cut it down."

Debbie nodded; eyes closed still, a mixture of sadness and awe written on her face. As the overlighting deva descended and the tree's elemental reached towards it we both opened our eyes. Loud, unsettling screeching pierced the air. Two seagulls flew in tight circles a few metres above the tree's tip, their calling raucous and insistent. Suddenly a black shape shot out of the top of the tree, a black bird perhaps. It joined the screeching seagulls and suddenly all three were gone.

Pat, who had arrived just in time to witness the birds' strange behaviour, called out as they disappeared. "It's done!"

It takes so little time and effort to move from mindlessness to gratitude and recognition of the sentient life within everything that grows. That it does not have a human *form* does not mean it is not in any way conscious or less important to the health of this great body we call Earth.

Screams

My friend Gale was most alarmed when she heard a terrible scream coming from the tree outside the window of her second-storey Sydney apartment. A few seconds later, a chainsaw started up and very quickly the treetop outside her window disappeared. She'd had no idea there was a plan to cut down the tree. When Gale told me about her experience it was one that was familiar to me.

I was lying in bed one Saturday morning, half way between sleeping and waking when I was disturbed by a heart-rending scream of distress. It was not a human sound and though I leapt out of bed and raised the blind to look down on the neighbour's property where the sound seemed to have come from, I could see no activity at all. Yet, within an hour or so, the ghastly whine of a chainsaw rent the weekend peace and a large part of a big old pohutukawa tree next door was cut away.

That plants and trees pick up our intentions, like so many other things I am writing about, is at present, "unprovable". If we could measure intention to the satisfaction of science, I'm sure a lot of lawyers and judges would be happy! I find it interesting that scientific rigour can be very selectively applied. In a talk in Scotland, former pharmaceutical research chemist and author, David R. Hamilton, pointed out that the measure of effectiveness for new drugs to be approved for production was commonly very close to the scores received by placebos used as the "control" in the trials. Science doesn't yet know how to deal with all the variables that go into why placebos are so effective, so that success is ignored and clearly, it is not in the business interests of pharmaceutical companies to make this clear to the public. Yet cocktails of prescribed drugs can cause real harm. Do we, as a species not have things somewhat upside down here? Science cannot currently deal adequately with the subjective phenomena that gives these kinds of results for the same reasons it can't deal with deva at any level. So no, I can't give you scientific proof of so much of what I am saying in this book, but if we waited for such proof before applying many of life's intangibles, we'd do very little that we consider humane or sensible.

Singing Them Home

Walking along a stony beach where the border of sea and land is narrow and steep, I came across a slender branch from a gum tree, washed up by New Zealand's vigorous West Coast tides. Leaves remained attached to its twigs, indicative of a short journey, probably from the nearby river. The distinctive blue-green leaves of the eucalyptus family were clearly still alive and clapping together in the wind. I stood in front of the branch tuning in. "Sing to us," was the message my heart received.

I don't sing, even in the shower, can't hold a tune. Fortunately, when singing to deva there are no human words and the tune is not a product of a remembering brain but a spontaneous composition of the heart and intuition feeding down from the planes above our normal consciousness. So, I sang softly, a song of gratitude to the dying tree, gratitude for its beauty, for its life, and in the light of this simple song the *breath* of the branch and leaves released their hold and floated away on the wind.

A decade earlier, I had discovered I could sing to deva. It was inland west of the energetic, sandstone, concrete and human jungle of Sydney, Australia's largest city. The heights of the Blue Mountains obscured the distant loom of the city lights revealing the stars above me in clustered mosaics. From a lookout above the Grand Canyon where I stood, the broad dark shapes of the steep, treed slopes below disappeared into shadow. Here at the canyon's head, the mountains rose in a soft, curving crook. I stood alone, just another shadow in the soft darkness of night.

My companions had set off along a pathway that began some distance away and ran alongside the canyon. They'd gone, perhaps in search of fireflies, leaving me safely alone, away from human eyes and ears. Quiet moonlight and starlight picked out the soft lumps of treetops and when I raised my eyes the cobwebbed light of the Seven Sisters of the Pleiades winked in the black night sky. In the shadows below, the presence of deva was palpable and spontaneously I began to sing. The deva gathered its elemental entourage and rose, floating up from the dark valley until it and I were level.

There was no command in it, no desire for anything, just a praise of Being itself. When silence settled again, I still buzzed with the crested energy. I gave my thanks and then, filled with gratitude for the joy of the experience, set off after the others.

It is well known that deva or faerie can steal the notion of time from the human mind and I thought only a few minutes had passed as deva, stars and I wove together in song. I found the trail they had taken easily enough in the moonlight but only a short way along I walked into a wall. It was as black as pitch, as impenetrable as a "real" wall, a force-field worthy of a sci-fi story. The message was clear, "Go back, you cannot enter here right now."

Somewhat unnerved, I found my way back to the unsealed road and walked alone up the long hill to the lights of the lodge, wondering why the way had been blocked to me and how long it would be before the others got back. I was astonished and disoriented when I found they were already there, well settled into the evening chat and activities of the larger group.

"We heard your singing," they said, "it was beautiful."

"You can't have!" Thinking I had been safe from human listeners, I was embarrassed.

"Oh yes, we did."

They assured me they had been back quite a while and I wandered off, mystified. It was not to be the last occasion faerie would play such tricks on me.

Time Tricks and Language

When we step outside the familiar three-dimensional perception of our world with its linear time, to move in more subtle planes of consciousness, our brain can no longer hold onto our structure of "time" because time *as we know it* doesn't function in that same way at the less dense levels of our physical universe. Perhaps this is why, on the edge of things, like the place where scientists study the movement of quantum particles, they cannot explain how a particle can be in two places at once.

To be fully connected with the world of faerie, elementals or the higher deva, it can be difficult to stay properly aware of the human world, so we blame the faeries for confusing us. It's not their fault we can have trouble holding our consciousness in two very different planes or perspectives at once.

The faeries don't really understand it either. They don't know what it's like to be a human, any more than we know what it's like to be them. One of them, a nature spirit from a small brown-trunked tree once asked me, "What's it like to be so big, heavy and dense?"

I'm translating of course. They don't use words like "big", "heavy" and "dense". They don't actually use words at all. They speak in thought-feelings that convey directly what they mean, which effectively gifts us the feeling they have. That, I imagine, is what it will be like when we too can develop such telepathy between us. We won't have to ask someone how he or she is feeling. We'll just *know* because they'll share it directly. When we're very "close" to someone, we do already get a sense of this. We call it empathy.

It's well known that among some of the Aboriginal tribes of Australia, mind or psychic messages pass between members over large distances so they know when their relatives are coming to visit from across a great expanse of desert even though no "normal" form of long-distance communication has been available or used.

When the nature spirit from the small tree asked me that question it showed me directly, how dense and heavy my body seemed to "him". As human bodies go, mine is not very heavy at all so to feel it the way he perceived it as "dense and heavy" was both a strange sensation for me and very amusing. The memory still makes me smile.

They are very curious about us, you see. It's because they see us all the time but we don't see them and of course, they know that. This nature spirit level of deva is very appealing to us and it's the kind most often written about in our stories. They resonate more closely with our emotional bodies than do their higher counterparts. They are change artists, shape shifters, mimicking our human form, fooling us into thinking they are some kind of cutesy little version of ourselves.

Elastic Form

It's not just their delight in mimicry that gives them a form that's sort of humanoid. Our brains have a need to recognize the familiar and if we experience something at a subtle level that doesn't *fit*, our brain will search for the nearest match, like a computer operating on "fuzzy logic". Shifting easily from slippery light to something we can recognize, it's easy to see why they have been depicted as creatures of trickery and magic. Compared with our dense and heavy forms they seem magical, moving with a freedom and speed our bodies cannot match.

Esotericist, Helena Roerich (scribing the wisdom of the Master Morya in *Leaves of Morya's Garden, Vol II*), says of the nature spirits: "Their main property is elasticity. Their form depends on the aspiratory conditions. Falling into the focus of human sight, they are sucked into human form. Men will see them in human shape and animals will see them as animals, because they have no shell." So, when artists like me depict them as forms that we can relate to we are being rather misleading. Now that you know the truth, I shall have to practise depicting them as streaks of light instead. However, if our anthropomorphizing helps us to acknowledge their existence and recognize the differences between them, perhaps that's not altogether a bad thing.

And then there is their joy. The nature spirits exude it. They move in trails of joyous light, spreading colour in their wake. In the world beyond our normal senses, sound and colour are one because light and sound are products of each other and colour is a quality of light. We can feel or even hear their laughter as they go about their tasks and their joy is infectious. Joy is as intrinsic to deva as pain is to a human being. In the splitting of our Oneness into many, we got the struggle side of the experience equation, along with "free will". Deva don't have our freedom to decide what they will do; they must follow the will that commands them but the gift of that lack of choice, is joy.

No wonder a healthy, natural, beautiful forest can bring me joy. It's crammed with it! Every space is filled with the dance of deva. Birds and plants sing to each other in a chorus of activity, thrusting towards the light, building, dismantling, recycling and building again.

Sound, Time, and Light

Sound, like sight and our other "normal" human senses that create, rule and limit our perception of "reality", affords us only one narrow band of reality's possibilities. We have expanded this perception a little. We realize animals can often hear sounds we cannot. Astrophysicists can now record the sounds of planets. Mystics and some religions talk of everything singing the Creator's praise.

In New Zealand, we have cicadas. Like crickets, they make a high-pitched sound. I always think of February as being "cicada month" because that's when our Southern summer is usually at its peak and the cicadas at their most vocal. Along that favourite riverbank of mine, the walkway wound through a grove of Karaka trees, their densely packed, deep green and glossy leaves created a dark tunnel overhead. Here a multitude of cicadas sang their praises to life, a song that to some was unbearably strong but to me it was a bath in sound that jiggled and cleansed every part of my field and left my heart bouncing with happiness.

When crickets rub their legs together, it sounds to our human ear, as a shrill, continuous hum. When that sound is slowed down to match cricket time to human time (using the life span of a cricket relative to the average human span of years), the crickets' song sounds like a chorus of angels; a beautiful lilting harmony in praise of Life.

Every atom is a vibrating energy and everything we see as physical is composed of atoms. Everything fizzes with lesser or greater energy. Everything has its own vibration and therefore its own sound. When we can raise our consciousness above the dense physical levels at which we normally operate we can get a sense of how everything is actually sound and light.

I was participating in a group meditation when I first experienced the two-sided nature of sound and light. I was often aware of the light generated by meditation and on this occasion, I was aware of the strong light emitted by the group. Suddenly, I could also hear that the light was making a sound. We can't really separate the two. At the higher levels that we rightly refer to as deva—beings of light or angelic beings—they are (to us) pure light and sound. The elementals are responding to the light and sound of their angelic overlords. They can't help but do so.

Chapter Twelve
Tree Harmonies and Jarring Notes

Pine, Oak, and Beech

Having spent a fair bit of time in Scotland, I've been lucky to spend time in some of its forests. They're so different from the youthful exuberant tangle of New Zealand forests, in which, until the arrival of the Maori people about a thousand years ago, there were no land mammals apart from a mouse-sized bat. There were no grazing mammals to squash and chomp on the vegetation of the forest floor as there were in Europe or even in Australia, which these days is about 2000 kilometres (1300 miles) away across the Tasman Sea. In New Zealand, there were only birds, some small reptiles, one of which is officially a left-over from the dinosaur era (no snakes), insects, spiders and the tiny bats.

In my favourite Scottish woodland in the Scottish Borders, the understory is sparse. Small deer wander through, grazing on whatever is available. The trees are a mix of youth and venerable age—magnificent smooth-trunked beech giants, dark-skinned horse chestnuts and brooding yews. An intricate deva song would tantalize, seeming far away and so lightly ethereal, it could hardly be heard but that doubtless just meant my inner hearing was insufficiently keen.

On one of the lower paths, there was a trio of trees that attracted me often, a Scots pine, a beech and an oak but it wasn't until a friend's prompting that I managed a good connection with them. It all had to do, in the end, with sound. The Scots pine, the beech and the oak were all tall trees and I was shown how their individual, etheric fluidity moved between them and how their roots, especially the

Scots pine and the beech were intertwined in the earth due to their physical proximity. (At this time, I hadn't read Peter Wohlleben's book with its information about root communication.) These factors along with their height gave them a communicative function that I intended to explore further but haven't yet had the opportunity.

The individual sounds of the trees I could not convey on this plane and can only describe in the words available to me. Not surprisingly, they were sounds that reflected the different energetic qualities of each species. The Scots pine sound reflected its crusty, strong endurance of harsh conditions along with the great beauty of its texture and shape. It was a more short-noted sound and though not at all grating on the mind was more piercing in quality than the others. There was great strength but no harshness. The beech was more musical to my inner ear, more graceful, more peaceful and yet dancing, while the oak had a deeper, lower note despite its slender appearance.

The deva revealed how the sound or song of each tree emanates from its own overlighting deva and is received and sung by its elementals as tunes. The elementals both receive the sound and emit it, taking it to every part of the tree where its different component tunes grow and maintain the many kinds of cells and systems. The sound both carries and emits the light of the tree since its sound and light are one.

Each individual tree spirit (elemental) will use the sound in slight variation as it accommodates the immediate environment, which creates the variation in form of one Scots pine to another. This "choice" (of a low order) is possible because even a minimal "creative choice" factor exists in all expressions of being and the choice widens as the level of consciousness rises. Compared with the so-called free will of a human being it is very limited and in the case of nature is an expression of the joy the deva has in its ability to assemble and maintain form.

Notes and Tunes

While to our inner ear each tree has a singular note, within that note is a tune that makes up the note. For those sensitive to the imprint of sound (both heard by the ears and sound that is heard on the inner planes), we can hear how the note of an idea contains its many tunes that express what it is. Although this idea was given to me in the text for *This World of Echoes* (variously quoted in this book), I didn't understand what it meant until one day when I was listening to one of my favourite pieces of music, "Pathfinder" from Medwyn Goodall's *Earth Healer* album. It begins with a long note and that note is held while the tunes of the theme begin to tumble "out" of it. Suddenly through this music, I realized the reality of sound as a manifesting mechanism.

So, it is the tune that tumbles out of the higher, inclusive note with which the deva and elementals can play to produce a measure of individuality in the variety of branches, shape, bark pattern, etc. We must also remember that the elementals are responding to the forces surrounding them with which they must interact—forces of gravity, wind, water and so on, all of which are also songs of the deva kingdom. The individual tunes are part of an orchestra of tunes dancing together within "the rules of the score", which is set by the originating note, and the Universal Laws under which they operate, thus creating variation of sound and movement that we perceive as nature's *appearance* and *activity*.

The transitional elementals (nature spirits) have more latitude to play with the potential of the tunes though they are still bound and driven by the primary sound emanating from the tree species deva. That deva is holding each form of the physical species within its primary sound. Think about this stupendous achievement and you'll begin to realize the level of consciousness of these angelic beings. It's easy to realize why they are called "higher deva", "angels of species" and perhaps most descriptively, "architects of form". In fact, it's really useful to think of the deva kingdom as a whole as the weavers or *builders of form*.

The material form of the tree dies when the overlighting deva withdraws its sound. Remember how in the little pine forest the overlighting deva formed a central column, like a trunk, that gently pulled back the life light of each tree via the remaining roots, thus extracting the elementals. It does this in a kind of reversal of the song, singing a song of withdrawal rather than one of infusing or outflowing. Now we can perhaps grasp why the branch washed up on the beach asked me to sing to it so that the leaves and the life left in them could more easily withdraw from the material form. The most important thing about that, I think, is that it was simply a song of praise, of gratitude for the beauty, and function of the tree during its life as a form. We can begin to realize why "Praise of Being" is an important concept, not just in the confines of a religious building or service but as a state of living. Now there's something worthy of both aspiration and practice.

Defying Gravity

When asked how a tree can make a branch that grows out at ninety degrees from the trunk, seemingly defying gravity, this was the response from a high deva, who at this level would rightly be called an angel.

———✳———

We are the architects of the physical universe. We command the forces that you cannot and gravity is amongst these. Because we have in fact created gravity, we know how to design to counteract it but also to cooperate with it.

We shape the cells for maximum joining and strength. Our cells are organic—they are flexible and growing, unlike your buildings and the materials you use for them. The growing outside cells of a branch can actively support it even while the inside cells are "dead" by your definition. They [the growing cells] create a strong and flexible "glue". Also, if you could see the true nature of a branch . . . you would see that it is an airy thing of flowing streams of light, not so very different from the air that surrounds it. You would see how in essence, air and branch work in harmony together.

When that life light is withdrawn, the "outer" shell survives and is susceptible to breaking because its fluidity is gone. Even a healthy limb can be broken by storm or lightning but this is always as a result of response to larger movements.

There were two statements of particular interest to me in this communication that I found worthy of further pondering. One was that deva had "created gravity". The other was that they were therefore able to design to counteract the force of gravity or to cooperate with it. This brings to mind some of the buildings designed in recent years that seem to defy gravity (or cooperate with it) in a similar way. These new, more organic shapes in large buildings give the human-constructed landscape a wonderful feel. They indicate that we are beginning to realize we can create cities that mimic, cooperate with or use deva in a way that could be more delightfully natural and perhaps healthier. Some include atrium spaces, along with structures and plants that render things like air conditioning unnecessary. They are examples of how the wisdom of nature can be incorporated into our constructions. We just need the will and commitment to make it so, more often. Often cost is cited as the reason such innovations are not yet mainstream. That's testament to our general stupidity as a society. What makes us healthier and happier is actually less costly to the society as a whole, in the long run.

Tree Life on the Inside

More than a decade before the communication on gravity recounted above, we were living in Sydney, Australia. I was working on illustrations for *The Children of Gaia,* my novel about the ecology of the forests of the world and the natural intelligence that drives them. Not too far from where we lived, there was a park and on a grassy flat at the base of the park's surrounding hills was a large white gum tree. I had made a couple of failed attempts to get "inside" that tree to research a piece for the book.

One morning, as I was exercising in the large attic room of our apartment, I became aware of a slender, pale blue light about a metre high, hovering in the corner. It wasn't the first time such a light had paid me a visit and my inner child had fondly dubbed it the "Blue Faery". By its presence I knew I needed to get down to that big white tree in the park and that this time my mission to connect would succeed.

I sat in the grass a short distance from the tree. Its trunk was large and its thick bark as white as bleached paper. What I found "inside" was extraordinarily beautiful. Pod shapes of light in soft clear colours were moving in a great river of liquid light. Branches felt like tentacles waving freely, as light and responsive as the air itself. Trees, or any other physical life form, are not solid at this level, but a moving stream of energy.

Whether it's a tree or a human being, there are different layers to everything in the physical realm. What level of reality we perceive depends on *the point of consciousness from which we perceive it*. We can look at a tree with our eyes in the normal way of physical sight or we can take ultra thin shavings from the wood and look at them through an electron microscope. Through this kind of microscope, we see an incredible labyrinth of cell structures as complex as any human city. If we could see at the atomic level, everything would look quite different; there would be buzzing clusters of energy with large gaps in between. These latter views are to one side of or "below" our normal physical perception.

If we look "above" or to the other, upper side of our normal physical sight, we see what metaphysics labels the *etheric* reality. It's still physical but it's a finer grade of physicality. So, what I've described here in the white gum tree is at a level *above* our normal physical perception, most likely at the etheric level. There are many levels above this again, each with their own characteristics and patterns as we saw in our earlier diagrams. What is important to understand is that the etheric levels contain the blueprint or the finer form of what we see in the lower layers. The physical tree we see with our eyes is the *result*, a manifestation of that higher-level blueprint. The overall design however, comes from even more subtle levels of reality, from the intelligence of a higher deva, architect of the tree species itself.

It is not only our physical eyes that determine what we see or perceive. Unless we are consciously aware at a more subtle level, we cannot perceive or "see" at that level. There are many variables that go into our ability (or inability) to go beyond "normal" sight—our own physical and subtle constitution, our natural endowments and perhaps most important of all, the training and nurturing of our consciousness.

I find that every time I experience a subtler level of the world around us it raises more questions than it answers, enticing me on to deeper and deeper understanding. This was never truer than one dark night back in suburban New Zealand.

Internal Realities for Suburban Trees

It was a still night and the neighbourhood was quiet. We had a mature plum tree in our back yard in front of my studio. I was crossing the back lawn on my way to fetch something from the studio when I was drawn to stop in front of this elderly tree. Its branches were black silhouettes in the night. Suddenly, without warning, I went from standing on the lawn to being conscious only of being *inside* the tree. Not with my body of course, that was undoubtedly still standing on the grass. I had somehow, unwittingly joined with the consciousness of the tree. It's a communion that is as close as we can get to know just what it's like to be a tree. It wasn't the only time it has happened to me, either spontaneously or deliberately but this time it was night, not day.

The sensation was strange indeed for I was instantly aware of all the television sets that were on in the neighbourhood. I did not hear them, I *felt* them, like a bizarre spatial map. I was aware of all those signals for about a hundred metres (or yards) in each direction. Unlike other trips inside trees, this time everything remained dark to my inner sight. I *felt* not saw where the TV sets were on as they received and emitted their signals.

Suddenly, I was out again, aware of standing on the lawn where there was just the stillness of the night with its dark muted shapes of the familiar. With normal hearing restored, I couldn't even hear our own television that was on in the lounge at the other side of the house and was certainly no longer *aware* of it.

Size and Awareness

The great stream of energy that circulates through a tree is stunningly beautiful and dynamic. It's a stream of awareness that while it is not human, it is nevertheless aware of the energetic qualities of what is going on above, below, around and through it. What especially interested me when I was communing with the large white gum in Sydney was getting a sense of how much of its environment the tree was aware of.

So far, my experiences suggest that generally speaking the small trees are aware of the ground beneath them and of their immediate surroundings, including above them but that range doesn't really extend very far. The larger and older the tree, the greater the awareness of its environment. The white gum, for example, seemed very aware of the part of the park it occupied, the sloping hill behind it and the houses rising up another nearby slope. Its awareness also included much of the sky above and the earth deep beneath its roots.

Coupled with their awareness of what is outside of them, there is also a constant flow of "knowledge" or "information" flowing through the tree's subtle structures. It contains information about the wider environment in which the tree is growing and at the same time, its internal environment. Scientifically, we also know that trees communicate with each other via the release of hormonal chemicals, via the symbiotic relationship between roots and the fungi that live on and around them and are directly affected by changes in the environment.

Written by biologist, David George Haskell, *The Songs of Trees* is a superbly crafted book that takes us on an incredible journey into the lives of twelve different kinds of trees and their interrelationships with their immediate and wider environment, including the local human populations. Quite early on in the book, Haskell makes the following observation about the ability of a balsam fir to modulate its behaviour: "When such processes run through animal nerves, we call them 'behaviour' and 'thought'. If we broaden our definition and let drop the arbitrary requirement of the possession of nerves, then the balsam fir tree is a behaving and thinking creature. Indeed, the proteins that we vertebrate animals use to create the electrical gradients that enliven our nerves are closely related to the proteins in plant cells that cause similar electrical excitation."

After years of research at the Damanhur Federation, Italy, a cell-phone-sized device is now available that converts the variations in electrical signals between a plant's leaves and its root systems into digital sound. From dandelions to trees, the music produced can be astonishing and delightful. Anecdotal accounts of how plants can respond to having a human musician play to them while the plant is hooked up to the device suggest some exciting discoveries ahead in the hotly disputed arena of plant consciousness. I wonder too, how attitudes to the vegetable kingdom would change if every child's classroom had one of these devices?

Trees as Meridians

The large trees are like meridians. They channel the life force that beats at the heart of the Earth up into the atmosphere. As mentioned earlier, science has shown that Pythagoras, the Ancient Greek Mathematician, was right, the vibration of stars and planets sound notes, great gong-like heartbeats that ring out across space, the outcome of a vibration that has reached the level of physical density. It comes from a point, that to us is "no sound" down to a level that *manifests* as sound.

What flows through the trees in a landscape is a *consciousness* of what is happening above, below and around them. It is not a human consciousness so it is not self-referencing. It doesn't "think" in terms of "I" or outside of "Me", rather it is a two-way stream of *information* and *impression* in the form of qualities of energy, so through them we can have greater access to the harmonizing life force at the centre of our planetary Being.

The largest, oldest trees in our lands, be they in cities, suburbs or countryside are worthy of protection for the very real contribution they make to our environment at subtle and physical levels and thereby also to our lives, both subtly and physically. We reduce the size and number of green areas in and around our communities at our peril. Yes, trees drop leaves, disrupt pavements as they grow and foul power lines when planted in the "wrong" place but such inconveniences are a small price to pay for the subtle and beautiful benefit they gift us just by the very nature of their being. Haskell's research indicates that when local residents feel a vested interest in the trees integrated into city pavements, those trees can actually act as catalysts for closer human interaction and the forming of social bonds resulting in an increased sense of community.

Trees in the Landscape

Where trees are sparse—in places like the dry planes of Western Australia—the energetic importance of trees such as the Boab, seem particularly obvious. In a very real sense, trees both anchor the landscape and bind both the physical and subtle layers of the planet's biosphere contributing significantly to its coherence. Carbon sinks and the forests' recycling roles are the results that we see from huge, integrated and interdependent systems of Life that we take for granted on planet Earth. At present, we seem to be blind to the fact that this Life is a totality, the body of one Being. We cannot dismantle or destroy one part of it without affecting the whole.

It's all about energy. Every naturally evolved place *where nature spirits thrive* displays a *synergy* of energy. It flows with ease from plants to trees, along slopes, circulating in glorious sweeps of colour and light. There is no jarring dead end to trap the flow. According to Peter Wohlleben, trees of different heights and species balance each other, protect and feed each other. Left on their own, the nature spirits, under the direction of their overlighting deva create a perfect balance in each place but it isn't static. It's a balance that shifts and changes in form through the long, evolving songs of planet Earth.

Through the natural evolution of landscapes, a balance is created via these flows of energy, which in turn creates an energetic harmony that enables the myriad lives existing in that ecological system to *thrive* rather than just survive. When a naturally evolved (and evolving) area is divided up for development, the human plan for housing or commerce is imposed on the landscape, usually with no recognition or consideration for the existing flows of energy. Mature trees, waterways and almost all aspects that remain of the original ecology are removed in one place but one or two trees, for example, may be left somewhere else. Collectively the original trees had created channels for energy to move from earth to sky and between each other in a matrix of patterns that increased the vitality of the entire area. Without that balance, the harmonic exchange of energy is lost and the landscape loses its "lustre". You may see a couple of lone trees on a hill but the trees that balanced them on other parts of the local environment have been removed and the energetic field is now one of weakness and dissonance, not harmonious vibrancy.

A Matter of Value

Unfortunately, too few people are attuned to these important influences so we easily and often suffer a loss of energetic integrity in our environments. Yet if you look at the most expensive suburbs around the world, you'll generally find they are the ones with plenty of mature trees. There is an instinctive recognition that mature trees and beautiful gardens add significant value to a property and not just a commercial value.

If we humans were smart, we would work with nature's natural abundance. Instead, we try to force the nature spirits into our idea of efficiency and form. The closest we have come to right relationship since abandoning our hunter gatherer lives to settle in villages, towns and cities, is the philosophy and methodology of Permaculture, where the gardener mimics nature and gives deva freedom to do what they have spent millions of years perfecting. Instead, we have all but declared war on nature, raping forest and sea in ignorance and greed. Permaculture has proved that when we truly mimic and work with nature we can feed large numbers of people from small pieces of land. We can even coax verdure from a desert without huge, expensive irrigation that may further rob the greater environment. Permaculture proves that our will and deva intelligence can work with joyous productivity when we are prepared to learn and cooperate. Articles on Permaculture can be found on the Internet along with Permaculture Societies in various countries.

A well-known pioneer working cooperatively and consciously with deva in a garden environment is Machaelle Small Wright who can be found at www.perelandra-ltd.com.

Botanical Breathing Spaces

In days gone by, especially during the 19th century, botanical gardens were created in many of our cities. They feed our dwelling places with energy and they balance somewhat, the dearth of energetic health generated by the concrete and asphalt jungles of our cityscapes.

Large green spaces feed a city with oxygen, energetic harmony and liveliness. Now that it has been restored and looked after, what a literal and joyful breath of fresh air is New York's heavily treed Central Park that takes up a large chunk of upper Manhattan. In Alexandria (Egypt), Montazah Park, the large gardens of King Farouk's former residence, is a favourite weekend treat for locals, especially for those who live in the big concrete suburbs that are devoid of vegetation. Madrid has its El Retiro, London its Hyde Park and so on.

In Melbourne, Australia, the botanical garden pulses steadily, sending wave upon wave out into the city that surrounds it. Its plantings, the choice and groupings of its trees is inspired, its energy steadying and calming. Dr Geo has run nature spirit tours of the gardens, not for the nature spirits—who clearly need no instruction—but for human visitors, coaxing them into awareness of these delightful beings that keep the garden so energetically harmonious and thus feed the city a diet of subtle health and joy. Dr Geo's *Angels of the Botanic Gardens*, is available on the Internet at the time of writing.

Out of Kilter

Sometimes we come across places that are distinctly "out of kilter", where it feels as if we have walked into an energetic war zone or where everything is sick. In Sydney, a city of varied, sometimes jarring energies, I found the botanic garden was not always so at ease as its Melbourne counterpart. When I walked into the cactus enclosure, it was as if the cacti were moaning in pain and the air criss-crossed with jarring currents through which there was no clear path. The entire configuration of the area was "wrong". The energy was unable to circulate in a healthy way and consequently the plants were struggling.

I wondered for a moment whether moving the plants into a different arrangement would solve the problem but actually, the sculpting of the land, the layout of the walking paths and lack of an energy circulation and exit were all problematic. My Chinese friend would have said, "The Feng Shui is bad, the chi cannot move properly." I had only taken a few paces into the enclosure when I felt ill and had to retreat. I sent the cacti what loving energy I could to relieve their torture and quickly left, selfishly, for my own comfort. As I turned out of the enclosure and walked up the main path, a man and a woman came out of the nearby administration building and walked down the slope towards me. The man was carrying a briefcase and from the body language of the two, I guessed that he was an official visitor. As they passed me, I heard the woman say, "The succulent garden is down here. It's not thriving and we don't know why."

Sorry as I was for the cacti, I was delighted at this chance confirmation that I had not imagined my experience. It was tempting to stop them both and tell them what was wrong. I would probably have the courage and experience to do that today but more than twenty years ago when this incident took place, I did not. I hope somebody got wise and relieved the poor cacti of their misery.

Geo Stress

In another part of Sydney, there is a magnificent Chinese garden. In the early 1990s, a large maple tree stood atop a high point of the garden. A friend told me it had been transplanted there but it was dying and a number of experts had been brought in to see what could be done. Indeed, the maple was obviously in trouble. Horticultural netting had been placed over its crown, whether in an effort to prevent distress from the hot Australian sun or to lessen the loss of water from the leaves, I don't know. The garden was quite crowded that day so I sent the tree some loving energy, being as unobtrusive as I could and then I moved on, wandering along the meandering paths, enjoying the rest of the garden.

At one point, I came to a narrowing of the path as it wound around the base of a small cliff. Suddenly, I felt nauseous. Wondering if I was suddenly coming down with food poisoning, I tried to recall what I had eaten that morning, but at that moment, the nausea vanished. I had reached the other side of that particularly narrow part of the path. I stopped, turned around and walked back the way I had come. Again, my body was flooded with nausea until I stepped off this narrow section once more. I searched, scanning the small area for the change in energy. It was underground, not close to the surface but not very far down either. It felt like an extremely toxic pollution of some kind and seemed to be confined to a relatively small area. Perhaps it was a pipe containing something foul or maybe a natural occurrence but energetically toxic. I glanced upward and saw that I was at the base of the rise on which the poor, sick maple was struggling to grow.

Can We Help?

People often tell me of similar experiences they have had. For example, a young friend recounted a time when she and her husband were visiting a park when they came across a large glasshouse containing a tropical garden. Once inside, they stopped in their tracks and looked at each other. "Something was very wrong," she recalled, "the plants were all growing nicely, they were lush and green, but the place felt awful. We just wanted to turn around and walk straight out again." But they completed their walk through the glasshouse and noticed that the other visitors were similarly subdued. There were no smiles of pleasure at this place. She and her husband left. As they walked away, she had second thoughts.

"I've got to go back in there," she told her husband. "I've got to try to help those plants if I can." So, despite her own discomfort, she returned to the glasshouse and sent out as much healing light as she was able. When she and I discussed it, we agreed that the problem in this case also seemed to lie within the land beneath the building. I suggested that on her return visit, or with remote healing, she bring a powerful column of loving light down from the higher planes, through the glasshouse and into the ground beneath. Our sense was that there was a malcontent energy beneath.

As we saw earlier, such energies can be old elemental forms that have failed to evolve or for some reason have become stagnant or they are elementals that have been energetically distressed by the placement of a building over the area through which they function.

Monocultures

Nature does sometimes produce monocultures but most often, that's our trick. Monoculture means having only one kind of tree or crop on a piece of land. German foresters told me that this practice leaves a forest much more vulnerable to storm damage because the roots all grow to the same level and the trees grow pretty much to the same height. Where the trees are of different kinds of foliage, different heights and root depths, the damage in a storm tends to be less severe. However, as we saw in New Zealand in the Easter storms of 2014, even very old, mature and naturally evolved forests, can be vulnerable to storms, especially if a very powerful wind comes from a direction that's not prevalent.

It's a common theme in metaphysics that forms—our bodies for example—are containers for the expression of spirit. The aim of evolution then, is to develop more and more suitable vehicles or forms so that spirit can be expressed with as little distortion as possible. I had known this in theory for a long time but it was through trees I came to understand it experientially. Monocultures, group plantings of just one kind of tree, can give a very special experience at the subtle level.

Cottonwoods

It was a sunny day in midwinter. Over the preceding weeks, I had come to know the distinctive energy field of a grove of middle-aged cottonwoods. They grew on the steep hillside of a large suburban park that is criss-crossed with walking tracks both undulating and steep. The trails were well patronized by locals yet I always found myself alone when I passed by these cottonwoods. Invariably I stopped to take photographs or just be with the trees.

On this particular day, I spent a little time with them and then walked on. About ten minutes later, I was prompted to take another path and found it took me back through the same cottonwood grove only lower down the hillside. This lower path had not been visible to me from the path above.

"Okay," I thought to the trees, "so you've called me back."

I found a perfect place to sit at the base of one of their number and soon fell to communing with them. I called upon their overlighting deva and asked if it would share with me or show me, its essence. What stillness there was in those trees. They held each other in a space of utter peace in being. It was a stillness that was beyond the light breeze, beyond the sporadic twitter of birds and the floating hum of distant traffic from the wide flat countryside that stretched below and beyond.

Though the trees were many, I experienced them as a unity because being a part of their overlighting deva, they are in fact one life. Their slender forms stood, open receptacles of Life. It flowed through them, not only from their deva but joined inseparably to a greater unity whose limits and boundaries, if it had any, I could neither see nor sense.

Above them, I could feel their deva's grace; an airy lightness that belies the appearance of solidity we think of as "tree". I could feel the deva's movement in branch, twig and leaf. Because it was winter, they were bare, their discarded leaves lying crinkled amongst the grass. Energetically though, in the deva's etheric blueprint for the cotton-woods, leaves were still there, in design and function. The movements of circulation and rebirth were there too in the essence of its being, in an extraordinary gentleness whose nature, through and through, was grace.

There was a continuous flow of spirit from Life to deva *to* the trees and *through* the trees, in an unbroken song of being. I saw that this held true for me and for all form, all these vehicles that exist solely for the expression of spirit, of Life, of Being itself. For a few measureless moments outside of time, I saw the simple truth of all things. Such glimpses are rare but entice us on in our journey of awakening to a consciousness that will eventually rest in continuous enlightenment.

Old Twisted Yews

In the gardens of one of Scotland's oldest homes is a line of extraordinary old Yew trees. Many are bent double, their bark striped with many colours. Wherever we go we can make a connection to the energy of the trees of that place, tune in to their deva and link to it again at a more convenient time when we can record the communication and follow a line of questioning. After a visit to these ancient trees, my friends and I did just that upon our return home. What follows is what the overlighting deva of the Yew told us in response to our questions . . .

———————✳———————

I put my roots deep in time and much passes if I am allowed to bring forth form without interference. My nature spirits delight in the slow forming of the twists and turns of the beautiful colours of our bark as you noticed today.

[X] is right in what [they] said about our trees being part of, or being plugged into a network. However, the nature of that network could well be clarified for you.

The network is both in time and space. Time is an ever present now and that is why we have our connection in both the past and the present. The past and the present are simultaneously with us and it is only creatures such as you who do not experience that as holistic oneness.

If past and present is now, then the past is here simultaneously with now. We are conscious of all our past and present at once in the endless now, but when you have gone to the next minute of your attention, for you the past is gone.

Q: Do you make anything like karma?

———————✳———————

Karma is the result of intention. We are subject in a strange way to the karma of others. We are subject to the karma of the planet itself for the planet is a Being of intention. Remember that we are part of the Mother [The deva kingdom] and the Mother must respond to the will of intention. Only in this way do we have karma.

My function is to design and bring into being a form, which expresses the energy I am. We unfold that energy; we unfold it from that part of the beingness of Earth that is given to us to express. We deva are merely serving that energetic intention of the planet. Do you therefore see that our involvement with karma must of necessity be different to yours; we do not decide the quality of energy that the Earth chooses to express, we merely express it.

It is important to understand the nature of deva. We are servants of Life and do not mistake our activity, as being that of initiators of Life. We may set the seed growing but the impetus for the seed's existence, comes from the Life of the planet itself, remember I repeat, we are expressions of Life.

The trees that are an expression of me exist in praise of the One Life.

Our sound is a celebration. When humankind hears our celebration, his heart is opened and as with you today his eyes will well with tears of joy and delight of this song of praise. When humanity fails to hear the chimes of those songs around them, they neglect to ensure the safety and health of those trees. This in turn adds to the diminishment of the energy of praise and celebration that we bring. Do you perhaps get a sense in this way of the interweaving of our lives with yours and the network that exists between us and with you?

Were you to understand the nature of rocks you would see that they too are a part of the network for all is One, is it not? And if you were to add your songs of praise that can resonate through your being when you are aware of your part of this network, you could set those very rocks ringing across the world with your songs of joy and gratitude for Life's tender compassion.

We deva find your thought processes very amusing and a trifle puzzling. Nay, more than a trifle! But we endeavour to understand that you are not in constant connection with this joy of being as we are. It is what you would call our consciousness and here, you will find the key.

When your state of consciousness can be maintained as one of connection and Oneness, that is when you will really be effective. In the meantime, find joy in everything and connect with that world of Oneness and deva as often as possible and of course you can share this joy with others for pure joy, undistorted joy, is contagious. Have you not all found the laughter of babies contagious? Do they not laugh with the sheer joy of being and the delight of Life itself? They seek no reason for their joy and neither do we. Joy is connection and connection is joy. Joy is the nature of Oneness.

Myths, Symbols, and Trees

The Yew tree deva referred to being part of the Mother. We can understand this as the idea that Will (Purpose or Intention) is seen as the active, initiating, "masculine" or "Father" aspect of creation. Deva is seen as the responsive, reacting intelligence, the "feminine" or "Mother" aspect. In this framework, consciousness—the result of reuniting the Mother and Father aspects—is the "Son". (You can see how this looks in the appendix at the end of the book.)

Once again, we meet the core behind the framework of understanding set out in this book; that everything that is manifested as form, at every level of density, originated as One. Such trinities are descriptions of or metaphors for the main aspects of that One.

There are a number of cultures whose creation myths centre on the idea that in the beginning the Mother and Father of the world were inseparable. Myths, teachings and religious scriptures help us to make sense of our experience and give us clues about the deep mysteries of life that we are trying to understand as we evolve.

Despite the varied versions, there are common underlying themes that lead us to a sense of the truth behind the stories. Really, these myths are *symbols* designed to give us insights into the nature of truth and as such, they are valuable and necessary. None may be wholly "right" and our desire to defend the truth of our own favourites can never justify the harming or domination of those whose stories and beliefs are different from ours. Instead, we must try to look underneath at the synthesis between apparent variations of "truth". Myths are appropriate for the society and the era that created them. As our understanding evolves, we need to modify those myths or create new ones to reflect our expanded understanding.

There's another catch to mythologies too. As societies become more complex and sophisticated, divisions arise between sectors of the population; clear "classes" may emerge, some more educated and more privileged than others. Ancient Egypt was a good example. The priestly class was initiated into the higher meaning of the mythologies, understanding them as metaphors for the deeper mysteries of the inner life of the spirit, of humanity, the solar system and the cosmos. But the stories told in the mythologies were retained for the general, barely educated majority for whom the concepts and language of the deeper mysteries were incomprehensible. So, mythologies can be used as *reflections* of higher truths as well as a *veil* over that truth so that the truth behind the mythological veil can only be understood by those ready, privileged and educated enough for the deeper meaning to be revealed to them. Great spiritual teachers have used parables in much the same way.

Different Cultures—Similar Stories

When the Maori arrived in what they call Aotearoa and the world knows today as New Zealand, the land was pretty much covered with forest. In the north were giant trees like kauri. With only a remnant left, the survivors are now threatened by a disease thought to be introduced and spread on the shoes of local and international tourists wanting to get close to these wondrous trees. There were also magnificent, magical swamp forests of kahikatea (white pine) their trunks so tall and straight the British Navy immediately saw their value as ship masts. Eventually, most of the kahikatea went to make parchment-lined butter boxes. With the trees extracted, the swamps were drained to create farms for imported breeds of cows and sheep. Kahikatea is our tallest native tree and believed to be the oldest kind, its origins going back 100 million years. Sadly, the fate of both kauri and kahikatea is common to tree species all over our planet.

Though the tribes differ a little in their versions, in the New Zealand Maori creation myth, Ranginui and Papatuanuku are the "parents", the Sky Father and the Earth Mother respectively. They lie tightly together in primordial darkness, their children cramped between them. As the children grow, they desire to live in the light so one by one the children try to push the parents apart. Eventually Tāne Mahuta, god of the forests (who has two enormous kauri trees for legs) succeeds. Ranginui is banished to the sky and the children remain on Papatuanuku, the earth, to be nourished by her. Thus, the airy atmosphere above the earth is created and the "children" are blessed with the light and heat of the sun thus giving rise to the wondrously varied life-forms of Earth. It's interesting that in this Creation myth, it is not the great mountain ranges of New Zealand that are described as pushing the parents apart, it's the forests.

There was a very similar cosmology in Ancient Greece where Gaia was the undifferentiated Mother Earth and Uranus was the Father. Here again the two parents were separated by their offspring and Uranus was likewise banished to the sky.

As we saw at the beginning of this book, in the Judaeo-Christian bible—in Genesis, the first book of the Old Testament—we find a Creation story that contains similar elements though more esoterically expressed:

"And the earth was without form, and void; and darkness was upon the face of the deep" (*King James Version, Genesis, Verse 2*) "And God said, let there be light: and there was light *(Verse 3)* . . . and God divided the light from the darkness." (*Verse 4*)

In all of these Creation stories, we find a version of our dark void in which all is contained and which can only be *revealed* by separation and the consequent *release of Light*.

Chapter Thirteen
Working with Nature

How Trees Adapt to Us

Trees are not just passive receptors or "victims" of our actions. We have been modifying the ways trees interact with their environments throughout our latter history at least. Not all of that interaction is negative. Haskell points out that the life opportunities of olive trees in the Mediterranean countries have been restricted to dry lands by our activities. Water, a scarce resource in the region has been reserved for thirsty, food-producing species, like citrus. The unique structure of the olive tree's leaves and its highly adaptive roots, enable it to be more tolerant of the hot dry climate. Generations of humans have taken advantage of this and thus confined the olive to the most arid of environments while at the same time big plantings, since Roman times at least, have ensured a large gene stock. Large areas of Northern Tunisia have been in olive plantations for over two thousand years.

In Israel, modern technologies have produced an adaptation of the olive that has a different shape and size that suits mechanized collection of the precious olives. The plant kingdom is as least as opportunistic as we are.

We have selected plants that we see as beneficial to ourselves and as a result have created great monocultures, often at the expense of the rich ecologies the Earth created. In *The World Without Us,* Alan Weisman points out that if we were all suddenly taken off the Earth, many of these monocultures (food crops especially) would not survive without us and would quickly be replaced by the plants and trees they ousted.

Without adaptation, there can be no physical expression of Life, as we know it and certainly no vegetable kingdom. A. G. Cairns-Smith (*Genetic Takeover and the Mineral Origins of Life*) points out that two things are required for life to unfold as form. It has to be able to replicate itself and it has to be able to incorporate something that modifies it. Replication of a cell on its own just gets us more of the same cell. The ability to incorporate something new that modifies the cell in some way gives us a new expression of life. These two fundamental abilities, to replicate and change are the basis for the glorious diversity we see in the world around us and in the extraordinary complexity of our human form. Life in our physical universe is in a constant state of change and we are part of that change, which makes our ability to discriminate, to decide which are the best choices for our thoughts, emotions and actions, whether singly or collectively, of critical importance.

Animals

Growing up, my brother and I had our share of pets through the years—a fluffy white Samoyed dog, cats, and a budgie and for a short time a rooster and hens. At this point, I do not subscribe to the belief that animals have an *individual* "soul". I believe that they are instinctual beings that are part of a *group* soul. I do go along with the view that they are evolving *towards* eventual individualization and that *devotion* is the pinnacle achievement or apogee of the animal kingdom on Earth.

Farmer Joe had flocks of domestic ducks that produced very tasty eggs. They were pretty, white ducks and their overlighting deva or oversoul had a wonderfully gentle nature, despite the incredible racket a flock makes when it's excited or their tendency to be extremely vicious to each other (in captivity at least). This deva was a very large being with the quality of gentleness and innocence, in its feminine side anyway. The design, structure and instinctual behaviour of this particular white duck "family" are held by this entity. Showing singular lack of imagination, I dubbed it the White Duck deva. I believe that whatever consciousness flows through the brains of these ducks emanates from this being, not from any individual duck's "soul".

Biologist and author, Rupert Sheldrake, postulates something like a group consciousness among animal species that he calls a "morphic or morphogenic field". With Pamela Smart, he has done interesting research on the ability of dogs to know when their owner is leaving work to come home, despite random variations in the timing.

There is much still to learn about the capabilities of the animal kingdom and I believe it is an important part of our human evolution to treat them well. Apart from a couple of encounters with a very large dog "over-soul", I really have nothing more to add on the subject at this point and will happily leave that exploration to those much better qualified. I might add though, that the few overlighting animal souls I've come across have been extremely large.

The Fungi Deva

Truffles (not to be confused with the dessert balls that sometimes also go by the same name), are a rare, strongly flavoured edible mushroom, very expensive and much prized by food connoisseurs. They form a symbiotic relationship with the roots of certain trees: oaks, chestnuts, elm, willows and pines. For many tree species, their relationship with certain fungi species is essential and there are other fungi that can be fatal to their host.

Like all natural processes, which are actually morally neutral, we humans can put a positive or negative perspective on it and the seemingly humble fungus is both revered and reviled. Mould in cheese can be valued as part of the flavour, as in blue vein cheese. On a different cheese, it serves as a warning that the cheese is no longer fit to be eaten. The fungus is of course, a life force as well but not always one that our bodies can tolerate, so fungi, in our living spaces in the form of moulds, can be toxic. Then of course there are the highly poisonous fungi that spell death to us even in the smallest quantities. Woe betide the uneducated mushroom harvester.

I love mushrooms and toadstools. I love the way they appear suddenly overnight and the subtle colours and soft textures of their moist flesh. I especially love the delicate flanges beneath their tops where the spores hide. And that little skirt they often have near the base of their stalks, I love that too. Then I observe, fascinated, as the days go by, how they change colour and shape, dying and shrivelling, fading into physical death and disappearance again.

It took me a while to connect with any of the mushroom deva and that puzzled me. Was it because, like their physical manifestations, they were hidden from view most of the time, doing their work in the secret dark? Mushrooms are a very "yin" thing; they grow in the damp and dark without sunlight. They are mediators between form or what we see as "life" and what we call "death" or the breakdown of physical form.

They live in a nether zone, transformative agents of regeneration and recycling. Fungi can break down cellulose, decomposing plant material (including wood) so that its constituent parts can be re-used. There are fungi that can neutralize and absorb pollutants and others that live in symbiotic relationship with trees, enabling the fine root hairs to absorb minerals and nutrients the tree could not get otherwise. Some, like penicillin are essential in modern medicine and of course, some make yummy and nutritious food for humans.

One day, I realized I had been concentrating on the outer form, which so entranced me and not the inner essence. Then, bingo, I was there. To meet the overlighting fungi deva was a little like moving into the void where everything exists in the darkness as a sea of potential. Though it was similar to begin with, my experience of the fungi deva was different from the void.

I was constantly aware of movement and the *unseen presence* of light within the darkness. This is one of the greatest beings I have had the privilege to contact. Its height and depth were immeasurable, reaching into the depths of involution, into the deepest solidity from a point of light so high and far away, I could not conceive the extent of its brilliance.

It struck me that this was a deva of great sacrifice; that it foregoes its birthplace in the light to descend into the depths of physical form where it uses all the power of its enormous intelligence to break up the material form and return it to its constituent parts. It never loses its link to the light and threads, most delicately, a cosmic light into its delving, sending it forth as the quick-lived fungal form we see as mushrooms, toadstools, etc.

I sent it gratitude and appreciation for its service, the magnitude of which I have only touched upon in my tiny way. To begin to appreciate the enormity and extent of this deva, we need to remember that it holds within it all the blueprints for its lesser angels, the deva of every fungal species. They perform a wide variety of specialist tasks on planet Earth. They have an especially close relationship with the water elementals, which they harness for their needs.

The fungi deva is a supreme alchemist, governing the magical process that turns what we think of as dead matter into rotting matter, making it available for use in a new form that can be inhabited by different kinds of Life forces. Just as form manifests into physical reality from the void of potential so the mushrooms and toadstools we see are a manifestation of new form life, an expression of the light that was unseen within the darkness of that alchemical process.

Crop Field Deva

On one of my early visits to Joe's farm in Scotland, he asked me to see if there was a deva on his land. By this, he meant a deva that had an overlighting and coordinating influence on the land where he grew grain crops. Although very sensitive to what he described generally as "the energies", Joe had not experienced the energetic supervisors we call the landscape deva or angels. I went up to a particularly pleasant energy point on the farm near the top of a slope at the border of a small wood of densely planted spruce trees. With my back to the trees, I prepared myself for a deva search.

It was not a very happy deva, in fact, it seemed huddled over and a bit miserable. Unusually, it was so low it was practically *in* the ground. I tried to hide my surprise and called it out, energetically speaking, with lots of love and joy at finding it. With deva, as with humans, unconditional love usually works a treat and the deva unfolded itself. It still seemed small as land deva go so, I just continued to flood it with love and gratitude for it being there and eventually took my leave.

On my next visit to Joe's farm, he asked me to check on the deva but it was a short and busy stay and it was the morning of my departure before I succumbed to Joe's entreaties and returned to the spot at the edge of the wood. What a change! The deva was now spinning gently over the field, a pale blue angel of swirling "skirts". It greeted me with joy. I asked if it had any messages for Joe and soon left it to its work.

"Well?" he said. I told him what I had seen and he reported with some pride that his crop yields were up a little. The farm assessor had asked him what he had changed in his management of fertilizer etc., but he had done nothing different except that he had regularly sent the deva loving positive thoughts and gratitude, even though he had to just trust that it was receiving them. Given the right kind of love, even where nature spirits are subjected to doses of chemicals that may make them feel the deva equivalent of a tummy bug or car sick, they usually respond to our approach and especially to our gratitude.

"The deva did have a request this time," I told Joe. "It said a little less fertilizer please." Farmer Joe frowned. This was not so easy. There were *rules*. To receive a subsidy for growing an approved crop one must use a specified amount of fertilizer. He couldn't go any lower without financial disadvantage. Ah! So, agriculture in the European world is not so much about producing healthy crops as providing financial opportunity to Agri-companies? I firmly repeated that this was the deva's only request, reminding Joe that it had requested a little less, not none at all.

The following summer, before harvest, I was there again. Joe pressed me to go and see how the deva of that field was doing. I did. The change was wonderful. The deva was dancing above the field as such overlighting deva usually do, tracing light around like a whirling dervish. When I returned to the house and reported, Joe was practically bursting to tell me that he had "fudged it" and used less fertilizer just as the deva had requested, not a lot less but less all the same.

"And . . .", Joe grinned, "my yields have gone up and so has the quality!" What could make a farmer happier than less money spent for more money earned!

On my next visit, I was intrigued to find that the deva had been joined by another that normally looked after a field on the opposite side of the farm. The original deva was a beautiful pale blue; this second one was rich shades of autumn colours. They spun together in a circling, spiralling dance over the land, quite close to the crops they were energizing. These crop deva stayed close to their fields but landscapes also have higher deva that oversee larger areas from above. It's hierarchical, with higher and higher deva intelligence overlighting and coordinating smaller, lesser and more numerous deva and elementals.

The Barley Deva

One day there was a message from the Barley deva.

———————✗———————

To bless the seed with the protective light of pale blue is indeed a righteous thing to do. You know well that the energies and not their manifestations in physical colour are what accomplish the task.

The same is true of the health of the soil. Were you to discover the energetic pulse that corresponds to the soil, when you plant you would have no need of sprays to kill the possibility of weeds.

There is an energetic frequency for everything that lives. The true mastery for man is the cooperation with those higher frequencies but even these must be protected from man's greed. You want the elimination of "weeds" but you must recognize the rights of deva to grow these weeds. Generosity in the dedication of space for what you see as Nature's whims would be all that deva need to carry on their task. Treat not all the land as thine. It does not belong to thee and should you abuse the privilege of its use, only a poverty of life shall come to thee. Begrudge us not our playgrounds.

To begin you can match the colour used to bless the seeds with that you use to energize the soil in which you plant these seeds. If you are afraid, try only a small portion this way until you prove what we say. Weaken or abandon the spray you would have put upon this experimental planting lay and work at the technique of energetic cooperation until you master and understand our way.

For the rest you could try both but give us the aid of your abilities and all can be rewarded.

There was a beautiful geometry about this Barley deva, full of angles and repetitions of shape, a wonderful example of sacred geometry in manifestation. It had a quick light, like the flashing of windmill blades in the sun. At its centre was a point of stillness. Upon reflection I wondered if this perhaps reflected the stillness of the plant's early development for after the initial pushing through the ground the stalks seem to be almost stationary for a while.

The Rape Seed Deva

What a summer delight these deva are! They create the most incredible yellow flowers that carpet the British countryside in summer. Their deva gave a very different impression to the deva of Winter Barley. It was like a kaleidoscope of butterflies, each flitting about its own spot while they all held a vague formation about a centre that seemed to be nothing but a bright pale-coloured light. Somewhere in this mass, hanging like ghosts, were small shiny, dark ribbon shapes that seemed twisted so that as they turned, they were like little propellers. I felt these were the leaf blueprints.

The "shapes" that seem to constitute the overlighting deva don't necessarily appear to be anything like their physical counterparts but energetically they make total sense. What if we taught the wonderful new children coming into the world to communicate with deva, to combine modern farming with a partnership with nature through communication with its inherent and knowable intelligence? The Steiner schools are aligned with such philosophy and perhaps there are others too that manage to combine science with more esoteric knowledge.

The Findhorn Community in Northern Scotland was founded on conscious communication with deva and their publications on cooperating with nature via the deva kingdom have much to recommend them. As I mentioned in the Introduction, it was a book about this community that enticed me into this field of study so many years ago.

A Bad Paint Job

My friend, Carron, never did finish her house. She was overcome by chronic fatigue and the recurring sense of hopelessness that accompanies (or causes?) that debilitating condition. In younger days, when life had a greater measure of hope, she wanted to paint her special reading room, and I offered to help her. Following my mother's example and encouragement, I had been painting rooms since my teens and the small, east-facing room at Carron's presented no great challenges. How wrong I was about that!

Carron had chosen a lovely, soothing shade of green, named on the paint chart "wood green". She had made all the necessary purchases and we were ready to start. It soon became apparent that something was very wrong; the paint, despite being a reputable brand and well stirred, was going on the walls in cobweb-like streaky globules. We had to go over it quite strenuously with brushes and of course that ruined the texture one should achieve with the rollers.

I suggested the paint and the room might be too cold so we put heaters on, and made a cup of tea while the room warmed up. It made no difference. Time slipped away while we battled on and the problem was still not solved. What should have been an easy morning's painting had turned into a nightmare. Carron was understandably close to tears.

We retreated to the living room for another cup of tea and some food. "What's going on?" we asked each other and ourselves. Then I realised a strange sensation had been creeping upon me for several minutes, a sense of change in the room and a disturbance in the alta major centre at the back of my head. Carron, who as I mentioned in the Introduction had grown up with awareness of nature spirits, also felt it.

Something was coming into the room, or should I say, some *things* were coming into the house. They moved en masse, like a low level grey cloud, through the closed ranch slider doors and across the floor. At first a coalescence, they quickly separated out into individual beings no more than forty centimetres (about sixteen inches) high. Their bodies were slim, a pale greyish green, and they were all "talking" at once. Their agitation was jiggling my subtle substance in that receptive area at the back of my head known as the "psychic gate" (see page 45 for further explanation). Their distress was palpable.

We checked with each other, as was our habit, to see if we were both seeing the same thing. There was no doubt that we were.

"Where are they from?" Carron asked.

From outside the window something pulled at my attention. I went over and looked out.

"From over the road," I said. "Something's wrong."

We left the house and walked across the road, followed by the agitated band of little creatures. On the other side of the road was an estuary, and when we got to the edge, I saw that below the road, edging the water was a narrow strip of reeds that grew into a wide band of swampy reed islands a little further around. These little creatures were reed faeries.

The estuary was a designated scientific reserve, a precious remaining piece of the area's original ecology where many bird species fed and nested. The reed faeries crowded around and surged in front of us, their agitation increasing the noise at the back of my head, an unpleasant hum, like sped-up radio static.

As Carron and I stood at the edge of the reeds that bordered the estuary, I asked them what the source of their distress was. As I looked down into the water, a dark chunky shape, an ancient elemental being came into sight. Was it symbolic, I wondered? Was this an ancient energy that needed to move on, or was it merely showing me that danger lurked for these reed faeries? I got no answers and could not unscramble the agitated noise I was receiving from the little creatures. Carron had no answers either. I promised to meditate on their plight, see what information came to me and what I could do about it. Perhaps a little reassured, they dispersed throughout the reeds and Carron and I walked back to the house.

The plastic sheath from one of the new paint rollers we had been using had blown onto the floor when we had opened the ranch slider doors to go out. Carron bent down and picked it up. A squeal escaped her when she looked at it.

"These rollers are for rough surfaces! I bought the wrong rollers!"

She was right, it was written plainly on the plastic sheath and when I considered the furry texture of the rollers we had been using, it was obvious they were inappropriate. Why had we not noticed before? Was it just eagerness to get the job done, or had we both been distracted by the growing disturbance across the road? We'll never know. Rudolph Steiner said that when we enter the realm of the elementals we cannot function as we normally do.

Carron rushed off to buy new rollers and when we put them to use, the paint spread smoothly across the walls. In a few hours the reading room was painted, a pleasant little cocoon of "wood green".

That night I meditated on the reed faeries. The dark shape I had seen in the water moved again before my inner sight. Was it time for this ancient elemental to move on? I surrounded it with light and it swam out to sea. Was it, I wondered, a shadow form created by negative human energy? Either way I was prompted that it was time for it to leave. I let the higher light of love and deva evolution take over the task, and handed the dark creature into their care. For a while, I could see it wending its way, just beneath the surface, its wide, dark serpentine shape wrapped in a guiding cloak of light. I sent the reed faeries some light before weariness overcame me and I lay down, drifting into sleep with the image of its swimming still in my mind's sight.

Verification

Midway through the following morning, I was taking morning tea with a visitor when the telephone rang. It was Carron and she was in tears. When we arrived at her house, she was standing outside waiting for us. Her son had been biking at the head of the estuary when he came across signs of an impending housing development. Earth-moving machines were parked and there was a new sign showing a subdivision plan. Carron had made inquiries. The sand hills that bordered the estuary would be removed, the land flattened and houses built.

No wonder the reed faeries were agitated! It transpired that Carron and I and the little reed faeries were not the only ones upset. A public meeting was organized by concerned citizens and though the sub-division could not be stopped, some small modifications were made to the plans. Local service clubs were invited to plant the strip next to the estuary as a buffer zone.

Before the earth-moving machines did their work, Carron and I took our four children there one evening. While they explored, she and I sat on top of those lovely big sand hills above the estuary, watching the birds in their busy dusk flight. In the reeds, the faeries glowed pale green tipped with yellow. Out in the sea the big island shrouded its feet in misty skirts. We watched the colours of Earth's aura shining from the dunes and lighting the gathering dusk. At last, the descending night sent us home with a shiver of cold.

The sand hills are long gone and so are Carron and her son. I think of her often, and picture her, head bent earnestly as she studies in the Halls of Learning on the inner planes. I've not been by for many years but the last time I looked her house was still there, visible across the estuary. My children are grown, with children of their own. One way and another, we have all moved on.

Applying the Learning

We thrive where light and energy flow, where the air is fresh and pure, where nature supports us with beauty and love, yet we take a piece of land created over many thousands of years, strip it of trees, suck out the waterways and sell the land for housing. Where energy once flowed, now there is struggle. Instead of understanding the wonderful flow the higher deva and their nature spirit servants have created and working with that flow, we carve it up, kill the life it had and plant a road and houses in its place.

Skills such as understanding the flow of energy, the creation and care and right placement of plants and trees should be taught in school. There is perhaps a step towards such learning in New Zealand's State Schools. At the time of writing, a third of all schools in New

Zealand—Primary, Intermediate and Secondary (High Schools)—are part of the Enviroschools project (www.enviroschools.org.nz). Here is part of their mission statement:

> Our aim is to foster a generation of people who instinctively think and act sustainably.
> – Sustainability has many different interpretations.
> – To us it means living in a country where people work with positive energy to connect with each other, their cultural identity and their land, to create a healthier, peaceful, more equitable society.
> – It means the regeneration of resilient, connected communities in which people care for each other and the environment.
> – It means valuing indigenous knowledge and celebrating diversity so that everyone thrives.

Sadly, many children grow up (in the West at least) knowing nothing about the origins of the food they eat. Fortunately, many schools and communities around the world are involved in programmes similar to Enviroschools, which is a start to turn the tide of our future into one that is mindful of our *interdependence* at all levels with everything else that shares the planet with us. Steiner schools, following the philosophy of Rudolph Steiner and many Montessori schools also try to inculcate an understanding of environmental interdependence in their pupils. A healthy, nurturing environment supports *our* health at all levels. Sickness of mind and body is paid for by all of us in dealing with crime, poor community health and the need for all manner of other social services.

As this book is being prepared for press, the world is witnessing the anger of youth, galvanized by the brave, outspoken young teenager, Greta Thurnberg. It's traditional for the "oldies" in every generation to bemoan the degenerative slide of the "young" but I think we are witnessing an unprecedented awakening and the dawn of a great promise. I pray they have the strength of purpose and clarity of intent to see that promise become reality.

Chapter Fourteen
Touching the Angelic Kingdom

Expanding the Picture

Back in Chapter One, we learned the basics of the deva kingdom hierarchy, from the elemental life within the most minute of substances to much more complex elementals of plants and trees and then to the overlighting or angelic deva who are the "architects" of the physical forms like species of trees. We've explored some of these overlighting deva: of landscapes, rivers, mountains and so on. They are generally referred to in the West as "angels" and as we learned at the beginning, the entire deva kingdom is called "the angelic kingdom". However, with the replacement of nature-based religions with Christianity, the lower, elemental levels of the kingdom have dropped into folklore or worse, treated as some kind of superstitious evil. We shall explore this further in Chapter Seventeen.

At the higher, angelic level, deva are well on the evolutionary path or *may never have descended further into matter*. Rather, the lesser beings (nature spirits and elementals) that they command may have descended while remaining under the coordination of their higher deva overlords. Bear in mind here what we have said earlier about the concepts of involution and evolution. Beyond these overlighting deva we met already, there are even higher levels of Deva life, rightly referred to as "Deva Lords". By now, you'll be grasping the idea that this hierarchy isn't really a series of groups, it's a continuum. Seeing it as separate groups is just a choice our brain makes as it tries to make order out of an unfamiliar complexity.

Now we can think of the deva kingdom more accurately as *a continuum of increasing intelligence infused into matter at all levels of density with corresponding degrees of complexity and power.* Yeah, we might need to contemplate that sentence more than once.

It's a very useful definition but how can we picture or understand it as a reality? In this chapter and the next, we're going to try to deepen our sense of what that reality is like, or at least, how we as humans can experience its complexity.

Let Them Seek You Out

Connecting with "landscape angels" (aka overlighting deva) can be a way of allowing the landscape to speak to us instead of imposing or projecting our cultural framework onto the land. The land deva are to the elementals of the rocks and plants what the soul or higher self is to the human being. An overlighting landscape angel/deva infusing a piece of land performs a similar function to the infusion of our personality with our soul or higher self.

I recorded the following around 2007 . . .

I am writing this piece by a beautiful little stream. It is what New Zealanders would inelegantly call "a creek". It runs down the crease of a small valley in the forest. Its little waterfalls are churning the water into bubbles leaving white cloaks of foam on some of the pools. Other pools are the colour of deep sienna from the tannin in leaves that shine from the bottom like coins.

This area is temperate rain forest. Vibrant green mosses and liverworts cover exposed roots, fallen branches and the bases of trees. Last night's rain is still caught in great shiny drops on the spider webs. They are suspended under nooks and crannies like trapeze nets or strung between tree trunks and ground litter in gloomy little ferny grottos.

Unpractised for a while in the art of faery spotting, I came up here after breakfast when the sun was picking out the greens and turning them to gold. Now another bank of cloud has chased its warmth away and the mosses are luminous in the gloom. Thinking to spot some nature spirits of the stream, I stood for a while, drinking in its beauty. Shining black Tui made a brief visit to the trees above me, singing their distinctive, throaty calls. Water dripped from the trees to the pools, circling them with ripples.

I saw no water sprites but a strong presence loomed behind me. I turned around to notice a young rimu tree, maybe eighty years old. Beside it, the stream descended beneath a guard of lesser trees; straight, bent, twisted, with branches both turned and straight. Moss, ferns and thick congregations of fallen leaves dressed the banks under a lacy roof of yellowy green.

An even stronger presence called from higher up the valley, coming down to meet me—an overlighting deva. At first, I thought it was the deva of the stream but it was larger than that, its consciousness embracing the stream, trees, the entire forest—an environmental angel. It seems to me quite a masculine presence that encompasses earth and forest, rising up on occasions to quite a height into the air.

The Emerald Forests

In 2014 chance and a generous offer from a man called Martin to be my driver and host found me stopping off in Japan on my way to Britain. When Martin's invitation arrived to explore an island off the southern tip of Japan, I looked at the photos he had emailed and said "Yes!"

Yakushima, I learned, is circular, an inverted cone shape that can be circumnavigated by car in about five hours. The climate is subtropical around the coast but snowy cold in the mountainous centre in winter. It has a couple of World Heritage sites venerating ancient cedar trees. I booked my tickets.

Above the Sea of Japan, the Earth revealed its layers. Nature spirits of the air were building and shaping with water, wind and particles of dust, creating puffball armies of clouds and marching them across the cerulean plains of the sky. Above, the high sun shadowed the otherwise perfect sheet of the sea below with the mirrored blotches of those puffy clouds. Here and there, the deva gathered their creations into thunderhead towers whose peaks were losing their form, spreading out at the top as if they had found a ceiling to leak across.

The wings of the plane shook a little, way out at their tips. Their metal sheeting looked vulnerable against the power and pressure of this beautiful sky. Eventually, the puffball clouds merged, melting into each other, turning into a bouclé quilt of white and grey before dissolving to a misty sheet.

Yakushima is a green jewel in the ocean, the glow created by its cedar forests, punctuated in the volcanic centre by sharp mountain peaks. Trees thousands of years old stand among younger sentinels, themselves hundreds of years in the growing. The trails were well populated with Japanese holidaymakers, restrained and respectful to each other, to me and to Martin and to this wonderful forest where Macaque monkeys and tiny Sika deer show little concern for human visitors.

The trails are steep and demanding but there were elderly walkers as well as the young and middle aged. It was midsummer when I visited the island and though it didn't rain that week, there was no lack of water for the beautiful boulder-strewn rivers and waterfalls that tumble down hills through lush emerald forests.

Sometimes, the forests of Yakushima are mossy and mysterious. Ancient cedars that have stood for thousands of years create great bridges from earth to sky, their roots deep and their channels of energy and knowing so much deeper and higher than their physical form. Elsewhere, Yakushima is youthfully fresh with young cedars thrusting tall and straight from gullies and hillsides.

Walking alone I could feel the presence of a *very* tall deva behind me, sometimes coming so near I thought it would surround me but it stayed behind, so close I could feel its presence as pressure on my etheric body. It was a column of intelligence and knowing, of the Earth yet of something much greater. Regardless of the time of day it had the feeling of reaching way up into the night of space, a powerful yet familiar presence I have often felt before. It is not just of the Earth but also of Earth's connection to its companion planets—a part of the vastness of great angelic life that surrounds and permeates our tiny part of this universe.

An Airy Water Master

We made a special trip to view one particular waterfall that cascaded from a great height above a large viewing space on the valley floor below. The presence of its overlighting deva was immediately apparent. It's a constant surprise to me how distinctive each of these overlighting deva is, even though there is a commonality arising from their function. "This waterfall deva is a power-flow opportunist," I wrote in my journal. It was like the conductor of an orchestra directing the watery notes with exuberant joy; how long each would play, where each would go. "It goes where it can, flows over, doesn't hesitate, doesn't care about resistance. It doesn't lose any joy for meeting an obstacle. It just flows over them, bouncing on. Being. Detached. Joyful. It wears down rocks, moves, overcomes stillness while at the same time its joy flows from its stillness."

This wonderful being was not the water nor the rocks that it flowed over, nor the air in which it danced. It was even more than their overseer. It was their composer and choir master, huge and "smiling" in the air above yet present in the swirling pool of amassed drops that gathered among the rocks below before rushing away to continue their voyage, no longer a waterfall but a river.

The Coral Deva

When I was urged to contact the coral deva, I knew these were not the deva of coral as in coral that grows in the sea but deva that had the vibration of a coral colour. I didn't recall having heard anything about them before so I was rather curious as to their role in the angelic symphonies of deva.

We work with landscape, with the particles of rock and soil at a molecular level, a level of arrangement.

We work with the forces to mould the landscape.

We are builders. We work with the forces, which are a result of the larger movements of deva within the system. When you move your body, it creates a force, does it not? But the elementals within your muscles and cells obey the commandment of your overall body elemental that is making the movement according to your conscious and subconscious will. No deva work alone, no matter how large or small.

By dealing with particles, we influence the shape of landscapes. Because our work seems slow compared with that of the plant kingdom, we are easily overlooked yet our work is critical in allowing other deva to do what they do. The shape of the land enables different kinds of energies to abide there. It's easier to demonstrate to you how we work in a desert-like landscape than in a vegetated one. You think of land, of rock being heavy and dense but the particles of which it is comprised are not.

The deva showed me then how they are operating at a high level of light.

"Ah! I see," I said. "Even though the land is solid and 'heavy', we partly see it like that because of the time span we're viewing it from?"

———————✕———————

Yes. If you view it from a perspective of thousands or millions of your years, you would see it as a thing of great movement and light.

We are light deva who are under command of the Planetary Being's bodily evolution of its substantial form. Although the outcome is a manifestation of solidity, its higher levels, its origination, is with us, high in the planes of Earth's etheric.

The Earth's Etheric is said to be the top four planes of our scheme of the Cosmic Physical Plane in Fig 13 on page 250 and Fig 9 on page 118.

Through these last few "travelogues", I hope you are gaining a sense of the increasing scope of these angelic deva. Their realm is an intricate network of connections and energy exchanges. You can imagine it like a multi-dimensional fabric and flow of energy, of light and sound, of colour and chords. It emanates from a high point though this may not at first seem obvious. That high point is an overlighting deva. Often, the sensed reality seems umbrella-shaped to me as the overlighting deva *holds* all of this complex sphere of its influence by its consciousness or *within* its Being.

It's a system in constant motion as energy moves and exchanges from one part to another. It is also the elemental intelligence within each component. The deva, no matter how small or large knows what energy is required and where to send it.

From the human perspective, it is plants and soil interacting with insects and birds. It is roots communicating with other roots and fungus, air and water elementals exchanging the energy inherent in substance and all of it driven by the underlying fire of our universe. It's natural, incredible and complex beyond belief. It makes our computer systems look like the simple toys of a primitive race, which, despite our pride, is what they are.

Overlighting Green Deva

The deva of the plant kingdom are generally described as green deva and the higher of these hold all that complex functioning in their being. They are the "system heads". Here's how a high green deva described what it does.

---✳---

I exist in service to the Earth but I am before the Earth. I serve the greater deva of evolution, of beauty in form. I govern the interface between the seeming parts of an ecological system. I create the pathways through which energy travels between all that you see as the separate things that make up a garden, a forest, all those that you describe as "nature".

Were you to see as we do, you would find all such things connected to each other in streams of light, energy and what you call consciousness.

Comprising this singing fabric of light, of energy, are rhythms that sing in harmony with the greater rhythms of climate, of seasons, of seeds sprouting when conditions are optimal and fruit falling when the tune has completed and is reabsorbed into the greater theme to be brought forth again when it is right or appropriate for its tune to be re-sung as part of the whole.

We serve in a partnership with the planetary Being. We serve it as your body elemental and its lesser elementals serve you. You are yet another seed in the Earth's garden, come forth in birth, to blossom, learn, wither and die to be reborn again as your own song has both evolved and contributed to the evolution of the whole—in your case humanity but of Earth also.

In times long past, humanity fitted well with us. We were sensed, felt and more or less understood in an instinctive way. Humankind has been passing through a stage of seeming "independence", a phase similar to what you call your teenage years. It is a mixture of arrogance, rebellion, a little knowledge, cleverness and erratic insights. Your imaginations are powerful but you need to choose carefully what to imagine for that is often the physical reality you create.

When humanity has true understanding of deva and can see the intricate fabric of a natural system, the energy and song we have created here, it will realize, sense, know and feel every effect it has on our effort.

Right now and for many thousands of your years, humankind has come under different influences, moving away from us to develop their mental equipment.

The Green deva work more with the lifeblood of the plants, the subtle channels of light and fluid energy that create the interrelationships of the vegetation of a place.

It feels to me that there is a great liquidity about these beings. It reminds me of that extraordinary sense of liquid light I have experienced *inside* trees. In the case of the overlighting green deva, I was told that sense of liquidity comes from the way their light moves in channels, in its circulation to and from and between each plant. The circulation *between* plants is of a different kind because always when energies are combined the result is something different and greater than the parts.

Through these experiences, we get a better sense of the overlighting or higher deva. Remember too that our collective activity can create deva as we saw in the Heathrow Airport example. The Findhorn Community in Scotland, which has been a conscious experiment in cooperating with Deva, has it's own higher deva known as The Findhorn Angel. Just as many Asian countries have village shrines built in honour of their versions of deva, similar shrines can be found all over the world.

At What Level Do We Communicate with Deva?

We will meet more members of the angelic level in the next chapter but now that we're beginning to get a better sense of the different levels of deva, it would be helpful to get an understanding of how our own levels of *consciousness* affect our ability to contact and communicate with those levels of deva.

In Fig 13 overleaf, we see the general idea of how this works. When we remind ourselves that few people are capable of reaching, let alone maintaining a level of Buddhic consciousness, we begin to understand how much more we have to evolve before we can safely work with deva in truly united partnership.

A Matter of Light

Don't try to figure out which deva is higher than another. It doesn't matter! That we even ask the question is just our intellect wanting to impose our idea of order on things. Remember that "deva" means "Being of Light" so when talking of the angelic level especially, we can think in terms of quality of light. It's no coincidence that the spiritual journey is so often referenced by light. Such light is an expression of power—the release of the potential that rests unmanifested in the original stillness of the dark. The alchemy of such highly evolved angelic beings is beyond our understanding but through openness, patience, trust, imagination and the gradual building of our subtle sensitivity, we can glimpse this angelic realm that builds the bigger structures and holds the great movements of our world with it's active intelligence.

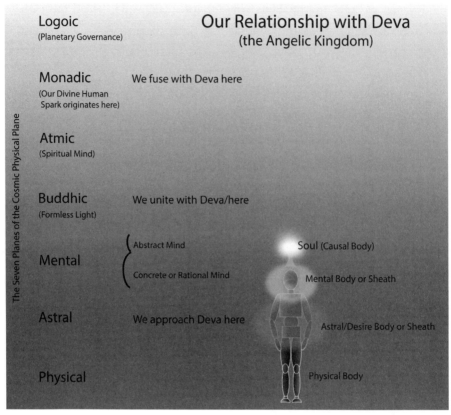

Figure 13 Where and How We Communicate with Deva
(Adapted from Ageless Wisdom Teaching and the works of Alice A. Bailey)

Everywhere, we can see how an idea has been manifested or *built* as form. You may sense it in the world around you, in the wonder of a sunset or the budding of leaves on the branch of a tree. When you see them, rounding with the moist promise of Spring, remind yourself of how, long before they even looked anything like leaves, their placement was arranged, not randomly bunched together but carefully set to each unfold at a different angle so each of them can catch their share of sun.

Chapter Fifteen
Experiencing Symphony

Loving the Forests

In whatever part of the world I've been able to experience the forests, I've loved them all. As a tourist and depending upon circumstances, it hasn't always been possible to spend time tuning in to the deva life. Often, it's easier for me to get to know some of the deva life of a forest when I'm in the company of a close friend on a similar journey but preferably just one companion or two as I find the individual energies within groups very distracting.

We've met the deva of streams, rivers, sea and landscapes and hopefully picked up a sense of their function and the complexity of what they do. What about the overlighting forest deva?

Language, linear logic and compartmentalization is a function that our "left" brain is very good at but it is our "right" brain that can experience the simultaneous complexity of deva. There's a point above the head that joins both right- and left-brain hemispheres, enabling us to experience *complexity with understanding*. We can access it via our higher centres (chakras) especially the crown from which we can build a bridge to a higher consciousness. (In Eastern teachings this bridge may be called the Antahkarana.)

When we experience the nature spirits of trees, we pick up their joy, their function and maybe the light and colour that they are. We begin to see the trees in which they work as vessels of light and conduits of knowledge of all that surrounds them and passes through them.

When we experience the overlighting deva of the forest, we get a sense of their height and breadth and their *holding* of all that goes on within the forest. We can also experience the simultaneous complexity of deva activity; what it is that the overlighting deva is coordinating.

In Peter Wohlleben's book on trees, he points out the differences between forests that have evolved naturally and plantations of trees. My experiences of deva reflect the science that is now emerging on the differences in cooperation and complex interactions that happen in the naturally evolved forests that are missing from man-planted forests. The differences are especially apparent, not just because the latter tend to be monocultures while nature generally favours a rich diversity of species. In New Zealand, we still have some large and ancient forests where we can experience the extraordinary life of a relatively pristine forest environment though these are under constant threat from introduced pests—animal, insect, microbial and human.

Ancient Forest Immersion

One of my favourite forests is exceptionally beautiful, very ancient and suffers minimal human molestation. Experiencing the deva of this glorious place has gifted me glimpses into the complexity of what these higher deva do and how they do it. This time, my friend Linda was with me, "holding the space" for me. Linda is an excellent gatekeeper. She makes sure I am undisturbed, somehow managing to create a tourist-free zone, so I can concentrate uninterrupted by the "outside" human world. Linda wasn't the only gatekeeper around that day. A large deva, who has been in the background of my interaction with this kingdom for many years, was there too. This Being has a very distinctive energy and I could feel it there, like a facilitator, a kind of diplomat enabling the meeting of foreign ambassadors. With the facilitation of this wonderful Being, I met the deva overlighting this ancient forest.

As usual for me, it was at once a visual, feeling and knowledge experience though I suspect that what I "see" is my brain's interpretation of what I am actually experiencing as *direct knowing* because it is the *knowing* that is paramount in the experience.

The deva of this ancient forest has an extraordinarily beautiful energy. It's no wonder they are referred to as angels. Though I know gender (as we understand it) is our projection onto deva, this deva's energy felt female to me so I'll refer to "her" that way.

Every part of the forest was held in her consciousness. I was well aware of her while at the same time experiencing the very active elemental life she coordinated. There was nowhere that was not filled with her glorious light—a pale golden green from which legions of nature spirits and lesser elementals danced in a moving body of complex connections. These connections are pathways of light that the elementals both take with them *and travel within.* The elementals *are* the light but they are also using or *trailing* the higher angelic light along with them as they move. The activity was extraordinary with countless elementals joyously delighting in this conscious connection between us.

I was aware (though vaguely) of the physical forms of the plants and trees as the recipients and channels for these streams of light and energy, in which and with which her elementals and nature spirits danced. The dance was at the same time a song, as each elemental sang their part of her note. This deva activity was revealed in light, colour and sound and in the nearly overwhelming impression of presence. *Every* thing was joined in flowing arcs of light and moving energy emanating from her overlighting position "above" the forest that left no space untouched. The "faces" of grinning nature spirits formed and dissolved as if saying, "Here you can recognize us, but now this is how we really are—intelligent light passing through all that grows."

Though I had sensed, to a degree experienced it and written of this kind of activity before, this experience was an almost total *immersion* into this glorious celebration of conscious life. I say "almost total" because I know there is always more for us to learn and higher states of consciousness to experience.

Enduring the Storms

This ancient forest had suffered a good deal of damage during a fierce storm a couple of years before that visit with Linda. The prevailing winds come from the West so the tree roots will have grown stronger on the Western-facing side. When this great storm approached from the East, there was not the deep root growth on that Eastern side to hold the very tall trees against its force. It took the humans who maintain the tracks days to clear them of the fallen giants after the storm. We came across many large trees that had crashed down amongst and upon their lesser neighbours. Sometimes all we could see were their roots upended, exposed in a large circular tangle of wood and soil. The trunks had already begun to disappear as other vegetation rushed to take advantage of the resultant gaps in the canopy.

Curious of the deva's view of this damage to trees that were often many hundreds of years old I put the thought to her. She seemed to have no real concerns about these losses. There was just a flicker of acknowledgement from her that their falling gave opportunity for others to grow in their place. This forest is purportedly thirty-five million years old but from a human perspective it will take a very long time for the new trees to reach the same maturity as those that have fallen, so meantime, we mourn their loss.

A Wall of Intelligence

I was house sitting for a friend, standing on the deck one evening before the light had gone from the day. Across a short space of lawn was a lush shrubbery. I was just admiring it, appreciating it, when the space between filled with intelligence. Now I know that sounds weird so I'll try to explain it better.

The air or space between the shrubbery and me was not empty; it was full of palpable intelligent life, so full in fact that it formed a *solidity* of intelligence. The apparently empty air was not empty at all. After a few moments, my brain began to "see" it as a multitude of "faces" but they weren't faces, rather they were entities of intelligence. Years before, I had written in *The Children of Gaia* that the sylvans inhabited the spaces of the world. Until this moment I hadn't experienced quite such a *full reality* of that statement nor that the "sea of deva" in which we live could be sensed so palpably and "solidly".

I believe we do get a sense of it in different ways at various times. Perhaps it's "The Force" of George Lucas's Star Wars movies. In the movie, *The Legend of Baggar Vance* it's the "field". It's the fullness of the *apparently* empty void. Perhaps it mimics the unity we will experience with deva when our consciousness sits in the Buddhic plane—the plane of formless light, the "raincloud of knowable things". I think animals, birds, trees—nature generally—live in constant awareness of this "field". It joins everything to everything else and our separation from it is an illusion.

The Myth of Empty Space

There is no part of the universe that is truly empty. Even the vast reaches of space are filled. The only reason science cannot agree with this statement is because it does not know how to measure the more subtle levels of Being. Perhaps one day Being or Beingness will be known as the Universal Principle of Completeness. (Orthodox philosophers would probably say there's a tautology here. So be it.)

When completeness is understood, perhaps we will finally abandon our doctrine of separateness, which has arisen out of the limitations of human perception and the evolution of self-awareness which governs so much of our thinking and action. This "error" of separation has arisen because to know oneself as "individual" we have ditched the reality of non-separation or completeness, at least temporarily. Hence, each human being passes through a stage that has us thinking we each stand alone. Aloneness is not always a safe or comfortable place to be and in place of completeness, we have invented our own mini imitations—family, village, tribe, nation. Here we meet another paradox.

These groupings, by their very nature contain the concept of separateness versus togetherness—my family is separate from yours. My tribe is separate and different from yours and so on. In this concept is the seed of discord and war, yet by belonging to such groups as family or tribe we also learn about loyalty, service and cooperation, all of which are watered down versions of true togetherness—Love. It's through these *reflections* of Love that we keep a tenuous hold on our original Oneness, strengthening that hold as we evolve to a more inclusive understanding of Love while at the same time bringing with us the consciousness we've gained *because* of our experience of being separate individual beings. It's no surprise then that in the higher planes—above those that we are normally aware of—we have a greater and greater experience of unity as the whole system works its way back to a synthesis and eventually to the original Oneness. On the return journey, however, through its experience as separate things, mineral, vegetable, animal, human, and whatever comes next, that Oneness is now *conscious* of all the parts of itself and its possibilities.

In a sense, the paradox doesn't exist because the giant illusion is that the Oneness has gone away. It hasn't. It is there in the synthesis behind our *perceived* separative reality. We get a glimpse of what such conscious synthesis is like when we come across that rare human who has conquered the challenges of their physical, emotional and mental bodies. We also get a glimpse of what it's like and how it feels when we meet the overlighting deva of large ecosystems.

Weaving the Songs

So, Deva fills the so-called spaces of the world. When humans understand this, we will realize that even across the apparent vastness of space all things touch each other and all things complete each other. Yet it seems that everything eventually dies—plants sprout from seeds, grow, mature, fruit and die and all life repeats this cycle of becoming and dying. This perception arises because we cannot see that the creation and cycling of *forms* is an *expression* of something that does *not* come into being and go out of being because it is Being Itself.

What is expressed as Life, is a glorious dance wherein all the ranks of deva respond to some level or other of Will. Deva manipulate matter in response to the force of Will. Like Captain Picard on the Starship Enterprise, Will says "Make it so!" and deva make it so. We do well to re-read what deva had to say about how they contact purpose in the chapter "The Joy of Deva" on Page 116.

As we have glimpsed in our encounters with the angelic level of the deva kingdom, when we experience deva as the weavers of Life's songs, we find ourselves in a sea of colour and light that is constantly moving, creating, building, flowering, changing, breaking down, building up. Movement and deva go together like water and wetness. A healthy land is one where deva radiate, spiral, circle and dance their songs, keeping the currents of life flowing, just as blood flows through the circuitry of our veins.

Deva sparkle the air with prana, spiralling this life energy of light from air into sea, from sky into mountains, across the surface of streams and through the breeze of deserts. Without the movement of deva, the Earth becomes as stagnant as a human body without exercise, prone to obesity and disease. In a healthy Earth, the movement of deva is critical. Nothing is wasted; everything is re-used again and again in different ways, producing different forms in the great experiment of Creation.

So much of the activity we see as life is so well practised it seems automatic, yet each event is the result of a force of Will and a response of deva to Will's *purpose.* It may seem minuscule like a weed pushing up through the gravel or it may seem mighty like the great storms that whirl across the lands and seas. Behind them all is a Being bigger than any of these smaller expressions—the Planet itself, which in turn is part of a larger Being, the Solar system.

If you consider this fanciful, think on this. Your body contains countless cells, channels, liquids of various kinds and untold microbes to whom you are a "planet". They are living out their lives of becoming and dying and the only knowledge you have of them is when something gets out of balance and your body does not work so well or your body *is* working supremely well giving you feelings of fitness and strength. Are all those tiny microbes aware of you as a conscious being? I think not.

At each level of Life there is not just a hierarchy of *form* but a *hierarchy of knowing.* Each step along the way we are asked to become aware of a larger and larger expression of Life and at each step we find larger and more powerful forces of Will at work and larger and greater intelligences of deva responding.

It is through joy they evolve and in joy that they fulfil their function. The untouched forest is a haven of deva activity. Rain in a jungle is a drumming song of deva that sets the forest to dance and its creatures to sing. Deva fill the air with song and sparkle the water, rocks and plants with their swirling. They are the circulators of life on Planet Earth. When we remove what has naturally evolved, turning a healthy forest into a limited monoculture, a wasteland, or fill the land with rubbish and the air with choking fumes from our factories and vehicles, the nature deva cannot function. That seemingly intangible thing called "life" disappears to be replaced by stagnation, illness and a foggy astral density that destroys the spirit and burdens body and mind.

Yet, it is not so long ago in our human history that sensitives were trained to understand the "codes" of edible plants that grew in the jungle and then used their knowledge to choose the right plant species and placement of crops to feed the cities. Today we use "science" but often without recourse to the wider environment and certainly with no regard for the complex energy requirements of a healthy land.

Are We Learning Yet?

If we could gift such experiences with deva to every human on the planet, would we treat nature with the respect and reverence it deserves? We each evolve at our own pace and in our own areas of challenge in a particular lifetime and I am not exempt from such challenges. However, with a few notable exceptions, we're pretty much all capable of coordination and cooperation. The only thing preventing us is the *motive* for what we do. Self-interested intention and misuse of Commerce will just keep us stuck for a long time to come. We advance through service intended to improve the lot of all of us, collectively.

It is not *escape* from this world that we need to "save" us but *unity with it.* When we are conscious of the life that flows through all things, we can begin to understand both our place in it and our responsibility to it. How we do it, by learning to see and communicate with deva, through studying ecology or simply developing compassion and respect for Creation, it is critical we mend this wound of separation before we completely destroy this beautiful world, our societies and ourselves in the process.

One day we will work consciously with deva to create beautiful, thriving environments for ourselves as well as leaving deva to look after the myriad plants and creatures who share the planet with us, creatures who by playing their part no matter how small, sustain us.

Science is discovering the interdependent complexities of nature. It is learning the way trees are able to "remember", how they have forms of communication, how plants, bees and birds have networks that keep the activity of Earth alive and healthy for the benefit of all of us who are supported by its body. How all parts of a natural environment are in communication with each other, via electrical charges, chemical and hormonal emissions and so on. They have discovered, for example, that as well as colour, pattern and fragrance, plants communicate with bees via electrical fields, sending out charges which apparently tell the bees whether a particular flower has available nectar or not. This way the bees don't have to waste energy going to flowers that have nothing to offer. (See paper by Dominic Clarke et al.) The scientific recognition of nature's complexity is growing. Just imagine what is going on at the deva/angelic level.

As the Coral Deva explained in Chapter Fourteen, Earth has a changing body. One night during the time I'd been putting this book together from earlier drafts, a stretch of the New Zealand seabed rose 5.5 meters (18 feet) to create a new rocky shore fifty metres wide. It took only *two minutes* for the Earth to do this and many hours for the sea to drain from the raised rocks. Think for a moment about the forces involved to accomplish this. Inland, a farm of undulating hills was split when a large portion of its land rose up, creating a high cliff. Meanwhile, along the coast the hills burst, spewing enough dirt to fill three hundred Olympic sized swimming pools onto the main highway and railway line. Seeing the newly raised seabed on television, I was reminded of the whale skeletons that lay on the desert north of Cairo and the beds of seashells on the desert near Egypt's border with Libya. The Earth is constantly shrugging and changing. It's all a matter of where we stand to view time. To the microbes in our bodies, an eternity has passed between our breakfast and dinner. To a planet, a thousand years is merely a day or less.

Climate Change

Climate can be thought of as a symphony of its own. Of course, I am concerned about climate change. It is obviously happening. Yet, something about it has always niggled at me. It is obvious from my writings that I feel humanity has been and continues to be, utterly foolish in our disrespect for and exploitation of the Earth and yet I feel that something bigger is going on with the planetary body than what we can tell from our statistics and data-gathering on global changes.

What follows is taken from my notes, written seven years before the earthquakes just mentioned.

While walking with friends in a very beautiful wood in the Scottish borders in 2009 I asked the deva what they could tell me about the climate changes the Earth appeared to be going through. What they showed me I found astounding and I have struggled since to put it into words. I can tell you what I saw, more or less, and describe how it made me feel, more or less, but I can't describe the understanding it gave me because I have no words for it. It just underscores for me how limited we can be in our ability to truly communicate knowledge and how our words can keep us imprisoned in our perceptual boxes, unconscious to one degree or another. The limitations of words notwithstanding, I'll do my best, however clumsy it might be.

The deva showed me a huge stream of particles spiralling to tremendous heights. They were different colours, some shining, some not, all individually swirling within the greater collective movement of them all. What are they? Prana, life energy of the planet? Behind the movement was a tremendous reshaping, a rearrangement into a new creation as if each expression of life on the planet was being infused with a new energy, a new consciousness, creating a totally new expression of the spirit within each Earthly form. It was awesome, terrifying in its scale and glorious in its aim.

But what does it mean in physical "reality"? I can't answer that with any certainty. Whether it bodes the upheavals of earthquake, fire and flood and the rising of lands from beneath the ocean and the sinking of others in the kind of doomsday scenarios that have abounded in recent decades or not, I certainly don't pretend to know.

I think that our human minds, egos and emotional bodies are very attracted to drama and fear, which is why doomsday films of great catastrophes do so well at the box office. There's the added ego attraction in these too, that in the end the "heroes" almost always survive. The human ego loves the idea of specialness, of being chosen above others, so in this respect too, such stories have great appeal to our lower nature.

Our understanding of the bigger picture of life on Earth is often built of a jigsaw collection of insights. This is true of both science and revelation. Maybe that's because an experience of truth as a whole would blow our mind fuses if we were to experience it all at once. Like Saul's (later St Paul) experience on the road to Damascus, the light of truth can be blinding (even if temporarily) to our relatively undeveloped subtle and physical body structures.

Opinion of our relationship with our Planet seesaws between a megalomaniac attitude that we can do anything we want, to the opinion that we are nothing to the Earth and it will crush us if it "wants" or needs to. As we learned earlier, Ageless Wisdom teaches that humans are each just elementals in the Earth's throat chakra. In humans, the throat is the centre through which we primarily express ourselves. It's also the seat of the thyroid which governs so much of our body's healthy function. (An interesting correspondence perhaps.) From the perspective of cause and effect, we don't need to postulate any of these correlations as explanations. What we do need to do is wise-up to the complexity of the mechanisms the Earth has developed, especially its ecological systems and in particular the vegetable kingdom. These have gone through millions of years of experimentation to reach the sophisticated stage they are at now. To act deliberately or with ignorance in ways that damage these systems is perilous indeed and that's pretty much what we are doing on a grand scale. If you want to know the physical implications of our attitude or if you doubt that collectively, we are doing serious harm, I recommend Alan Weisman's superbly researched and beautifully written book, *In the World without Us*, investigating what would happen if humanity were suddenly not here.

Planetary Deva

We have seen throughout our meanderings in the deva kingdom, that there are great deva who coordinate the activities of the planetary body, governing weather, the seas, forest systems and so on. There are others who are mediating between the planet and its wider Solar environment. These great deva are responding to the Being of the planet itself just as our body elemental coordinates the lesser elementals of our physical being in response to our conscious and subconscious will.

As we evolve it is likely we will be able to have greater contact and understanding of very large overlighting planetary deva but it would be foolish to underestimate the height above us in consciousness from which these great angelic beings work or to assume their consciousness is even within our reach. When questioning our relationship with deva, I was told:

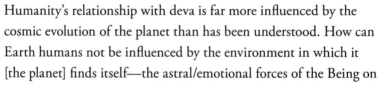

Humanity's relationship with deva is far more influenced by the cosmic evolution of the planet than has been understood. How can Earth humans not be influenced by the environment in which it [the planet] finds itself—the astral/emotional forces of the Being on which it lives?

This is not to say that there are exact correspondences between the evolution of humanity and that of the planet! We are simply saying that humanity is, of necessity impacted upon and influenced to one degree or another by the planetary Being's stage and state of evolution. How could the lesser not be influenced by the greater?

That's something that in our arrogance, we so often forget or choose to ignore.

Chapter Sixteen
Meeting the Singers

The Gateway to Deva

The gateway to deva is inside us more than in our looking outside ourselves. It was my friend Grace, who partnered with me to relieve the slaughtered young pines (Chapter Eleven), who wisely observed, "We *know* deva from the inside of us." Yet we persist in thinking of deva—the angelic kingdom, faerie and higher such beings—as "out there" in the world outside us but Grace is right and the opposite is true. Deva are part of the subtle world so it's through the seemingly "non-physical" subtle part of ourselves that we connect with them. When we theorize, we are using our intellect. When we *experience* we are feeling or using something subtler.

Imagination can be your gateway. Imagination takes us out of our intellect and puts us into that seemingly nebulous universe of ideas where *inspiration* triggers our invention of new things in a seeming "magic" of creation. To be inspired is not just to take in air but to "breathe-in spirit" and that is the essential key to the realm of deva.

We discussed imagination somewhat in Chapter Nine. When I say "imagination" it tends to suggest something that is not true or real but to think of imagination in that way is to totally miss its higher function. Imagination is a form of inspiration and a practice approved and suggested by spiritual Masters who have gone before us. It connects us to the subtle, that which is not physically seen— yet. It is also a form of Will and where there is Will there is a devic response.

Imagination is your gateway to the realm where creation *happens*. Whatever we see or experience in the physical realm or plane manifests or solidifies out of the subtle from the realm of idea and possibility—the metaphysical "void"—into form. Deva is the intelligence that enables idea to emerge as a physical object or form of some kind, yet we set about trying to see deva objectively in the physical world. Instead, we need to look in the subjective, subtle world of non-solid matter.

If you really want to connect with deva, begin with the traces of those times when they've knocked on the edges of your consciousness. They are the joy in the rain, the magical way a bud unfolds itself to reveal a beautiful flower. They're the flash of lightning and the whisper in your mind when for an instant you feel that all around you everything is alive and it connects with the aliveness within you. It's that sense of aliveness we need to re-awaken, that subtle but very real heightened awareness that we need to be able to connect with deva. Allow that sense of aliveness to reach out from you to the aliveness in the trees, the flowers, the sky, the building in which you live, whatever it is you have available to you to connect with. Such as these are your gateways to deva.

That means if you live in the heart of a city you can still experience deva. They are in *all* matter, not just in the plant kingdom. It's usually easier in nature, that's all. If you don't have access to a lovely garden, park or forest, remember there are always the overlighting deva of houses, buildings and organizations you can seek out. Cities have transport systems, religious and civic buildings whose deva you can discover. You may be surprised at what you can learn about the relationship between humans and deva in this way. In his online articles, Dr Geo offers a fascinating account of his long and detailed study of the deva involved in the political centres of Australia's capital city.

What Will They Look Like?

We pretty much covered this earlier but let's recap. Faerie folk are often depicted as humanoid with skinny limbs and pointy ears. Why? It may just be the artist's interpretation but there may well be deeper reasons. It is frequently reported that transitional elementals, the faeries, gnomes, pixies etc., imitate human form, both out of fascination for our costume and our denser and heavier physical body structure. It may also be an attempt to appear "normal" to us. Perhaps it is for their amusement or perhaps just to get our attention. It is reasoned that they have tended to copy the dress of earlier times when faerie was so much more a part of human folklore and experience. Most often though, faerie is simply an etheric or astral light—coloured, moving, shape-changing. It is knowable and communicable because it is an active, responsive intelligence despite the fact that it doesn't have a solid appearance.

Solidity is an illusion however, both science and sages tell us; matter is actually a buzzing energy when examined at its smallest parts. It is assembled and moves in ways that may be most appropriately described in terms of frequency and resonance. I tend to experience deva more as having a distinctive quality of energy than a particular form. I do feel that our perception is greatly influenced by our social and cultural conditioning, just as our idea of beauty can be very culture-based. What I think is an ideal womanly beauty or male handsomeness, for example, may seem rather ugly to someone of a different ethnic background.

If faery appear to be similar to us, we may accept them more easily. We'll find it easier to relate to them. When I was illustrating and writing *The Children of Gaia*, this was a familiar challenge. It's much easier to draw or paint something that is meaningful to us than to represent them more accurately as fast-moving light, colour and shape. Nevertheless, I have often seen them just as they are depicted with humanoid form that can easily slip back into slithers of light and colour. The tendency to mimic human appearance is mostly confined to the nature spirit level. I don't see that in the higher organizing deva.

Where Do We See Them?

If you don't recall it, turn back to page 45 to the chapter "Subtle Connectors" for my description of how I experience "seeing" them. I also see or sense the nature spirits en masse as light moving over beds of plants and flowers but I experience the nature spirits of trees as more individual. The higher deva, such as the landscape, mountain and air angels I often see as swirling, usually spiralling energies that are distinctive in colour. Deva of plant species, the plant's architectural deva if you like, appear to me as complex patterns of light and colour, often with a strong sense of geometry.

Unlike many writers in this field, I don't often see a face within these higher deva but if I look for a face within the form, I will usually "find" one. Either I am imposing one or the deva is responding to my "desire" to see a face, or there actually is a core that to us is face-like.

Having said all this about their appearance, very often I don't see them so much as *feel* their presence. What is more important to me is that these are beings of lighter substance than our bodies and in this hierarchical world it is the quality of energy that is important, not the form. That is true for humans too but alas, we often judge people on the perceived beauty of their form rather than their truer nature, which is expressed better in their subtle energy field.

What about the practical aspects of conscious communication with deva? Maybe you have already established a good rapport with them or perhaps you are wondering, "How does one even begin?"

Seeing Nature Spirits

"How do I see them?"

That's the most frequent question I'm asked about communicating with the deva realm. In *To Hear The Angels Sing,* a delightful account of co-creating with the deva kingdom, Dorothy Maclean, one of the three founders of the Findhorn Community in Scotland, also says seeing deva is the main thing people want to be able to do with regard to deva. Mostly they mean they want to see faeries. Her answer to them may surprise you.

What is my technique? Their awe of me rapidly expires when I flatly reply that I have never seen them either, or that astral vision is a retrograde step for mankind, or that I don't believe it matters.

What did Dorothy Maclean mean when she stated that astral vision is a retrograde step for mankind? As we have seen, the astral is the plane of the elementals of desire and emotions. It is also the plane of psychic phenomena (such as pre-cognition). Often what we think of as psychic is actually instinct, which is an inheritance from the animal kingdom. Higher "intuition", on the other hand, in our present framework, has its source at soul level and filters down into the mental planes (remember Diana's diagram, Fig 12 on page 182).

We saw in Chapter Eight how the astral plane of emotion and desire is currently our biggest challenge as a kingdom and that we are trying to rise above it to a higher plane of consciousness. It's no accident that the illusions we are subjected to at the astral level are called "glamours". They are such a big problem for humanity, Alice A. Bailey devoted an entire book to the subject. It's a very appropriate label and tells us a good deal about the pitfalls of this desire level of consciousness.

We also saw that the elementals of that plane are still on the involutionary path into denser and denser matter and our task is not to join them but to elevate them. It is said that when we see things like visions, faeries and so on, that we are operating at the astral level, hence Dorothy Maclean's comment.

While she is right to caution us about the lure of the astral plane, the danger is specifically our *identification* with that plane and its elementals. Remember though, that we *approach* deva at the level of the astral plane (Fig 13 on page 250). Roc, the gentleman who spent quite of lot of time at the Findhorn Community and who was a close and influential friend to its three founders, related his encounters with nature spirits in *Encounters with Nature Spirits*. He was also visited by the great Being we know historically as "Pan", who has oversight of nature spirits at a planetary, angelic level and plays something of a mediating role with the human kingdom. We'll learn more about Pan in the next chapter.

How should we go about approaching deva so as to avoid the "step backward" into astrality Dorothy Maclean speaks of?

Engaging Our Upper Centres

Perhaps the most important thing I can suggest to you, around this question of the astral plane, is to engage your highest centres or chakras, not your desire elementals. By using those higher centres—heart, ajna, crown—you are *not identifying* with the lower, solar plexus centre, which is the focus of your astral/desire body.

Like Dorothy Maclean, my contact with deva has most often been at the level of overlighting deva who are higher up. However, there are many grades of such beings and some may appear to occupy the high astral level but maybe are higher, into abstract mind or Buddhi. Does that mean when I tell you what they look like to me it's because I am accessing the astral plane? Not necessarily. Because their presence *impresses* upon me the quality and nature of their being, part of me interprets that in ways that lead to what sounds like a "physical" description. Sometimes, as with the Barley and Rapeseed's Species Deva, I will be treated to a strong flash in the ajna centre that depicts the deva's energy visually or that *my brain interprets visually.*

I haven't physically seen nature spirits very often and those occasions were mostly confined to the time of my research for *The Children of Gaia* as if those views were gifted to me solely for the purpose of writing and illustrating the book. Most of us have been raised with tales of faerie. Movies tend to reinforce the images—delicate creatures with frilly dresses and wings or caricatures of goblin-like beings. Please put aside those storybook or movie-maker preconceptions of how they will look. One day you may see a nature spirit that looks the way you expected but don't begin with that expectation.

Take little steps in this, as in any new endeavour and they will eventually lead you to competence. So here are my suggestions as to how you can work towards your goal.

Gentle Persistence

The qualities of awareness, joy, knowing, love and respect will draw a response sooner or later. Sometimes, they can be jumping up and down in front of us and we're not aware of it because we are so nervous or trying so hard to get it right! (Whatever "right" means.)

Don't be discouraged if you cannot see little pixies or tinker-bell-like faeries floating about in organza skirts and dragonfly wings. These are constructs rather than accurate realities. Also, some people are more kinaesthetic than clairvoyant so they *feel* their subtle experiences rather than *see* them. For others, their internal *hearing* may be their door to the internal kingdoms.

What is important is to recognize the signals you are receiving from the subtle realms. Then gradually explore other nuances of perception. Remember that at the beginning new skills can seem difficult and frustrating but the more we *relax,* yes relax (!), *allow* and pay close but floating, gentle attention, the quicker we learn. Forcing these abilities does not work especially when higher, subtler functions are involved.

What Can You Expect?

I can't answer that for you. What you experience is for you to find out. In fact, it's better not to have any expectations save that you *will* succeed, if not immediately then at some stage in the future. Remember how Elizabeth's assumption that I could easily meet with the elemental in the hill and *her* obvious confidence in me, virtually assured me success, yet I had no preconceived idea of what I would find.

You may not see anything in the normal sense of standing and looking. Grace Bell, who is an extraordinary channel for communication with beings in higher planes, recounted that she experienced one of her most immersive contacts with the deva kingdom while walking really fast along her favourite bush track. She said that walking faster and faster somehow got her thinking brain out of the way. Perhaps because vigorous walking gave her energetic physical body something to concentrate on.

Remember too, that it takes time to develop the subtle structures that enable such experiences. As a baby and young child, your neural pathways and strategies had to be progressively built to enable you to think and experience the world in your new, human body. There is a similar process that happens in the subtle bodies as well. Some children retain links to the higher, subtle levels of consciousness but they are often gradually shut down during the processes we call socialization and enculturation.

You may just become aware of a presence that is not you. So be aware of the very subtle things you experience and don't give up. Watch out for the signals your body is already giving you. Keep respecting, keep loving, improve your awareness, be joyful and above all, relax both body and mind!

City Bound?

If you live in the heart of a city and don't often get to a green space, there are other options. Your house, apartment, building, organization etc., will have some kind of deva development as a result of the collective matter, emotions and thoughts they are imbued with through human activity. That's an easy place to start.

Learn to feel the deva of buildings, especially those that are used by the public a good deal. See if you can sense an overlighting deva— of the subway perhaps or of your own living space. In her books on de-cluttering our living spaces, Marie Kondo gives insights into recognizing the life within our possessions and our houses. Ms Kondo is from Japan, which has a philosophy known as Shinto that acknowledges the elementals of trees and sees intelligent life residing in all things. It's no surprise then that Marie Kondo emphazises the role of appreciation and gratitude in raising the tenor of our daily existence, our interaction with the things we live with and how to keep only what we really love, or appreciate for its service. Assume your home has a deva. Take her advice and say goodbye when you leave it and greet it when you return. Be as joyful towards it as you would be to a nature spirit should you find one in a garden or on your walk to work or school.

If you belong to a group, business or organization, sense the collective energy it has created. How strong is the deva thus created or assembled? How does it reflect the purity of intention and purpose of those most active or influential in the group? Remember too, Dr Geo's important and informative work on the deva that work with government in Canberra, Australia that can be found online under *Angels of Canberra*.

So, if you live in the depths of a city where there are no beautiful gardens handy it does not mean you can't experience deva. Deva are in all matter, not just in the plant kingdom. It's just easier to find the transitional elementals and their higher coordinators in nature.

As for the concrete devas, I suggest you try to connect with the overlighting deva of concrete—it's architect rather than the elementals within the concrete itself. Don't *expect* the overlighting deva to be heavy because it may not feel that way at all. Why do I suggest the overlighting deva? You may recall the warnings given earlier about the perils of engaging with the level of elementals that are still on the involutionary path, that is, those heading into a greater and greater density of matter rather than those evolving towards less dense or higher planes. If you try to communicate with a drop of water, for example, you are more likely to find yourself feeling the great deva essence of water, not the elemental within the drop.

Listening to the Whispers

Appreciate the small as well as the large—the beauty of leaf and stone, the way the light catches where it can, how joyful a healthy garden or a naturally evolved forest feels. It's the life in things that sings. Listen to the birds—how they chatter to each other and to the trees and plants. *Perhaps above all listen to the whisper of your heart.* Notice when and how it tugs you to pay closer attention to the Life you're passing through when you're walking or travelling by vehicle. (Safer when being driven rather than doing your own driving. I don't think "being away with the pixies" will cut it with the traffic police if you have an accident.) By paying attention to the life around you, eventually you'll feel, hear or see the tunes the nature spirits dance or sense the long inclusive notes of the higher deva from which all the lesser activity tumbles forth.

Remember that people are collections of elemental deva too and each human being is learning, albeit slowly, to master them, to turn their activity towards a higher state that serves us all in better ways. Question not only your own intentions but also the purposes and intentions of your leaders, administrators and all those who are influencing the general trend of human affairs. What kind of song do those intentions sing—harmony or discord, fairness or self-interest, constructive or destructive?

Close your eyes at a live concert and see the light and colour of the music. You may be a person very much more sensitive to the subtle sounds of the universe than to how things *appear*. Don't force your learning or your subtle senses. *Let* them develop. With intention and openness, it happens naturally. With the encouragement and shared experience of like-minded friends, it quickens.

Drugs do not feature in a natural approach to deva. Drugs may give you a paranormal experience but they do not give you mastery. Mastery is a development of your own higher potential through your own higher faculties. Mind-altering drugs, especially when taken by the young, can have disastrous effects on the developing brain and psyche. They can damage, often irreparably, our ability to build and develop the subtle structures that lead to contact with and understanding of our higher self. Take a lesson from the plant kingdom—it is Light we need to strive for and it is Light that *reveals* the next stage of our natural development. After all, that's why the higher achievements are called en*light*enment.

If your home environment is less than pleasant, try an energy cleansing. I know people who have used Machaelle Small Wright's cleansing methods from her *Perelandra Garden Workbook* to very effectively rid rental houses of the lingering negative energies of drug use that have been left behind by previous tenants.

Fair Warning

We have learned that the distress of a tree severely mutilated or murdered without warning can be registered on our subtle senses as a scream. Intention is not just a thought or feeling that remains in the confines of our own mind or emotional body, at least not if it is a strong and purposeful intention that has the full force of our will behind it. The intention of a playground bully can be *felt*, evoking fear in a targeted classmate. Similarly, our intention to harm a tree can be felt by the elementals within the tree, but how?

Our strong intention ripples through the elementals in our own emotional and mental bodies, stirring them into activity that sends out waves of vibration into the surrounding environment. The deva kingdom is ever responsive to the force we call "will" and we humans are a kingdom of which *Will* is the primary, intrinsic characteristic and function. So, our will, our intention to cut down a tree, along with the *energy of the purpose or motive* behind our actions, triggers the elementals of our subtle bodies, and they in turn send out waves of energy that are received by the tree's elemental. People who cannot countenance suggestion of such communication forget that it is not words but vibration and resonance we are talking about here. Whether our concrete, rational mind wants to accept it or not, vibration and resonance *contain environmental information* that can be picked up both by sensitive humans and non-human life forms.

We don't have to cause anguish in the world around us, mindlessly maiming and murdering that which grows and lives beside us. If we warn a tree that tomorrow we need to prune its branches or cut it down altogether, we send a different quality of intention. We can warn it to withdraw its "consciousness" into the roots for example or if it is to be cut down, ask it to vacate the solid physical body of the tree and return to its overlighting deva.

Why would we not warn a sentient being of something that can cause it such extreme distress? Giving the tree time for the elemental consciousness to withdraw is like giving a human an anaesthetic before surgery. If the pruning is major or if it is to be cut down completely, give the tree at least twenty-four hours warning. Remember to give your gratitude and thanks for its growing and the beauty and function of its form.

Is It All Sweetness and Light?

Not all the elementals are delightful little lights buzzing around the flowerbeds. On very rare occasions, I have come across trees that exude a very negative energy towards human beings. Other people I have talked to report similar and equally rare experiences of nature's resentment. Sometimes, I have sensed that there has been a very unpleasant incident committed at the site involving humans. It feels as if the land has been deliberately or accidentally "cursed" by whatever took place there. Linda and I experienced a very negative energy while walking the rim of an abandoned quarry in Western Australia. Sometimes such situations are complicated and dealing with those kinds of problems is outside the scope of this present book. There are others who specialize in such matters that you can research. I would recommend Marco Pogačnik's book as well as in the works of Machaelle Small Wright and Dorothy Maclean already mentioned. (You'll find them all in the Bibliography at the back of this book.)

Usually, I apologize for whatever harm we have inflicted on the trees or the area, doing my best to be centred, non-judging and detached at the same time as holding a vibration of love, without forcing it upon them. Always, I am cognisant of the need to keep a respectful physical and psychic distance, allowing the Nature Spirits to approach me if they wish, just as we would want to be respectful of other humans. If we ask permission to approach, it is normally granted with gladness. However, if the negative energy is particularly potent it may be best to ensure the protection of your mind and subtle bodies by closing down your "openness" and physically leaving.

As we saw in Part Two, just being human gives us plenty of elemental challenges to deal with. You don't have to do anything special to know what an emotion or a thought "looks" or feels like. We're using them all the time so we are intimately familiar with their character and quality. We just have to decide what quality we want to transform them into and then make a habit of doing just that.

Remember it's not so much trying to be a saint (whatever that means) as ensuring that our lives are not *driven* by our physical, desire or mental elementals.

The Sad Reality

I've just used many thousands of words to entice you into the glorious reality of nature spirits and higher deva. Now, I've got to burst that bubble, a bit. Yes, the deva kingdom is the kingdom of Substance so one level or another of deva is all around us. But . . . the nature spirits are the beings that are trying to evolve into a higher level of their kingdom, just as we in our quest for higher consciousness are doing in our own kingdom. Nature spirits leave the land, fields, gardens, forests and so on when human influence means they can no longer abide there. The webs of life are fine and work in ways we are often ignorant of. Our wilful imposition of poisons, fertilizers and "efficient" methods destroy those once vibrant webs. Land no longer glows with deva's presence and no amount of wishing, aligning or whatever will bring you a nature spirit contact. They are no longer there.

The plants may keep growing and even look pretty healthy, pumped up with nutrients and with no bugs to bother them because they've all been killed off with pesticides. Their cellular elementals are still doing their job. However, there may be little or no energetic interplay between the planted area and its surroundings. The larger environment does not thrive either when all its parts are low in their natural "life force". Remember farmer Joe's field deva? When first found, it was not at all happy, even though the barley was growing and apparently fine. There was a big difference when it was acknowledged and its request for less fertilizer was granted. Not only was the deva energising the crop as it was designed to do, but the yields had gone up and the measurable quality improved.

When the nature spirits have abandoned an area, you may still be able to contact a landscape angel though they may also be somewhat diminished. If you find one, ask what is needed to bring more vibrancy into the area. I believe that with the right attitude and the cooperation of other humans we will find we can quickly heal our dead or dying environments if we are prepared to accept the reality of what nature spirits and their higher commanders actually do in our world. This kind of healing will only have a chance if we cease the practices that led the deva to abandon the land in the first place. To bring our Earth back to its natural state of abundance and health, we need to change our mindset and be clear about the effects of vested political and commercial interest that control our agricultural and forestry practices. Only with sufficient public and political will, education and pressure can we achieve the ultimate goal of healthy and harmonious cooperation with nature. The biggest challenge will always be the Ancient Fires of the long-held beliefs and thought forms of our fellow humankind, not to mention our own.

Chapter Seventeen
Deva, Religion, and Pan

Culture Clashes

The world with deva in it is a world replete with meaning. It is no longer a world of random events that have piecemeal explanations. To commune with deva is to be immersed in a sea of intelligent interaction that flows and spirals and streams with sound-filled light and colour. It cycles, dances, creates, breaks down, repels and forms anew. It's vibrant, exciting, always moving and full of joy. It is Creation itself, the act of appearing from the "no-thing" of potential into form—a seemingly endless parade of becoming, being, passing and becoming anew.

What we are taught to expect to see, we do see. When we are told often enough that something does not exist, we stop looking for it, yet there are many who do see or sense the more subtle layers of the world, who have not become blind to those more subtle levels of perception or who have learned to see them. Regrettably, such abilities and experiences are constantly ridiculed by mainstream media who, in the Western world at least, mostly live in boxes constructed of the limitations they have placed upon the world. The rest remain, for the large part, ignorant of the subtle realms, similarly scoffing or afraid of them.

On the other hand, the beliefs of indigenous minorities about the subtle worlds are tolerated because they are "traditional beliefs", though they may not actually be considered by outsiders as describing anything *real*. Further, it is forgotten that not so long ago the world of deva was seen and accepted as part of *all* cultures, albeit usually confined to the realm of nature.

To many indigenous cultures around the world, probably little of what I'm saying about the deva of nature would come as a surprise. The rise of science, in the Western world, has edged out general acceptance of deva. It began with the takeover of Pagan shrines all over Britain and Europe as the new Christian religion spread out across those lands. It's a normal process of cultural conquest—replace the centres of worship, which are the focus for a culture's belief systems, with your own. You can see it clearly in Central America. For example, just out of Mexico City at Teotihuacan, we can go beneath the newer temples to see how they have been constructed over top of the older ones. It's a strategy we see repeated in the old Mayan sites right through the countries of Central America.

We can argue that many of these older religions and customs contained superstitions and practices that were better supplanted with a more "rational" approach to the world. The downside (and it's coming home to haunt us now) is that the so-called rational approach also removed our reverence and respect for nature. Thus, we have given ourselves permission to manipulate and destroy what took the planet millions of years to evolve, with all its complexities and interrelationships. We do these things on the assumption that our self-interest is more important and worse, that we somehow know better than nature.

Out of the Closet

Although it usually *appears* that knowledge of the deva kingdom has largely disappeared from "European" cultures (in which I include Britain and Ireland), this is not in fact the case. It persists in folklore, children's books and in a very distorted way survives in fantasy book and movie genres. Wicca and Druid societies still practise their rituals and beliefs and doubtless, there are many similar cultural practices I know nothing of.

I am constantly surprised at how many people are now coming "out of the closet", where they have kept their interests in nature spirits or deva generally, hidden away for years. When I have given talks on the subject, I have often been astonished at the interest. Sometimes, there has barely been standing room in the venue and it has been particularly gratifying that there have been a high percentage of men present.

If you think such sensitivities are confined to "tree-huggers", "hippies" and "New Agers" you'd be wrong. A middle-aged Swedish forester was keen to tell me about his experiences of the "lady of the forest"—an ethereal light that appeared among the trees. My recollection is that he said it was blue but my memory may not be trustworthy on that point. Although in translation the light was described as a "lady", he indicated clearly that he related to my depiction of the nature spirits I was illustrating for *The Children of Gaia*.

I come from an increasingly multi-cultural nation where the indigenous Polynesian people have fought hard for official and general recognition of their language and culture and for the redressing of past wrongs by the British colonial conquerors and subsequent governments. The race of Maori currently accepted as being the indigenous people of New Zealand, arrived about a thousand years ago. Their culture, including its cosmological beliefs and practices are officially accepted and generally tolerated. I notice that acceptance of indigenous cultures is gradually increasing in other countries colonized by Europeans in recent centuries. Yet, if a European descendant talks of the kinds of experiences I have related in this book (which as part of my ethnicity go back a *very* long way) they are derided as "woo woo" or flaky. It's enough to make one wish for browner skin and fuller lips!

Deva and Religion

This is such a big topic it can be a book on its own. We've touched on it now and again and by now you probably have an impression of where I stand. I don't think that at this stage of our evolution any one single religious system, philosophy or science accounts for *all* of what our universe and the Life it expresses *is* or can *be*.

Perhaps a "one-size" view can never fit all because each plane of being has its own pattern of matter or substance, its own rules or laws of arrangement or defining characteristics. Consequently, each requires a different set of senses and level of consciousness or it cannot be known. Probably we cannot have the experience of being a single atom because we cannot function at the level of consciousness of an atom. We now have the consciousness that results from an enormous, intelligent assemblage of atoms.

Fortunately, in many countries today we can pick which system of thought, religion or philosophy we follow, without being tortured, killed or in other ways punished for it. Unfortunately, that is not the case everywhere. At its roots, the current world battle with fanaticism is about dogmatism versus the freedom to have our own understanding whilst at the same time, not forcing our understanding on others. By this definition, terrorism comes in many guises.

We are referring to the higher levels of deva as "angels" but these days "angel" is more often associated with religion. However, the angels of religion, from a metaphysical standpoint, are only a relative few of the deva of this level. In popular terminology and various cultures, there are plenty of references to the function and attributes of these angels of religion. Often they are named (and titled) and people may talk about their functions in very similar terms to the way we've talked of the higher deva here—as an angel of communication for example.

A religion that accepts the existence of "angels" at this level but rejects the rest of the deva or angelic kingdom as an anti-religious evil, misunderstands the nature of deva and their role in creative activity. Writer and healer Joel Goldsmith famously declared, "There is not God *and,* there is *only* God manifesting as . . ." [My italics.] Again, we meet the precept that all Life began and still is, only One Life that *appears* to have split into countless manifestations "while still remaining Oneness".

Many religions and philosophies throughout the ages speak of a trinity, the "three faces of God" or the three dynamic components of Creation. In Hinduism, it is Brahma, Vishnu and Shiva. For a long time in Ancient Egypt, it was Amun, Ra and Ptah. In the Christian tradition, it is the Father, the Son and the Holy Spirit. In the schema we are using, in the parlance of Ageless Wisdom, The Father (masculine) is Will, Deva the responsive, active intelligence within matter is the Mother or Holy Spirit (Feminine) and Consciousness or Love (the Son) is the result of the "marriage" between the two. (See Appendix for Diagrams.)

If you meet resistance or horror from your religion or religious friends, remind them that Divinity is omnipresent, which means it is in matter too. Point out that the deva kingdom *is* the angelic kingdom. If angels—deva of a higher order—are acceptable but not the elementals, remind them gently that even the lowly serve. Without our cells, we have no body for our consciousness to command. The elementals are the cellular equivalent in the wider context of life. Even the human distorted by "evil" can be "saved" by conquering their baser selves, that is, by lessening the distortion of their divine Self. Down at this level of personality we all suffer from the distortions of density. So it is with the lower elementals; they too have their path of learning and service and can be elevated over time. To paraphrase *A Course in Miracles*, if God is omnipresent, then there is *only* God and something that is not God cannot be real. To claim that Divinity is not in all things, great and small, is surely blasphemous under the paradigm of an omnipresent, omnipotent and omniscient deity. I say that God, the Oneness, the Great Spirit (whatever you want to call It) is experimenting with possibility, including playing at being human.

Aside from the political aspects, which we shall look at below, I believe that at the base of the Judaic-Christian relegation of deva to the ranks of devil-worship is the fear that it may amount to *worship* of deva. This comes from the determination of these religions to *replace* the Pagan beliefs (which revered and, in many cases, seemed to worship nature) with Monotheism, the recognition that there is only One originating God. In the sense that this signals a desire to return to the original state of Oneness from which we set out on this journey into density, that's a laudable goal.

Unfortunately, it has led to and justified the shocking attitude of abuse towards nature that we find ourselves in today. The irony is, as we've said, an Omnipresent Deity does not just reside in those aspects of Being and Creation that humans decide it does. All must, by the very definition of these religions, be a part of the One God. Let me be very clear that I am *not* advocating a worship of nature as a replacement of monotheism. I am suggesting it is time to have a more balanced view. We cannot exist here without the greater Life and its multitudinous expressions. We need to be mindful of treading the Middle Path between the extremes of *seemingly* alternative belief systems that are presented as mutually exclusive.

Echoes of the Past

What older nations do not have a tradition of faerie? So important were the nature spirits to the people of the past, shrines were built in their honour. These sacred places were usually sited on ley lines— pathways of recognisable energy flows that criss-cross every land. These sacred places were understood as the energies that made the land abundant, without which nature could not thrive. In Britain and Europe, deva was personified as the Green Man. Take a look at the Gothic Cathedrals and you will see that sculptures of the Green Man were *incorporated*, not excluded from Orthodox Christianity of the time. What happened between then and now? How did these beings get so relegated that their existence was not just denied but labelled as some kind of evil?

There are several things to consider in answering this question. Before the rise of modern science and modern medicine, many, if not most, of the healers were women. They were primarily herbalists who understood the healing properties of various plants. The word "witch" originates from this time and its original meaning had to do with this function of healing. It meant "wise woman". When science and its offshoot—scientific medicine—arose, it was the province of men not women. The wise women came to be seen as competition and an impediment to the advance of this new field of exclusively male endeavour. With the aid of the Christian churches, this cartel of early scientists and doctors launched a brainwashing campaign to destroy the female competition. Thus, the "witch hunts" were begun and included some men and children considered evilly cursed by abilities that were considered a threat to the new authorities. (See the National Film Board of Canada's excellent documentary, *The Burning Times*.) To this day, we feel the influence of this pogrom against both women and the naturebased healing arts. Nowadays orthodox medicine is aided by the commercial power of the pharmaceutical industry to establish and maintain legitimacy and to discredit and lobby for the abolition of more nature-based solutions.

Because orthodox medicine does not recognize the existence of a subtle body or bodies, it has no way to understand or appropriately measure the effect of more subtle forms of medicine or healing generally. So, how can it accept that for people who are very aware of their subtle bodies and different states and levels of consciousness, subtle remedies can be more effective than orthodox ones? Integrated medicine can bring modern science and our ancient knowledge of nature together, without the blind dogmatism of one or the out-moded superstitions of the other.

A Banished Deva "God"

Who is or was, Pan? He is said to have originated in ancient Greece, in the more rustic, rural areas. He was worshipped mostly in caves or at small shrines rather than in temples because he's always been associated primarily with the earth and with forest and trees in particular. It's very important that we understand how deva and forces we don't fully understand have always been personified into something ordinary human folk can relate to. While those with etheric vision or those with the ability to connect telepathically to such energies may not see them as partly humanoid, they still have the challenge as we've mentioned more than once in this book, first of relating to the deva they have connected with and secondly, of explaining what that being is like, to others. So, the qualities of the deva get distorted in the translation and often its essential purpose and nature is "lost".

There's no doubt from the historical record that Pan was originally felt to be "of the earth" and in Ancient Greece was depicted as an upright goat. I suspect that his presence was known long before then but here's the problem; how do you describe such a being as this, whose influence is so pervasive, so elusive and yet so palpable to those who glimpse or feel "his" presence? How to share with others his earthiness, his ability to appear and disappear, to be in different places at once, pervading earth, air, water and fire all at once? Such powerful mysteries have to be interpreted, reduced to a form that even a simple or uneducated person can understand. Over time, this great "god" of nature became the half-man, half-hoofed and horned creature of Medieval Europe and Britain. Understandably revered by the peoples who understood the land and their reliance upon nature, he became a symbol of Paganism that stood in the way of the Church's complete takeover of the old gods. For any new religion to succeed completely, it must be able to replace the old. The people must be convinced that the new gods or singular God is more powerful and more worthy of their worship or must appear more useful to their leaders. Hence, the Divine Right of Kings that the Christian Church espoused, made Christianity very attractive to ambitious leaders of Pagan tribes so that in the end, even the fiercely pagan Vikings were converted to the new religion.

Pan's image was increasingly morphed to convey a negative being that eventually came to epitomise "Satan", who, in later versions had set himself up as the destroyer of all that was good in the works of the Creator, like Tolkein's Melkor. One doesn't need to look far into the history of mythology to see the political-religious forces at work in this demonization of Pan, as the new wrests power from the old and in its turn becomes the new "ancient fire" that opposes the next turn of our evolutionary spiral.

There comes a time when we have to revisit the truths inherent in the old but to understand them in new ways, ways that are more appropriate to our changed perceptions. In the nineteenth century,

Pan received something of a cultural revival and not just amongst neo-Pagans. We already mentioned R. Ogilvie Crombie (in Chapters Six and Sixteen) who encountered Pan.

A Sense of Light

Pan has long been associated with sound; his name given to an instrument of reed pipes. As we said right at the beginning, deva means Being of Light and light has sound. Deva sound is sometimes perceived as an unusual vibration in and around our heads. At other times, we may feel it in our subtle field, impacting on our etheric body—that gossamer shell laced with beads of light that is the higher blueprint of our physical body. Sometimes I hear the song of deva in a forest. It is not the elemental notes but the song of the forest as a whole or sometimes a small, energetically special grove.

Even when we do not hear or feel the sound vibration of deva, we can often see their light. Those balls of light that dance about the ceiling and zip with lightning speed across the room like some small alien space craft exploring the upper reaches of your house, are deva. In our previous home, which had two mature trees close by, youthful visitors often commented with some delight on these phenomena. One of our sons also had a cat that would sit very alert in front of plants, moving her head as she watched something that was quite invisible to the rest of us. That "something" seemed to be dancing around the upper parts of the plant in a motion that I later came to recognize as that spiralling movement of deva. Sylphs, the nature spirits of the air are often described as streams of light particles flying, twisting and turning like flocks of birds. Why do we not all see and experience the deva life that's all around us?

As the nature spirit observed in conversation with me, our bodies are heavy and dense. Our conscious mind is primarily identified with these denser, heavier levels. We *cannot* experience a more subtle level of being without engaging a different set of sensors from a more subtle part of our being. If you want to listen to an FM radio station you can't hear it if your radio is set to AM, can you? Yet, we are so ready to dismiss as nutters and frauds, anyone who has developed their inner senses that are tuned to the finer frequencies, which can pick up the presence and activity of deva. Some of our inner senses develop faster than others and sometimes we just have to stop *trying* and allow those senses to open. Some of us are better constituted to tune into particular aspects of the deva kingdom, like Joe with his ley line walkers.

When the Whispers Become a Song

When we first begin to sense the songs of deva or the sight of them, they can seem faint, just beyond reach. The impression is general, like the first time we hear a symphony or a new song on the radio. When we hear it again and again, we get better at picking up the nuances, the subtlety of the tune and its phrases. It's no different when encountering the subtle world. It can take time and a number of visits, to become familiar, to notice the details, to see and feel more on each encounter.

I've suggested that when you get the tug to go to the park and enjoy the trees or drive through the countryside or stroll on a beach, you listen out for the whispers. They might come through the pattering of leaves, the swish of waves on the shore or the way the sun lights the edges of the clouds. When you take a walk, feel your way into the landscape. What does the land feel like? Which trees are channelling large amounts of energy from earth to sky? Is there a link of energy between different groups of trees? Don't ignore the little stirrings of joy that nature gifts us but follow them and see where they take you. Life may never be the same again. You could find yourself staying in one place while travelling into planes of understanding that you never knew existed, to levels of being that the wise have always told us are there if only we would be still and listen.

Go half way and then let it come to you. I've found this works better than trying to bore your way in like a miner with a jackhammer. In the subtle world, you have to *be* subtle. Going half way with heart and crown open and inviting, creates an edge, like the zone we talked about at length in Chapter Ten. When you go half way and then wait at the edge, deva will come to meet you there. You are both inviting them and being respectful of them. They will respond. Sometimes it just happens spontaneously.

Healthy Nature

I love to watch the recuperative powers of a garden. When the tomato plants of summer have turned to dry brown tangles hanging mournfully from the stakes that supported their growing and the cooling days kill off the rest of summer's bounty, a treasured carpet begins to appear amongst the dying plants. Miners' lettuce thrusts elegant stalks upwards, each offering a sweet, heart-shaped leaf at its end. Corn salad appears, in tiny clumps at first, then lengthening its narrow flat elongated leaves into a delicate fan of tastiness. Mizuna shoots in all directions amongst wandering stems of thick, arrow-shaped leaves of New Zealand spinach. It's riotous, disordered, joyful and highly productive. Personally, I think we should garden the ancient Japanese seedball (or seedbomb) way—throwing mud balls full of seeds around and letting the elementals choose which of those seeds is most suitable for any particular spot.

If you want nature spirits to abound in your own property, it's very helpful to set aside an area where they can do as they please. Don't spray it with chemicals. Just plant it with trees and/or shrubs that need little or no maintenance and leave them to grow whatever they want. When your neighbours frown at the riotous disorder that results, just smile tolerantly and tell them you're running a botanical experiment. On the quiet, you can stop by regularly and tell the nature spirits how delighted you are and ask them if there is anything they need. More water perhaps?

Subtle Signals

Every thought we have, every action we take, every emotion we feel, ripples out as energy, as a wave or vibration. The waveform is the energetic chord of the universe. Whether we like the idea or not our *intention* has an energetic motive that affects the world around us. Each of these waves has a quality of its own. Just as we can often sense an evil or benign intent from our fellow humans, so can the elemental intelligence within the plants and trees sense our intentions be they loving or destructive. Yes, in their own way trees can scream.

There are many subtle senses that we possess besides our five physical ones. We pick up anger, joy and discomfort from others just as easily as we see what they are wearing or the shape of their hands. To one degree or another we can be trained to perceive the subtle world and a sceptic is simply a person with limited perceptual ability and/or a firmly closed mind.

People raised from childhood to perceive the subtle world of faerie, like my friend Carron or Dora Van Gelda, develop a very finely tuned sense of the world. The rest of us can often still learn to experience a wider range of frequencies, albeit slowly with a good deal of patience and openness. It is a matter of what sort of sensory equipment we are born with as well as what we are sensitized to through natural inclination and training.

There is a lot of agreement among people who do experience the world of faerie or deva as to what it is like. In fact, I am still surprised by this level of agreement. When we lived in Australia, I noticed the nature spirits seemed to be predominantly blue. I told myself I was just imagining that because much of the vegetation has a blue tinge. When I discovered Dora Van Gelder's *The Real World of Faeries* I was delighted to read her description of the nature spirits of Australia (around Sydney at least) as being blue. Perhaps, I wondered, it is not just the blueness of the trees but also the blueness of the nature spirits that we are seeing in the bluish haze of the Australian bush.

"See" is one of our problem words because often what we experience is not so much seen as felt or sensed. Sensing deva may include a sensation of seeing but it may simply be a change in our own subtle field that registers the activity of deva.

Our survival as social animals has been finely tuned over millions of years to pick up subtle clues from each other. Clairvoyant people—those who can *see* these subtle layers—often report seeing emotion as waves or emissions of colour coming from the person experiencing or emanating those feelings. The colour or feeling impact we sense, visually or physically, is the activity of astral elementals. So actually, all but the emotionally bankrupt (psychopathic) recognize and respond to such elemental activity.

When we pay attention to these more subtle areas of our anatomy, we increase our awareness of the activity there. It's an awareness of the subtle that we can use to feel the presence of nature deva as well. Becoming very aware of changes in your own field, your own subtle body, is a big step to becoming sensitized to the subtle world that connects us to every other sentient being, to the intelligence that dwells, no matter how small or big, in all and every part of the world around us.

Even physical seeing is dependent on many factors. If you grew up as a Kalahari Bushman of Africa, you would be taught from a young age to distinguish, even from quite a distance, one kind of grass from another. If you were raised in an igloo among the Inuit people (in times past anyway), you would quickly learn to distinguish many different kinds and properties of snow. Whereas, if you were raised in a Western city and were taken to either of these other locations you may never learn to see these fine distinctions no matter how much tutoring you receive. There appear to be critical periods in early life when such learning takes place.

Chapter Eighteen
Consciousness

Why Is Consciousness So Important?

Why is our understanding of consciousness so important? The journey we have taken together through these pages has said as much about us as it has about deva. Underlying both the anecdotes and the metaphysics is the concept of consciousness. I believe that at this time, how we understand consciousness is the key to our prospects as a kingdom on this beautiful planet we call Earth. That understanding underlies our choices every day in every interaction we have—with other people, with the world around us and especially, with nature. How we view consciousness determines the science we undertake, the products we make, how we practise medicine, government, social welfare, agriculture, business . . . in short, it determines how we live our lives.

Back in Figs 5 and 6 (pages 59 and 61) we saw a model of the process by which consciousness is created. Fig 14 opposite reminds us how that process becomes a waveform that produces all the symphonies we call Creation, spilling forth from an originating point. That Oneness or Stillpoint—at whatever level we recognize it—apparently splits into a Purpose (Will) and a Response (deva) but because they are actually still One, they are drawn back together, thus creating a third point—love or consciousness—that mimics the original Oneness.

So, to one degree or another consciousness retains the light of the original Oneness that *appeared* to split and in that splitting, created

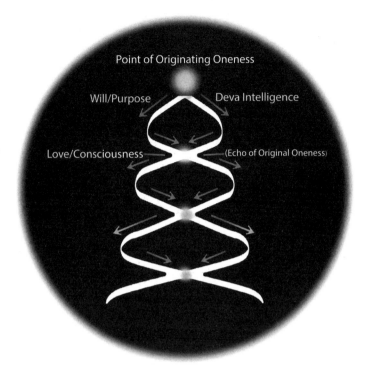

Figure 14 The Unfolding Song of Creation

our universe. It is the separation that is the illusion as nothing *ever actually left* the Oneness. Consciousness is the "memory" (however tenuous) of that Oneness that reappears when the "separated" parts reunite. That is why consciousness is able to exist in all regions of the Oneness at the same time. That is why it's Light is faster than the speed of physical light. It is also why so many spiritual texts say that everything we experience down here in the physical realms is an illusion. *Creation is simply a reforming of what appears to have been dissembled.*

Why did I say consciousness *mimics* the original Oneness? The "memory" of Oneness experienced by consciousness is not the same as the original Oneness. Why? The unfolding sound or song of Creation shines the Light only on those possibilities the Oneness contained that have been revealed by the "journey" into separation so far.

Without the participation of the deva kingdom, we wouldn't have been gifted this knowledge that is now "our" Consciousness. By our partnership with deva, they too have gained experience of the possibilities of the Oneness from which we both descended.

Our Bungee Jumping Journey

Consciousness, like everything else we've talked about in this book, has layers or levels. Not every part of us has "descended into matter". In Fig 9, page 118, showing our place in the Seven Planes of the Physical Universe, we saw that the second to top plane is labelled "Monadic" and beside that is the description, "Divine Human Spark". Ageless Wisdom says this is where we have descended *from* in our incarnational journey. If you look further down in Fig 9, you'll see that in the upper part of the mental plane there is a disk of light representing the soul or causal body.

So, you can think of our Monad or Divine Spark as being like a bungee jumper. The bungee cord is fixed securely at that Monadic level and we, the jumper (each one of us alone) jumps down to that soul level, anchors another bungee cord and from there, plunges into an assemblage of bodies (physical, emotion and mental) we call our human "personality".

When, for whatever reason, we have to vacate those three bodies in a process we call "death" we return to the soul or causal body. We get to process what we've learned and prepare for the next bungee jump into a new collection of bodies as a new personality to continue our learning through the human experience. Each of these lifetimes in different bodies and situations offers us the experience of different levels and qualities of consciousness.

Our Ladder of Consciousness

We saw in Fig 6 (The Creative Trinity on page 61) how consciousness (or love) is the result of the creative dance between Purpose or Will of one sort or another and the response of Deva. Although this creation of consciousness is happening all the time, we can also understand that at key points or levels, our human experience of consciousness has earned us an accumulation of learning that now makes our consciousness qualitatively different from what it was at an earlier stage. Our journey from birth to adulthood mimics or "recapitulates" those stages.

The usefulness of this framework can be seen in how it enables us to understand consciousness. Now let's impose the stages we go through as we evolve, onto the same schema we just used in Fig 14.

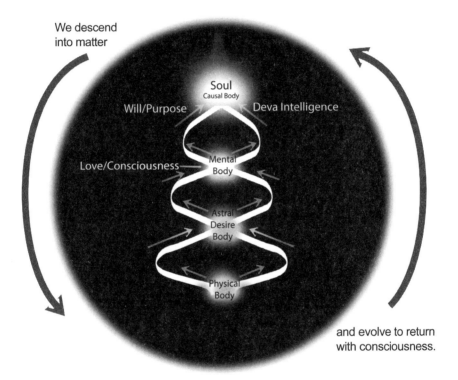

Figure 15 The Human Ladder of Consciousness

We can see in Fig 15 that there is a new "birth" or creation of consciousness at each level. Let's just look at the soul for a moment. It is conscious at a much higher level than where our emotional (astral) self is conscious. Our soul is "meditating" on its own plane up there in the substance of Abstract Mind and it also from time to time meditates or connects with us, it's personality extension. (When that happens, we experience true intuition and soul-infused love.)

There's a continuous dance between these levels of being and our awareness as we explore the substance (deva) that we are using. As we go through our experiences as John, Jacquelyn or whoever, we are doing two important things. *We are becoming conscious of the nature of life at these lower levels* (physical, astral and mental) *and we are learning to raise that manifested life (form) to a higher level.* So, we experience different *qualities* of consciousness at the various levels of the dance between deva and our will-based self. Together, we and deva are exploring the possibilities of being. Obviously then, what we are *conscious of* is going to be different as we begin to use higher levels of deva. Our human brain is an important part of this journey.

The Brain—Bringing Past and Future Together

Throughout our long evolution, our form has gone through countless stages of change as our developing bodies (physical and subtle) are continually modified. Those stages of changing form are visible in the development of the human foetus as it "relives" our evolutionary history from a small single cell to a swimming multi-celled creature to a reptilian-like amphibian and on to the gradual building of the sophisticated, complex biology that is ours today.

Our brain has its own elemental intelligence. Though we talk of the right and left sides of our brain as having primarily different functions—linear logic on the left and holistic conception on the right—those two sides of the healthy brain are constantly working with each other. Their interactive singing enables skills like language and speech as well as emotional processing. Stimuli from our environment trigger different parts of the brain. A shocking, traumatic circumstance may call our earlier or older brain into activity, triggering survival responses developed countless ages ago. Trauma can also interrupt or prevent the normal communication between different parts of the brain.

When we pick up a phone to call someone or search for information on the Internet, we call upon our newer brain where the elemental songs of speech and language skills have developed. New technology forces our brain to learn and process new things and in doing so, expands the opportunities for our conscious awareness to grow.

Slowly, science is piecing together the roles played in this symphony of our Earthly experience. We have body systems that have been with us for a very long time along with newer tools of a complex and somewhat "plastic" brain. Metaphysicians also look at how, for some, there is not only an active mental body but also a growing influence of the higher, abstract mind where the soul or causal body resides (Fig 9 on page 118 and Fig 15 on page 293).

Our will drives us to learn more, to experiment, invent, to experience new ways of being and doing. It calls forth a response from the substance we are using be it our body, brain or emotions and in this dance of our will with that substance, we and deva create new songs, build new structures, physical and subtle and thus create new experiences.

Where We Focus, We Become

Our brain is the physical instrument we use to store, process, access and interpret experiences of the physical, emotional and mental planes but it's the level of consciousness we often call "mind", that uses and interprets that brain activity. Thinking about the nature of zones we discussed earlier, it may be useful to see our "mind" as the interactive zone between our brain and our consciousness. However we choose to understand or label it, it's our consciousness that sets humans apart from the other kingdoms but our mistake is to assume ours is the only kingdom that *is* conscious. Actually, *what distinguishes each kingdom is the quality, nature and level of its consciousness.* We are so arrogant we think ours in the only kind of consciousness there is but that's a modern, and perhaps primarily Western, idea.

We've looked at how the solidity of our world only holds together in a narrow band of perception. We have known for three quarters of a century that at a different level of perception our world is one of energy. Yet, the grip of material thinking, the hold of those "ancient fires" of our created thought forms is very resistant to change and most of us remain imprisoned in this tiny but seemingly reliable 3-D world of the physical senses.

Today, visual technologies, fantasy and sci-fi films, books and video games, indulge our imagination and hint at other planes and worlds that are less materially dense. Nevertheless, they are still a dramatized distortion of the wider reality in which we exist. Our addiction to dramatic stories is very satisfying to our astral elementals. Those elementals *embody* drama and we all know people who seem to take tortured delight in lurching from one life drama to the next, while their excited elementals do their best to lasso those nearby into participating.

This addiction to drama isn't confined to individuals. It plays out in groups too. In the business world, managers and staff can get hyped up by the dramas of late deliveries, stalled production, cancelled orders, etc. Calm and rational examination of the where along the series of events the problems were caused, can disappear under power games and blame games. There are potential dramas involving our emotional elementals wherever we find group activity and in them, we can see the fog created when our emotional elementals are unleashed. Once under our higher control, their gift to us is the development of empathy and compassion.

On the other hand, if our lives focus primarily in the concrete, rational thinking of the lower mental plane, we may reinforce our perceptual prison with the surety of our assertion that the "reasoning", "logical" intellect is the pinnacle of human achievement and all there is left to do is to be more and more clever with our materialistic thinking. Actually, even this is just another necessary stage and the eventual and lasting gift of the elementals of concrete reason is *discrimination*, which can lead to quick problem solving and the dissolution of astral drama.

It's a song that's playing at every level our personality being inhabits—physical, emotional and mental—and in between each. Our *Will to Be* triggers the songs of elemental response. At each level, the substance we are using provides the material for our Will to dance with and in that dance our consciousness of the substance we are using develops.

As our consciousness rises above these three personality "worlds" however, the sense of duality reduces into a more simultaneous whole because, as we saw in Fig 10 on page 136, the distortion is less and less the higher up we go and eventually we are able to reconnect consistently with our soul consciousness. It is said that when humanity—as a kingdom—functions at that level we will become the Kingdom of Souls on Earth. Clearly, we have a good deal of self-mastery to accomplish first.

The "Where?" Trap

It is because conventional science paradigms do not generally see consciousness as separate from and *using* the brain that it gets stuck on *where* seemingly non-physical or so-called paranormal phenomena take place. There is a feedback system between consciousness and its physical instrument—the human brain and body—because what are we doing? We're learning to evolve ourselves via the matter or substance we are using. We, and the elementals we are using, are creating a new song as we work together, in a partnership that is far more equal than we, in our intellectual arrogance suppose.

Clearly, I do not believe our brain is solely responsible for consciousness, though it is an essential *instrument* we use in the *development* of consciousness. The brain ceases to function correctly when consciousness deserts it. The experiences of people during near death experiences (NDEs) have often been dismissed as hallucinations produced by the brain's lack of oxygen, chemical changes, etc. I sense a tautology lurking here.

When neurosurgeon Eben Alexander's brain completely shut down during an attack by a rare disease, his consciousness still had a powerful NDE. He was so impressed and changed by the experience that he wrote a book about it, called *Proof of Heaven,* and devoted himself to convincing his fellow doctors and scientists of the validity of other people's reported near death experiences. He feels that the medical conditions under which his experience took place, proves that consciousness is independent of the brain and its functions. Such claims are often highly contested. Nevertheless, NDEs so often have profound and positive life-changing effects on those who experience them.

Towards Synthesis

Of course, what I'm asserting in this book is not new to the sages of Eastern and some other branches of philosophy or to some religious teachings though the terminology may differ, along with the depth of their exploration.

Metaphysics would say that any physical thing is simply a *vehicle* for consciousness, whether it is our human body or a tree. The vehicle does not house the consciousness so much as sits *within* consciousness. Our soul does not so much inhabit our body but surrounds and interpenetrates it. Sure, we may access our soul by building our antahkarana (the bridge from personality to soul) over many lifetimes but then we become aware that our soul also surrounds us as a finer, lighter, less dense "body", not in some far-off dimension but in a plane that interpenetrates and overlays our physical world. We describe it as being "higher" but perhaps it is also accurate to describe it as "finer" or "lighter". At other times, it may feel as if the soul is deep within, in that inner "space" where we move past the veil of the physical and enter the formless.

Ageless Wisdom teachings bring us an important concept as we try to understand how all these different stages of learning and states of being lead eventually to a state of enlightenment. It is a state whereby "three minds unite"—the concrete-rational, the soul-causal and the abstract (see Fig 11, The Seven Subplanes of the Mental Plane, on page 154). Once we have integrated those three minds into a synthesis, we free ourselves from the thraldom of the lower elementals we have been using and our consciousness can ascend to the plane of formless light we call Buddhi, aka Nirvana.

Deva Know We're Here

Meanwhile, down here in our current reality . . .

Deva of nature are not shut off from us. We know, at least from the nature spirits up, that we are as visible to them as our seemingly solid world is to us and they are sometimes surprised and usually delighted to be recognized and acknowledged.

Communicating with deva is a two-way affair. The nature spirits and the lesser overlighting deva seem to have a genuine need and desire to figure out our contradictions. They puzzle as to why a human buys flowers to put in their home to enjoy and admire and yet we will chop down a bush in full flower. They cannot understand why humans don't wait until the nature spirits have finished pouring energy into the plant's flowering and the flowers have died. Don't we humans experience a deep grief when a young person is killed just when their youth is flowering? Why do humans cut down the forest and then wail and weep when the rains come, washing away the soil and flowing unimpeded to destroy homes and crops? The nature spirits cannot understand why we ignore the rhythms and cycles of energy and complex interrelationships that sustain the life we depend upon, not only for our very survival but also for our general health and wellbeing.

You may find, however, as others and I have done, that some higher deva have little interest in us or in our affairs, like the river and storm deva we met earlier. Regardless of our personal concerns, they will do whatever they must according to an overriding, more powerful theme in the great symphony of Earth.

We cannot expect to create a better world unless we work towards a higher consciousness. How do we do that? We do it with honest examination of the purposes contained in our intentions and patient training to gain a higher understanding. We need to stop and ask, *"What quality of energy is behind our motives? What level of consciousness are we operating from?"* That will entail that we focus on the big picture and along the way, learn how, as a kingdom, we rightly fit into that picture.

It is also important to take note of the warnings as deva are using forces beyond our comprehension in their power and complexity.

The Circulating Song

Spirals, circles and wave forms are the signature movements of deva in nature, particularly overlighting deva. Nature thrives when the energy of all its different components or systems can *circulate*. Why, when I first encountered the deva of farmer Joe's field in Scotland, was the deva all but stationary but when I called back on the third visit it was swirling around happily and despite a lessening of fertilizer application, the crop yields had improved? Was it simply being acknowledged that spurred the deva into greater activity resulting in a more abundant, healthier crop? Or had the fertilizer levels been interfering with its work? The deva's request that the fertilizer levels be reduced suggest the latter but I also suspect our recognition and appreciation of its role contributed.

Spiralling, circulating movement is also the signature movement of a healthy human energy system. Our chakras are vortices that wind up our etheric spine as a caduceus of energies circulating from the subtle to the physical layers of our bodies. Healthy, even-handed circulation of goods and services between individuals and groups is also key to healthy commerce, government and the overall welfare of our societies and nations.

Since Charles Darwin, there has been much emphasis on the fierce competition within nature but that is also a projection of our human predilection for competitive models of behaviour. It is a very cultural judgement based on separation thinking that ignores the interactive, cooperative, interdependent patterns of activity and energy between plants, trees, birds, insects and animals. Thanks to a wider variety of observation methods and a rising consciousness, this interdependent perspective is now acknowledged more and more by ecologists, biologists, biochemists and others. We also have much to learn about the quality, levels and possible sharing of consciousness that may occur in nature.

At a physical level, every atomic component is a minute fiery energy. When atoms combine, they create a new physical structure and a new energetic signature arises from that new combination. Like a minute DNA marker, a trace of the original quality of the component energy remains. The tendency to group together continues at every level of physical activity, creating the multitude of different forms or distinctive energies that constitute our physical world. At the same time, there is a hierarchy of subtle command or coordination behind these joinings. It is intelligent activity we're describing here, intelligent form building, *commanded from the top-down but carried out from the bottom up.*

Essentially, we can think of the angelic level of deva as the architects of form, the overlighting deva as the builders and their elementals as the workers that follow the plans to create that building. It's a constant movement, coming into and going out of form, spiralling, circulating, culminating, disintegrating and creating anew. Such movements apply to our own lives too.

Dangerous Attitudes

Imagine if you were aware that you are filled with and surrounded by intelligence, that even the air between you and the objects or plants you see is not empty but full of this intelligence. And you probably thought the world crowded already! If we lived with higher awareness of the greater Life in the world around us, we could not live in a bubble of isolation, treating everything around us as inert, mindless matter. When we do not recognize another person, or the group or race they belong to, as being as human or as "legitimate" as we are, it gives us licence to act as if that person or group is *not human*. This advanced stage of cultural blindness justifies any cruelty towards "not me" or "not us" and leads all too swiftly to the countless abominations of injustice, inequality, war and genocide that humans have inflicted upon each other for countless millennia.

The label "not human" has also justified our treatment of the Earth and its non-human inhabitants—land, forest, animals, water, air—everything we depend upon for our health and sustenance. What insanity is this? So much of it can be attributed to lack of *awareness* of the very Life that surrounds us and the intelligence of that Life that permeates every kind of matter at all levels of density.

We know the "mood" of the planet is changing. Great swathes of elemental life are massing in tumultuous response to something deeply disturbing—Change (with a capital C). Be it the Earth's response to human folly, its own evolutionary thrust, response to forces from its wider solar environment, or any other type of force we are unaware of, we are witnessing uncomfortable and ominous change. Melting ice, rising seas, frequent severe storms, tornadoes, earthquakes and fire. These things have always happened, just not recently with such fury or frequency. They coincide with a huge and relatively sudden loss of habitat and species worldwide.

What if we followed the advice of the highly advanced deva of the plant kingdom to right the wrongs we have wrought on nature on whom we *depend* for our health and well-being and our continued existence on Earth? My computer dictionary wants to correct me when I refer to nature with "whom" instead of "which". Perhaps if we talked of nature, not so much as a mythical Mother to be acknowl-edged at certain times of the year with ritual and ceremony but as having the status of a vastly Intelligent Being, deserving of *who* not *which*, we would start treating "Her" rightly too.

In 2017, after a battle of more than 140 years, the local Maori people in Whanganui, New Zealand, won the right for their river to be recognized as a living entity. In what is believed to be a world first, it means the river has the legal status of a person under a special bill passed by the New Zealand parliament. The story appeared in a number of newspapers around the world, including The Guardian, The Telegraph and the Independent in the United Kingdom.To some this legal status may seem bizarre, yet we happily grant businesses and organizations this right under law. A spokesman said, "We have always believed that the Whanganui River is an indivisible and living whole—Te Awa Tupua—which includes all its physical and spiritual elements from the mountains of the central North Island to the sea."

In Iceland an Act was introduced in 1990 to protect sites known, for at least 100 years as having "supernatural significance". Iceland, it seems, has had trouble with the elves of rocks. Apparently they have caused inexplicable, often bizarre accidents involving machinery when road workers have disturbed rocks that are important to the elves. This sounds similar to the problems with Taniwha in New Zealand (see page 121 under "Ancient Water Elementals").

Becoming Aware

We have barely skimmed the surface of deva in this collection of anecdotes and metaphysical discussions. Metaphysicians and spiritual masters, far, far more advanced than I, have written of these things and I commend their works to you. (You will find them listed in the Bibliography.) My aim has been to stimulate your interest and to encourage you to seek your own experiences. Stop in the busyness of your days to contemplate, appreciate and connect.

Each living thing on this planet has evolved, refining its physical form in the process. It is said that our bodies evolve to house greater and greater *expressions* of our originating spirit. We've seen that over the epochs, an emotional body has been developed as an addition to our physical body and the majority of humanity apparently still runs primarily on emotional activity. Now a mental "body" is being developed so we can use a new level of elemental intelligence, mostly at the level of concrete, rational thinking so far. Eventually we will all evolve into beings governed by the much loftier abstract mind of the soul that lives in a state of conscious awareness with other souls. After that, there are even loftier states of being and mastery to look forward to.

For now, most of us are prisoners of a fixed perception. I certainly do not personally claim to have overcome all the challenges of the astral and mental elementals! However, I do know that when we step out of this prison of "solid matter", we enter a set of unfamiliar realities. As our consciousness rises, we see and understand the levels we *used* to identify with differently. We see the illusions, the distortions of those levels because we *no longer identify with them*. We no longer define ourselves by our physical body, our emotions or even our thoughts. We recognize that we are not the equipment we are using just as we are not the car we get into to drive somewhere. For the duration of our incarnation on Earth, our physical, emotional and mental vehicles are just that, vehicles. Together, they are our personality, the vehicle we are driving through this particular lifetime. It's a vehicle we will vacate when, for whatever reason, we can no longer drive it. At that time, we return to the launching pad we call "soul" or "higher self" from which we bungeed down here. Our consciousness will remain at a higher, less dense level, to absorb the lessons of the journey until we are ready to return. And that, as I recall is where we began this account of my journey with deva.

The Other Half of Us

Our journey is a great song from the silence of unknowing Oneness to separation and re-joining, each stage carrying us on the gradual path of return to Oneness again, only we will return (eventually) with full awareness of all that comprises our Oneness. Deva makes this long symphony through space-time possible for us. It is the other half of ourselves with which we will one day reunite in the consciousness of Buddhi and then eventually, at the Monadic level, fuse. Why? Because we and deva are two halves of the same Being, like two sides of a piece of paper. In learning of deva, what to master and when to cooperate, we hasten the day of our reuniting as one conscious whole.

We don't all have to be clairvoyant, clairaudient or telepathic. We don't all have to see or experience deva directly. We just have to understand that we are partners with this "other half" of us— the intelligence embedded or infused into matter or substance that we are using at all levels of density. Without that intelligence, we have no *experience* of being here, of living this life at any level. It doesn't have to be an argument over divinity, religion or science, just simply a growing consciousness of the life that surrounds, enfolds and sustains us.

Who Are the Singers?

In Chapter One, I posed the question, "Who are the singers?" By now, you've probably figured out that they *all* are. At the beginning, I told you faeries were slithers of light and that the word "deva" means "being of light", and light as we discovered, has sound. Light sings.

Large beings, like our Planet Earth, has a body that sends out its note, both physical and metaphysical, into the Universe. All the symphonies of the lives created on this great being are contained within that note. They tumble out of it—all the songs of Earth's deva singing into form all that we call "kingdoms"—mineral, plant, animal and human. Most of us (humans that is) are so hearing-impaired, we have no idea there is music all around us. When we do chance to catch a devic tune, we are entranced by the beauty and joy of it.

The songs of deva have webbed our planet with their light, adding tunes, themes and symphonies over many, many millions of years but because of our blind, clever selfishness, we are pulling this beautiful web apart, destroying both the light and its song. Where we have done this, the song is no longer a praise of Being but a discordant agony of destruction and disconnection. It doesn't have to be this way and a change of mind, a change of intention and rightful clarity of purpose, will give deva the chance to do what they are destined to do—build anew and sing the song the Planet intends. If we are indeed elementals in the throat chakra of the planet, our job is to *help* the planet express its songs, not remove its larynx altogether.

In Closing

We have glimpsed the deva kingdom at many levels, from those who inhabit hills to the beings of great mountains, from those who energize streams to the masters of great waterfalls, from the beautiful deva of bays and coves to angelic hosts that mediate between the great oceans and the plane of formless light.

We have met trees, inside and out, sensed their light and their songs. We have talked of the great deva whose consciousness pervades the very life-fire of nature. "He" is one with the soil and all that lives therein and grows therefrom. His presence can be felt everywhere on this Earth where nature is allowed to flourish, in the soil, water and air that enables growth. He oversees the deva who stand at the point of death where the motion of life turns and the builders become the dismantlers, as they guide the death of form to a new resurrection. His elementals are legion. His distinctive presence shows us that Oneness is not just a seven-letter word; it is the state of Being we are so dangerously ignorant of that we are obliterating its evidence. In its place we are creating artifice designed to fill our endless desire, not realizing our desire cannot be quenched except by the Oneness whose evidence we have extinguished.

The Great Song dances out of the One from highest to lowest. We can see its effects all around us in every kingdom beside us. We can hear it directly when we cease to place our individuality before that One Life. Yet, from the beginning it has called on our inner ear relentlessly until we have learnt to listen and, in the listening, we hear the song of our own Light as well.

To conclude, is a little more of deva's description of who they are and what they do that was quoted near the beginning of our journey together (page 31). As you discover or continue your own journey with the songs of deva, I wish you joy and the courage to share your experience.

Together again, we will play the world, our words tumbling forth in harmony and not at war. And you will hear our song again in every breath of wind, and see our light in every flower, in every beast, in bird and fish and tree.

You will, each one, choose aright; rediscover that each of you owns a path that pours in light, a trail from what you are to where you now have come. Turn around and see us there beside you, creatures of the playful air, of liquid life, of flame, of stone. We make you, breathe you, servants all of Life. Come dance with us and know we all are One. *(WE I)*

Appendix

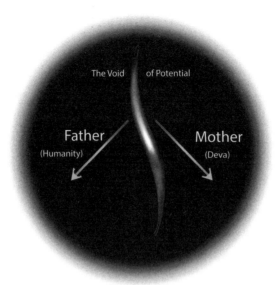

Figure 16 The Apparent Split of the Original Oneness:
Releasing the Light Contained in the Darkness of
the Void (aka The Big Bang)

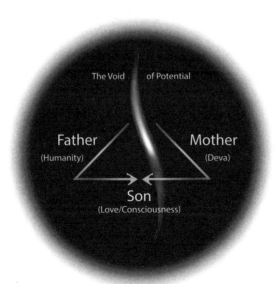

Figure 17 The Creative Trinity as It Applies to Humanity and Deva:
The "Re-joining" of the Apparently Separated Parts of Oneness

Illustrations

Appendix

Bibliography

Books

A Course in Miracles. Tiburon, CA: Foundation for Inner Peace, 1985.

Alexander, Eben. *Proof of Heaven*. NY: Simon & Schuster, 2012.

Bailey, Alice A. *A Treatise on Cosmic Fire*. NY: Lucis Press, 1982.

Bailey, Alice A. *Glamour—A World Problem*. NY: Lucis Press, 1995.

Bailey, Alice A. *Letters on Occult Meditation*. NY: Lucis Press, 1993.

Bolte Taylor, Jill. *My Stroke of Insight*. NY: Penguin, 2009.

Cairns-Smith, A.G. *Genetic Takeover and the Mineral Origins of Life*. Cambridge, UK: Cambridge University Press, 1982.

Cairns-Smith, A.G. *The Life Puzzle*. Edinburgh: Oliver & Boyd, 1971.

Carson, Rachel. *The Sea Around Us*. Oxford, UK: Oxford University Press, 1951.

Covey, Stephen R. *The 7 Habits of Highly Effective People*. NY: Fireside, Simon & Schuster, 1990.

Crombie, R. Ogilvie. *Encounters with Nature Spirits*. Rochester, VT: Findhorn Press, 2009/2018.

Doidge, Norman. *The Brain That Changes Itself*. NY: Viking, 2015.

Goldsmith, Joel. *The Thunder of Silence*. London: HarperCollins, 1993.

Greaves, Helen. *Testimony of Light*. Walden, England: Neville Spearman Publishers, 1985.

Hamilton, David. *It's the Thought that Counts*. Carlsbad, CA: Hay House, 2005.

Haskall, David George. *The Songs of Trees*. VIC Australia: Black Ink, 2017. (The quote in Chapter Twelve is reprinted by permission of Black Inc., an imprint of Schwartz Publishing. First published in the United States by Penguin Random House.)

Hawken, Paul. *The Magic of Findhorn*. NY: Bantam Books, 1976.

Hodson, Geoffrey. *The Kingdom of the Gods*. Adyar, Madras, India: Theosophical Publishing House, 1999.

Holy Bible, King James Version, Genesis Chapter 1. London: Collins.

Hunt, Roland. *Fragrant and Radiant Healing Symphony*. H. G. White, 1949.

Knight, Sirona. *The Complete Idiots guide to Elves and Fairies*. Indianapolis, IN: Alpha—Penguin Group 2005. (If you want to know what names humans have given all the nature spirits.)

Kondo, Marie. *The Life-changing Magic of Tidying*. London: Vermillion, Penguin Random House, 2014.

Lane, Jacquelyn E. *The Children of Gaia*. Second edition. New Zealand: Tall Pixie Publishing 2013.

Lane, Jacquelyn E. *This World of Echoes—Books I, II & III*. New Zealand: Tall Pixie Publishing, 2012. Carlsbad, CA: Balboa Press, 2013.

Lipton, Bruce. *The Biology of Belief*. London, UK: Hay House, 2008.

Lovelock, J. E. *Gaia*. Oxford, UK: Oxford University Press, 1987.

Maclean, Dorothy. *To Hear the Angels Sing*. Hudson, NY: Lindisfarne Press, 1990.

McTaggart, Lynne. *The Field*. London: Element, HarperCollins, 2003.

Miller, Hamish and Barry Brailsford. *In Search of the Southern Serpent*. Wellington, New Zealand: Stoneprint Press, 2006.

O'Leary, Brian, Christopher Bird, Jeane Manning, Barry Lynes. *Supressed Inventions and Other Discoveries*. Auckland Institute of Technology Press, 1994.

Ostrander, Sheila and Lynn Schroeder, with Nancy Ostrander. *Superlearning*. London: Sphere Books, 1981.

Pearce, Stewart. *The Alchemy of Voice.* Scotland, UK: Findhorn Press, 2010.

Pogačnik, Marko. *Nature Spirits and Elemental Beings.* Scotland, UK: Findhorn Press, 1997.

Roerich, Helena. *Fiery World Books I, II and III.* NY: Agni Yoga Society Inc., 1969.

Roerich, Helena. *Leaves of Morya's Garden Book II.* NY: Agni Yoga Society Inc., 1991.

Samanta-Laughton, Dr Manjir. *Punk Science.* Alresford, UK: John Hunt Publishing, 2006.

Shakespeare, William. *Hamlet* (1.5.167-8) Hamlet to Horatio. NY: Simon & Schuster, 1992.

Sheldrake, Rupert. *The Presence of the Past.* Rochester VT: Inner Traditions, 2012.

Small Wright, Machaelle. *The Perelandra Workbook II.* Jeffersonton, VA: Perelandra Limited, 1996.

Steiner, Rudolf. *Nature Spirits—Selected Lectures.* Forest Row, UK: Rudolf Steiner Press, 2007.

Strauch, Barbara. *The Secret Life of the Grown-up Brain.* NY: Penguin Random House, 2011.

Tharp, Twyla (Author) and Mark Reiter (Contributor). *The Creative Habit.* NY: Simon & Schuster, 2006.

Tolkien, JRR. *The Lord of the Rings.* Illustrator Alan Lee. London: HarperCollins, 1991.

Tolkien, JRR. Editor, Christopher Tolkien. *The Silmarillion.* London: George Allen and Unwin, 1977.

Tolle, Ekhart. *A New Earth.* VIC Australia: Michael Joseph Ltd, Penguin Group, 2005.

Tompkins, Peter and Christopher Bird. *The Secret Life of Plants.* Australia: Penguin, 1974. Note: The experiments on the ability of plants to respond to different music, which became synonymous with this book, have been hotly disputed over the years. Science now seems to be confirming that from its perspective, plants do in fact respond to what to us are minute vibrations.

Van Gelder, Dora. *The Real World of Faeries*. Wheaton, IL:: Quest, The Theosophical Publishing House, 1977.

Watson Lyall. *Lifetide*. London: Hodder & Stoughton, Coronet Imprint, 1980.

Weisman, Alan. *The World Without Us*. NY: St Martin's Press, 2008.

Wohlleben, Peter. *The Hidden Life of Trees*. VIC Australia: Black Ink, 2016.

Wray, William. *Leonardo Da Vinci—In His Own Words*. Slough, UK: Arcturus Publishing Ltd, 2005.

Articles and Papers

Clarke, Dominic, and Heather Whitney, Gregory Sutton, Daniel Robert. "Detection and learning of floral electric fields by bumblebees." From an original study at Bristol University. *Science Express* (2012).

Dr Geo. "Angels of the Botanic Gardens and Angels of Canberra." http://devahome.net/Level%204%20files/Angels%20of%20 the%20Botanic%20Gardens, accessed 23 February 2020.

Early Environmental Education. www.enviroschools.org.nz

Laibow, Rima. "Qantitative EEG and Neurofeedback." Research Paper.

Permaculture. An internet search shows up many links. You could start with: https://permacultureaustralia.org.au

Selk, Avi. Quoting Spahr Webb in: "Scientists are slowly unlocking the secrets of the Earth's mysterious hum." *Washington Post*, December 8, 2017. The information also appeared in the UK in *The Guardian, The Telegraph* and *The Independent*.

Sheldrake, Rupert and Pamela Smart. *Journal of Scientific Exploration* 14(2000): 233-255. www.sheldrake.org

Tugend, Alina. "Praise Is Fleeting, But Brickbats We Recall." *New York Times*, March 23, 2012.

Webb, Spahr. On Earth Sound in Selk, Avi. "Scientists are slowly unlocking the secrets of the Earth's mysterious hum." *Washington Post*, December 8, 2017.

Webb, Spahr. On Earth Sound in Selk, Avi. "Scientists are slowly unlocking the secrets of the Earth's mysterious hum." *Washington Post*, December 8, 2017.

Viewing and Listening

Down the Rabbit Hole is the full version of the popular movie/documentary, *What The Bleep Do We Know?* It's a fun way to challenge our "normal" perceptions of the world. Not surprisingly it is much disputed in some quarters. Revolver Entertainment, 2006. www.thebleep.co.uk

Ghost. Director Jerry Zucker, Paramount Studios, 1990.

Goldsmith, Joel. For recordings and quotes as well as his books: www.joelgoldsmith.com

Earth Healer, Medwyn Goodall, New World Music.

The Burning Times. National Film Board of Canada Documentary, 1990.

The Legend of Bagger Vance. Director Robert Redford, Dreamworks.

The Lord of the Rings. Film trilogy. Director Peter Jackson, New Line Cinema & WingNut Films, 2001, 2002, 2003.

The Lost Interview with Steve Jobs. Magnolia Pictures, Nerd TV, John Gau Productions. Currently available on YouTube and NetFlix.

The Sorcerer's Apprentice. From the original Fantasia, Walt Disney Studios.

Why Am I?, also known as *Why Am I?: The Science of Us* and *Predict My Future: The Science of Us.* Four-Part Documentary from The Dunedin Study. Razor Films, Auckland, New Zealand, 2016.

Acknowledgements

Truly, giants have walked this way before me, bringing us their observations of the deva kingdom. In their footprints, my own hesitant steps often seemed too tiny to merit your attention dear reader. I hesitated often, in writing this book, wondering what I could contribute but friends, bless them, disagreed and often reminded me that each perspective is unique in some way and has something valuable to offer and that mine was no exception. And gosh, they had not realized that airports had deva nor that great golden beings accompany passenger jets or that they personally, could make a difference to how a tree experienced being pruned or even cut down.

Clearly, this book has not come about without the contribution and support of others. I have had a wonderful team of Beta (or test) readers in different parts of the world, who made a real and very positive contribution to the final form of the book. They each brought their own skill and areas of expertise to the task. So, my deep appreciation and gratitude for their time and effort go to Yvonne Oliver, Diana Polkinghorne, David Young, Jennifer Klassen, Sally Burgess, Georgina May Scott, Deane Keir, Robert (Bob) Smith, Karly Oliver, Joy Brealey, Grace Bell and Linda Crowe. An extra thank you as well to Diana Polkinghorne for her thoughtful and valuable contribution on How We and Deva Create a Building (page 181) and the associated discussion.

My deep gratitude also goes to Linda for her wonderful friendship, so full of love, warmth and understanding. Linda heads another group of people who have over the years, at one time or another, either shared or in some way enabled my journey through the Deva Kingdom. Some have also been mentioned in the text. Thank you to Biannca Pace, Elizabeth Crennan, Grace Bell, Rosemary Coombs, the late Leon Kalili, Isobel McBeath, farmer Joe, Carol Druce, Martin Clegg and the late Carron Forster. William, who shared some special Northern Hemisphere forests and Sean Jamieson for his expert guiding in untracked parts of New Zealand forest so many years ago. A warm thank you to the late Lawson Bracewell for his recognition and support. There are many others who have attended my workshops and shared their own experiences with deva. If I have overlooked anyone who deserves to be acknowledged, I apologize, it is not deliberate. Please consider yourself appreciated.

There are of course many on the Inner Planes who have shared their wisdom over the years, in particular the higher deva who contributed chapters to *This World of Echoes—Book I,* from which I have quoted liberally.

It is clear from the selected book list that there are many wonderful authors who have also contributed to this journey. Importantly also, there are individual teachers to whom I am most grateful. Lani Murphy introduced me to the principles of Esoteric Healing. Two years after completing *This World of Echoes,* I began several years of esoteric study workshops with William Meader and later (all too briefly), with Michael Robbins. These teachers of esoteric philosophy added a wider understanding to earlier decades of experiences and received wisdom. As I wrote this book over a period of many years, I thought often of a paradox frequently repeated by William Meader that, "We're not as far advanced as we think we are and, at the same time, we are further ahead than we think we are."

Heartfelt thanks go to Sabine Weeke for taking on this book and guiding it expertly to publication. And my deep gratitude goes to my editor, Michael Hawkins, for his encouragement, wisdom, and skill in showing me where we could still polish and improve the manuscript. Undoubtedly, the best I've ever worked with. Thank you, Michael!

Last but never least, my heartfelt love and gratitude goes to my husband, Rick, who has provided so many opportunities for travel to places I never dreamed I would get to experience and who, in so many other ways, has generously enabled this journey.

About the Author

Photo by Cristina Longo

New Zealand author, artist, and educator **Jacquelyn E. Lane** supports her work with nearly fifty years of metaphysical studies and a wealth of overseas living and travel. She has a social science degree but opted to pursue careers in art and writing.

Deva was shortlisted for the 2019 Ashton Wylie Unpublished Manuscript Awards in the Mind Body Spirit genre. Jacquelyn has also written and illustrated an eco-spiritual novel on the forests of the world, illustrated a children's book, and scribed *This World of Echoes,* an integrated trilogy of practical wisdom. An accomplished artist, she shares both her understanding of metaphysics and artistic expertise via various workshops.

For more information, visit: **www.jacquelynelane.com**

Also of Interest from Findhorn Press

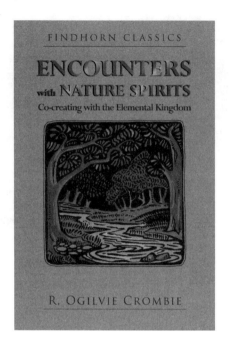

Encounters with Nature Spirits

by R. Ogilvie Crombie

A fascinating and charming first-hand account of the vast powers and true nature of the Elemental Kingdom. In R. Ogilvie Crombie's conversations with Pan, the faun Kurmos, elves, and other nature spirits it becomes apparent that the elemental realm is vastly more powerful than our human kingdom and possesses an ability to create far beyond our human means. True co-creation with nature, working *with* rather than against the elemental kingdom, is what will bring about vital positive change to our endangered eco-system. The elementals are open to this – are we?

ISBN 978–1–62055–837–9

Also of Interest from Findhorn Press

The Findhorn Garden Story
by the Findhorn Community

Founded more than 50 years ago in the north of Scotland, the Findhorn Community became famous for their co-creation with nature, growing vibrant vegetables on barren sand dunes. Guidance by God and absolute faith in the art of manifestation led the founders Eileen and Peter Caddy and Dorothy Maclean. Their discovery of how to contact and cooperate with the nature spirits and devas that made the garden possible sparked a phenomenon that continues today, as Findhorn has grown into an internationally recognized spiritual-learning center.

ISBN 978–1–84409–135–5

FINDHORN PRESS

Life-Changing Books

Learn more about us and our books at
www.findhornpress.com

For information on the Findhorn Foundation:
www.findhorn.org